Lincoln, Congress, and Emancipation

Perspectives on the History of Congress, 1801–1877
Donald R. Kennon, Series Editor

> *Congress and the Emergence of Sectionalism:*
> *From the Missouri Compromise to the Age of Jackson,*
> edited by Paul Finkelman and Donald R. Kennon
>
> *In the Shadow of Freedom: The Politics of Slavery in the National Capital,*
> edited by Paul Finkelman and Donald R. Kennon
>
> *Congress and the Crisis of the 1850s,* edited by Paul Finkelman
> and Donald R. Kennon
>
> *Lincoln, Congress, and Emancipation,* edited by Paul Finkelman
> and Donald R. Kennon

Lincoln, Congress, and Emancipation

Edited by Paul Finkelman and Donald R. Kennon

PUBLISHED FOR THE
UNITED STATES CAPITOL HISTORICAL SOCIETY
BY OHIO UNIVERSITY PRESS • ATHENS

Ohio University Press, Athens, Ohio 45701
ohioswallow.com
© 2016 by Ohio University Press
All rights reserved

To obtain permission to quote, reprint, or otherwise reproduce or distribute material from Ohio University Press publications, please contact our rights and permissions department at (740) 593-1154 or (740) 593-4536 (fax).

Printed in the United States of America
Ohio University Press books are printed on acid-free paper ∞ ™

26 25 24 23 22 21 20 19 18 17 16   5 4 3 2 1

Library of Congress Cataloging-in-Publication Data

Names: Finkelman, Paul, 1949– editor. | Kennon, Donald R., 1948– editor.
Title: Lincoln, Congress, and emancipation / edited by Paul Finkelman and Donald R. Kennon.
Description: Athens, Ohio : published for the United States Capitol Historical Society by Ohio University Press, 2016. | Series: Perspectives on the history of Congress, 1801/1877 | Includes bibliographical references and index.
Identifiers: LCCN 2016036283| ISBN 9780821422274 (hc : alk. paper) | ISBN 9780821422281 (pb : alk. paper) | ISBN 9780821445761 (pdf)
Subjects: LCSH: Lincoln, Abraham, 1809–1865—Views on slavery. | United States—Politics and government—1861–1865. | Slaves—Emancipation—United States. | United States. President (1861–1865 : Lincoln). Emancipation Proclamation. | United States. Constitution. 13th Amendment—History. | Lincoln, Abraham, 1809–1865—Influence.
Classification: LCC E457.2 .L823 2016 | DDC 973.7092—dc23
LC record available at https://lccn.loc.gov/2016036283

Contents

Paul Finkelman
Introduction: Freedom, Finally ... 1

Seymour Drescher
Legislators and Peoples: Emancipations in Comparative Perspective ... 8

Amy S. Greenberg
The Ranchero Spotty: An 1848 Perspective on Abraham Lincoln's Congressional Term ... 39

James Oakes
"Disunion . . . Is Abolition" ... 61

Orville Vernon Burton
Lincoln, Secession, and Emancipation ... 81

Beverly Wilson Palmer
Stevens, Sumner, and the Journey to Full Emancipation ... 105

L. Diane Barnes
Frederick Douglass and the Complications of Emancipation ... 123

Michael Burlingame
Abraham Lincoln: Reluctant Emancipator? ... 143

Paul Finkelman
Lincoln's Long Road to Freedom: How a Railroad Lawyer Became the Great Emancipator ... 162

Jenny Bourne

Double Take: Abolition and the Size of Transferred Property Rights ... 211

Matthew Pinsker

Mr. Spielberg Goes to Washington ... 236

Contributors ... 259

Index ... 263

Paul Finkelman

Introduction

Freedom, Finally

IN 1776 THIRTEEN American colonies declared their independence from Great Britain and formed a weak confederation called the United States of America. The American colonists offered an elaborate explanation—the Declaration of Independence—for why they were separating from their mother country. Much of the Declaration is a laundry list of specific complaints against the king. But the Declaration is mostly remembered for its stirring language about liberty and fundamental human rights:

> We hold these Truths to be self-evident, that all Men are created equal; that they are endowed by their Creator with certain unalienable Rights; that among these are Life, Liberty, and the Pursuit of Happiness—That, to secure these Rights, Governments are instituted among Men, deriving their Just powers from the Consent of the Governed.

The great problem with this brilliant endorsement of liberty, equality, and justice is that neither the primary author of the Declaration—Thomas Jefferson—nor most other leaders of the nation were willing to apply its principles to the 700,000 or so African and African American slaves living in the United States. The right to "liberty" may have been "unalienable," but the governments of all thirteen states denied this right to the slaves in their jurisdictions. All people may have been "created equal," but in the new United States all slaves and most free blacks were denied legal equality.

By 1787, when the Constitution was written, Massachusetts and New Hampshire had ended slavery and Pennsylvania, Connecticut, and Rhode Island had passed statutes to gradually end slavery.[1] But the institution was alive and well in New York and New Jersey, and in all of the states from Maryland to Georgia. The new Constitution explicitly supported slavery in a number of ways.[2] Although the Constitution authorized Congress to regulate all international commerce, the document specifically prohibited Congress from banning the African slave trade before 1808, and did not promise that the trade would ever be ended. Although the system of federalism created by the Constitution empowered the states to regulate the status of all people within their jurisdiction, the Constitution specifically prohibited states from emancipating fugitive slaves and required that such people be returned to their owners.

The political structure created by the Constitution both explicitly and implicitly protected slavery. Under the three-fifths clause, slaves were counted in determining how many representatives each state would get in Congress. The Constitution did not count any other form of private property in allocating representatives in Congress. Counting slaves for representation gave the South a bonus in the House of Representatives that provided the margin for passage of numerous proslavery laws, such as the Missouri Compromise of 1820 and the Fugitive Slave Act of 1850. Electoral votes were based on a state's congressional representation, which meant that seats in Congress created by counting slaves also gave the South extra electoral votes. In 1800 the slaveholding Thomas Jefferson would not have been elected president had slaves not been counted for representation and thus affected the Electoral College.

The structure of the Senate indirectly protected slavery as well. Each state had equal representation in the Senate, and thus even though the northern states had nearly twice as many residents as the slave states, the South had as many or more senators for most of the antebellum period.[3] In the 1850s the North had a slight majority of states and thus a majority in the Senate,

---

[1] See generally Arthur Zilversmit, *The First Emancipation: The Abolition of Slavery in the North* (Chicago, 1967).

[2] For a full discussion of the proslavery elements of the constitution see Paul Finkelman, *Slavery and the Founders: Race and Liberty in the Age of Jefferson*, 3d ed. (New York, 2014), chap. 1.

[3] For example, at the time of the Mexican War the South had a two-state majority and thus four more votes than the North in the Senate.

but there were always a few northern Democrats who were willing to vote with the South on issues affecting slavery. Thus, even with a northern majority in the Senate, that body passed the Kansas-Nebraska Act in 1854, which allowed slavery in western territories where it had previously been banned. The constitutional structure and the political realities of antebellum America made it impossible to imagine any federal laws impinging on slavery.

Slaves were the only form of privately held property that the Constitution acknowledged and protected. Thus, in 1857 the Supreme Court could explicitly hold that property in slaves was uniquely protected by the Constitution and Congress had no power to ban this property from any federal jurisdiction.[4]

Even if the northerners in Congress had united to oppose slavery, it is not clear they could have accomplished much. The Constitution of 1787 had created a government of very limited powers, and almost every serious constitutional theorist, lawyer, judge, and politician believed that the national government had no power to interfere with the "domestic institutions" of the states. Because the Constitution created a government with limited powers, Congress had no power to end slavery in the states. As General Charles Cotesworth Pinckney, the head of South Carolina's delegation, told the South Carolina House of Representatives after the Convention,

> We have a security that the general government can never emancipate them, for no such authority is granted and it is admitted, on all hands, that the general government has no powers but what are expressly granted by the Constitution, and that all rights not expressed were reserved by the several states.[5]

At least on its face, the Constitution left the regulation of slavery (and the status of people in general) in the hands of the states.

Thus, short of a constitutional amendment, Congress simply lacked the power to interfere with slavery where it existed, except perhaps in the federal territories and the District of Columbia. But in the antebellum period a constitutional amendment that harmed slavery was more than unimaginable—it would have been simply impossible to achieve. The Constitution is

---

[4]*Dred Scott v. Sandford*, 60 U.S. (19 How.) 393 (1857).
[5]Jonathan Elliot, *The Debates in the Several State Conventions on the Adoption of the Federal Constitution*, 5 vols. (1888; reprint ed., New York, 1987), 4:286.

extraordinarily difficult to amend. An amendment must be approved by two-thirds of each house of Congress. Until the Civil War the southern states always had enough representatives in both the House and the Senate to block any amendment. But even if somehow an amendment limiting slavery in any way had been voted out of the Congress, it could not have been ratified without substantial support from southern state legislatures. The Constitution requires that amendments be ratified by three-quarters of the states. In 1860 there were thirty-three states, and slavery was legal in fifteen of them. Thus, if all the slave state legislatures had voted against a constitutional amendment, it could never have been ratified. To understand the stranglehold that the slave South had on the constitutional structure, it is worth noting that in 2016, in a fifty-state union, the fifteen slave states could *still* block a constitutional amendment on slavery or anything else. It would take forty-five states to outvote the fifteen slave states to ratify a constitutional amendment ending slavery.

This short lesson in constitutional history and constitutional law helps us understand the problem of emancipation before and during the Civil War.

Thus, when Lincoln took office, in March 1861, the national government had no power to touch slavery in the states where it existed. Lincoln understood this, and said as much in his first inaugural address, noting: "I have no purpose, directly or indirectly, to interfere with the institution of slavery in the States where it exists. I believe I have no lawful right to do so, and I have no inclination to do so."[6] The most Lincoln could do, which was all he intended to do, was make sure that no new slave states entered the Union. Other than that, the new president had absolutely no power to affect slavery in the nation. This was his official position as president and did not reflect his personal view. Lincoln hated slavery and had always hated slavery. As he noted, "If slavery is not wrong, nothing is wrong."[7]

But Lincoln's personal views of slavery were not on his agenda. When he entered the White House Lincoln's main goal—his only goal—was to preserve the Union. He took office during the greatest constitutional and political crisis in the history of the United States. Seven states, fearful of Lincoln's known personal opposition to slavery, had declared they were no

---

[6] Abraham Lincoln, "First Inaugural Address—Final Text," in *The Collected Works of Abraham Lincoln*, ed. Roy P. Basler, 9 vols. (New Brunswick, N.J., 1953–55), 4:262–63.
[7] Lincoln to Albert G. Hodges, Apr. 4, 1864, ibid., 7:281.

longer in the Union. Lincoln used his first inaugural to assure Southerners that he was not a threat to slavery and would not harm their most important social institution. He understood that the root cause of secession was slavery and the fear that his administration would harm slavery.

The secessionists had made this clear when they left the Union. The leaders of these states simply did not want to be in a nation where the highest officeholder made no secret of his hatred of slavery, even if, as he said in his inaugural address, he had "no lawful right" and "no purpose" to interfere with slavery. But throughout his career Lincoln had also made it clear he opposed slavery, and in his famous "House Divided" speech, in 1858, Lincoln had declared that he thought slavery should ultimately be put on a "course of ultimate extinction." This was enough for Southern slave owners to attempt to destroy the nation. As the South Carolina secession convention put it:

> A geographical line has been drawn across the Union, and all the States north of that line have united in the election of a man to the high office of President of the United States, whose opinions and purposes are hostile to slavery. He is to be entrusted with the administration of the common Government, because he has declared that that "Government cannot endure permanently half slave, half free," and that the public mind must rest in the belief that slavery is in the course of ultimate extinction.[8]

Since 1788, Southerners had dominated American politics and particularly the presidency. Ten of the previous fifteen presidents had been slave owners. They had held the office for fifty-four of the seventy-two years since the Constitution had gone into effect. Lincoln was the first president to hold office who publicly opposed slavery and expressed any hostility to its expansion.[9] Thus, Southerners left the Union rather than remain there to see what Lincoln might do to slavery.

---

[8] Declaration of the Immediate Causes Which Induce and Justify the Secession of South Carolina from the Federal Union, Dec. 24, 1860.

[9] President Zachary Taylor, a sugar planter who owned hundreds of slaves, opposed the spread of slavery into the New Mexico and Utah territories because he believed the institution was not economically viable there and thus agitation by southern nationalists was foolish and dangerous. But he was an avowed supporter of slavery itself and even purchased more slaves while president. Two northern presidents, Martin Van Buren and William Henry Harrison, came from slaveholding families and owned slaves as adults. An eleventh president, James Buchanan, grew up in a slaveholding family in Pennsylvania, and his family held slaves and indentured blacks (whose mothers were slaves) until his death in 1821. There is no evidence James Buchanan personally owned slaves.

Lincoln believed that most Southerners did not actually support secession, and that in the end the people of the South would reject disunion. Thus, he promised in his first inaugural to do nothing coercive to end the crisis, while at the same time promising not to harm slavery. Even after the Civil War began, Lincoln believed and hoped that disunion was just a passing fancy among a minority of hotheads, and that the war and secession would soon be over. Thus, when the war began he refused to lift a finger to end slavery and rejected the advice of his political allies, some generals, black leaders, and white abolitionists to turn the war for the union into a crusade for freedom. He also understood that any attack on slavery would push the four loyal slave states into the arms of their fellow slaveholders in the Confederacy. When a group of ministers told Lincoln that if he ended slavery he would have God on this side, the president allegedly responded, "I would like to have God on my side, but I *need* Kentucky."

Slaves and opponents of slavery would not wait for Lincoln, however. Almost immediately slaves began to leave their masters and escape to U.S. Army camps. Some commanders gave sanctuary to these escaping slaves, others returned them to their masters. Some military commanders tried to move aggressively against slavery, while others rejected any attempts at abolition. In the summer of 1861 Congress passed the First Confiscation Act, which provided a process, however cumbersome and unwieldy, to free slaves owned by rebel masters. Meanwhile, the secretary of war, with Lincoln's approval, authorized commanders in the field to give sanctuary to slaves escaping Confederate masters. By the spring and early summer of 1862 Congress had moved further, ending slavery in Washington, D.C., and the federal territories, and promising to provide funds for compensated emancipation in the loyal slave states. In August Congress passed the Second Confiscation Act, which provided more opportunities for the army to emancipate slaves, and more importantly authorized the enlistment of black troops. Meanwhile, unbeknownst to all but a few trusted advisors, in early July Lincoln drafted what would become the Emancipation Proclamation. Lincoln had now determined that as commander in chief of the army and navy he had the power to end slavery in the states that were in rebellion, even though he could never have harmed slavery if there had not been secession and civil war. When he issued the preliminary Proclamation, on September 22, 1862, the War for the Union became the War for Freedom.

In the next three and a quarter years, slavery would come to an end. The United States Army would smash the Confederacy, and in the process liberate a million or more slaves. In the loyal slave states black men would be enrolled in the army and their families would become free. Some of those states, as well as the new state of West Virginia, would abolish slavery outright. In January 1865 Congress would pass a constitutional amendment—the Thirteenth—to completely end slavery in the nation. This was possible because eleven slave states were no longer in the Union and thus were unable to block the amendment. Indeed, the great irony of this monumental constitutional change is that secession made emancipation possible; had the slave states remained in the Union, Lincoln could never have taken steps to end slavery and Congress could never have passed the Thirteenth Amendment and sent it on to the states. In December the amendment was ratified.

The essays in this book flesh out and explore this history. They help us understand the nature of emancipation, the route Lincoln took to achieve it, and how it is remembered both in the United States and abroad. The book takes us from Lincoln's career in Congress in the 1840s to Stephen Spielberg's movie about the sixteenth president and his role in the passage of the Thirteenth Amendment.

Seymour Drescher

Legislators and Peoples

Emancipations in Comparative Perspective

WITH FEW EXCEPTIONS slavery has existed throughout the world, embedded in various societies and cultures. For millennia the practice was justified in legal codes as a quasi-universal condition. As recently as two and a half centuries ago, even those who were hostile to it on moral, political, or economic grounds could foresee no end to slavery. As he cast his philosophical gaze over the world a decade before the American Revolution, Adam Smith cautioned his students at the University of Glasgow: "We are apt to imagine that slavery is entirely abolished at this time, without considering that this is the case in only a small part of Europe; not remembering that all over Moscovy and the eastern parts of Europe and the whole of Asia, that is, from Bohemia to the Indian Ocean, all over Africa, and the greatest part of America, it is still in use. It is indeed almost impossible that it should ever be totally or generally abolished." Moreover, since the persons who made the laws were slaveholders, in a republican or free government, "it will scarcely ever happen that it should be abolished."[1]

Even among philosophers, for whom the rapid expansion of European-sponsored slavery aroused distress and anger, the prospect of alteration appeared bleak. The Abbé Raynal's famous diatribe against European overseas slavery foresaw only two meager hopes for change. It might issue from

---

[1] Adam Smith, *Lectures on Jurisprudence*, ed. R. L. Meek, D. D. Raphael, and P. G. Stein (Oxford, 1978), pp. 181–82, 451–52.

decrees by an all-powerful enlightened philosopher king. "Kings of the earth," he pleaded, "you alone can make this revolution." If the voice of humanity failed to move the mighty, humanity had but one other hope. As in ancient Rome, a new Spartacus might arise from the ranks of the runaway slaves." Elsewhere in the same work the author forlornly asked, "Isn't the future splendor of these [European] colonies a dream, and wouldn't the happiness of these regions be a still more amazing phenomenon than their original devastation?"[2]

By the end of the century that followed, slavery would be legally abolished throughout the Americas. All nations and empires once unquestioningly dedicated to the imperial expansion of slavery in the New World had pledged themselves to build empires of antislavery in the Old.[3] This metamorphosis occurred where free men in republican or free governments mobilized to initiate the termination of the institution. In this global process of emancipation the United States obviously played an important role. It might be fruitful to view this process within a broader comparative context.

The Economic Context of Antislavery

As late as the 1780s, the rulers and dominant elites of slaveholding societies and empires assumed that the institution was and would continue to be a significant contributor to their collective wealth and power. Dreams of tropical expansion continued unabated even during the period that is conventionally called the "Age of Revolution." In the Atlantic world as a whole the decade between the end of the American Revolutionary War and the Saint-Domingue Revolution was the peak decade of exports of enslaved Africans to the Americas. Within the New World empires, the most decisive assaults against the slave trade and slavery in the Anglo-American, French, and Iberian orbits all occurred at moments when their overseas economies promised maximum future economic advantages from their respective slave systems.

---

[2] G. T. Raynal, *Histoire philosophique et politique des . . . Européens dans les deux indes*, 4 vols. (Geneva, 1780), 1:14–15, 687–88; 2:3, 294, 358.
[3] Seymour Drescher, *Abolition: A History of Slavery and Antislavery* (New York, 2009). For slave trade figures, see "Voyages: The Transatlantic Slave Trade Database": http:www.slavevoyages.org/tast/index.faces.

During the decade before the British legally abolished their transatlantic slave trade (1807) and began their long campaign for international abolition, the British slave trade and British tropical sugar production dominated the Atlantic system as never before. Likewise, during the decade before French slavery was devastatingly assaulted by a slave uprising, its slave and slave trade systems both reached their own historic peaks. In 1790 nearly fifty-five thousand enslaved Africans were disembarked in the French colonies, ten thousand more human beings than had ever been delivered annually to any colonial economy. French domination of slave-produced commodities was also at its all-time peak.[4] Similarly, prior to the upheavals that shook the Spanish South American slave systems after 1810, the scale of their slave trade had expanded dramatically. On the eve of their revolutions, South Americans were sure of one thing: their "South Atlantic system and colonial political economies did depend on the survival of slavery."[5]

Later in the century the same economic context persisted. Just before the first great interruption to the growth of the institution occurred in Brazil (1850), its slave importations reached their triennial peak. During the decade just before the abolition of its slave imports, Cuba, with its sugar-producing regions, "must have ranked among the top half dozen of the world's nations," with a per capita income just below the level of the United States South. The United States South fully conformed to the hemispheric pattern during the decade before the Civil War. That nearly two-thirds of the richest Americans in 1860 were slaveholders in the South would have come as no surprise to their counterparts in Cuba and Brazil. On the eve of secession, the value of southern U.S. slaves was equivalent to nearly ten trillion dollars in today's prices and to 80 percent of the nation's annual gross national product. Contrary to the assertions of many antebellum abolitionists and later Southern apologists, free labor was not more productive than slave labor for producing many commodities for the world market. In short,

---

[4] In 1789 the French tropical colonies were producing 45 percent of the Atlantic world's sugar and probably half of the world's coffee. See David P. Geggus, "Sugar and Coffee Cultivation in Saint Domingue and the Shaping of the Labor Force," in *Cultivation and Culture: Labor and the Shaping of Slave Life in the Americas*, ed. Ira Berlin and Philip Morgan (Charlottesville, 1993), pp. 73–98; and Seymour Drescher, *Econocide: British Slavery in the Era of Abolition*, 2d ed. (Chapel Hill, 2010), p. 48, table 11.

[5] Jeremy Adelman, *Sovereignty and Revolution in the Iberian Atlantic* (Princeton, 2006), pp. 99–100.

throughout the century after the 1780s, capitalist slavery remained economically viable and competitive in every major colonial or national economy in which it was permitted to continue without legal impediment. The fundamental point of this survey is evident. For the slave Americas, "there was a profound incompatibility between economic self-interest and antislavery policy."[6]

In those economies where the institution endured into the second half of the nineteenth century, capitalist industrialization was quite compatible with slavery. Cuba inaugurated Latin America's first railroad line in 1838, only a few years after Britain's first commercial rail line began operating between Liverpool and Manchester. The first railroad in the United States was also constructed in the slave South. On the eve of Southern secession the region's 9,500 miles of track was greater than its counterparts in France, Germany, or Great Britain. Railroad construction got under way later in Brazil, but its first network was also developed in its most dynamic slave zone. As contributors to economic growth, the U.S. South was a major supplier of cotton to both the American North and Great Britain. By the late 1840s free-trade Britain became a source of demand for Brazil's cotton and sugar as well as coffee. Not only did Cuba become a supplier of sugar for Britain, but its sugar and slave trades were crucial to Spanish industrialization in the nineteenth century. The significance of slavery in the whole Atlantic economy indicates why the battle to abolish the slave trade and legislate emancipation extended over more than a century.[7]

If the economics of New World slavery presented common economic difficulties for antislavery proponents, the opposite was true as regards slave demography. Politicians, slaveholders, and abolitionists alike recognized a persistent problem in the reproduction of the institution. Except in the case of the United States, all slave systems depended on a steady stream of

---

[6]On the slave trade, see Slave Trade Database. For comparisons between the three major Atlantic slave systems in the nineteenth century see Laird W. Bergad, *The Comparative History of Slavery in Brazil, Cuba, and the United States* (New York, 2007). On Cuban productivity, see David Eltis, "The Slave Economies of the Caribbean: Structures, Performance, Evolution and Significance," in *General History of the Caribbean*, ed. Franklin W. Knight (London, 1997). On the comparative proportion of wealthy Southerners, see David Brion Davis, *Inhuman Bondage: The Rise and Fall of Slavery in the New World* (New York, 2006), p. 184.

[7]In addition to sources cited in note 6, see Bergad, *Comparative History*, chap. 6, and Robert W. Fogel and Stanley L. Engerman, *Time on the Cross: The Economics of American Negro Slavery* (Boston, 1974), pp. 247–57.

recruitment both for the growth and for the very maintenance of slave numbers. Almost everywhere on both sides of the Atlantic, attacks on slavery began with campaigns to curtail or to abolish trading in slaves. Owners and rulers clearly recognized that prohibiting the traffic would render their institution increasingly vulnerable to antislavery projects.[8]

Only in the United States did slavery grow primarily through natural reproduction. Long before the American Revolution, the slave population was capable of increasing without the aid of further importations from Africa. Between 1790 and 1860, the U.S. slave population rose from seven hundred thousand to four million, with a corresponding spatial expansion of the institution deep into the heart of the continent. Even in the United States, after the abolition of further African imports in 1808, the proportion of slaves to the American population diminished in every decennial census.

Comparative Antislavery in Political Perspective

Whatever the impact of economic or demographic trends, what ended all major New World slave systems was not the working out of market forces or reproductive patterns but political or military intervention. We must therefore attend to the behavior of both legislative and nonlegislative actors in the unfolding of Euro-American emancipations. This aspect of the antislavery process most effectively explains the dismantling of Atlantic slavery. Comparative analysis requires attention to both the domestic and the foreign aspects of the process of abolition. Domestic interventions include the balance of forces within each society and the condition of the public sphere within those systems. International interventions include the complex of diplomatic, economic, military, and economic pressures that could be brought to bear against slavery in each society.

In an earlier comparative analysis of European antislavery, I developed the notion of two variants of European abolitionism. The first, or British,

---

[8] Almost everywhere the abolition of the slave trade preceded the emancipation of slavery. On the magnitude of the transatlantic slave trades and the impacts of their endings, see David Eltis, *Economic Growth and the Ending of the Transatlantic Slave Trade* (New York, 1987); and David Eltis, "Was Abolition of the U.S. and British Slave Trade Significant in the Broader Atlantic Context?" *William and Mary Quarterly* 66 (2009):717–36.

variant stemmed from a broad and durable national social movement. It seized opportunities to bring massive popular pressure to bear on British imperial slavery for half a century (1788–1838). Thereafter, for yet another half century, Britain remained committed to furthering slave trade abolitions around the world. The other variant of European antislavery I term "continental abolitionism." It also began in the late 1780s. For most of the century that followed, continental antislavery activity was, with very few exceptions, confined to small political and cultural elites. These elites were unable, and usually even reluctant, to seek mass recruitment or large-scale mobilizations in the public sphere. Their political culture was embedded in political systems that constrained rights to public associations and to print publicly.[9]

Consequently, overseas slavery could rarely become an object of widespread popular discussion and contention in Europe. In minor imperial slave systems, antislavery initiatives were often the result of executive initiatives. Sweden, Denmark, the Netherlands, and Portugal all offer examples of this variant of antislavery. In some instances it was external pressures on governments that led to major curtailments of slavery. Alternatively, revolutionary upheavals, civil wars, or foreign interventions could occasion dramatic lurches toward slave emancipation and reversals or suspensions of antislavery initiatives. The effective endings of transatlantic slave trading by Europeans in Portugal, the Netherlands, Denmark, Sweden, Spain, and Brazil were all effected by external (i.e., British) interventions. In every international treaty negotiated for the purpose of ending the transatlantic slave trade, Great Britain was the initiator and a signatory.[10] The comparative analysis of paths to the legal termination of the transatlantic slave system therefore properly begins with British abolition.

Britain: People and Parliament

In order to illuminate the role of civil societies and legislators in determining the different roads to emancipation, this chapter will compare three

---

[9]Seymour Drescher, *From Slavery to Freedom: Comparative Studies in the Rise and Fall of Atlantic Slavery* (New York, 1999), pp. 35–56.
[10]Eltis, *Economic Growth*, pp. 85–101.

cases: those of Britain, France, and the United States. In contrast to all of its continental European counterparts and most of the Americas, the British Isles never suffered revolutionary upheaval, civil war, or foreign invasion during the entire period from the rise of political abolitionism in the late 1780s to the termination of its transatlantic, South African, and Indian Ocean slave systems. The emergence of British abolitionism was occasioned by neither defeat nor self-doubt following the American Revolutionary War. The abolitionist breakthrough in 1788–92 occurred in the wake of an astonishing economic and international rebound during the decade that followed the end of hostilities. British abolitionism emerged during one of the most benign economic and political junctures in British history. Britain would not again feel herself so prosperous and secure until the 1850s.

The British takeoff into abolition was not a compensatory response to the loss of the thirteen North American colonies. Nor was it a response to any internal political challenge. By all available empirical evidence, abolitionism emerged during a decade when a nation at peace reveled in its prosperity, security, and power. The wartime fires of partisanship and demands for reform subsided. British external trade in manufactured goods was winning out from one end of Eurasia to the other—from Calais to Canton. Britain simultaneously recovered her commercial primacy in the ports of the new American republic.

In international relations and security, the picture was equally bright. Britain's former enemies were all in disarray. In the late 1780s the Netherlands was wracked by civil war and Prussian occupation. France was descending into bankruptcy and revolution. The United States was in the midst of the political crisis that led to the reconstitution of its federation. Britain's relative security, both foreign and domestic, permitted the emergence of its distinctive antislavery process. The only major interruption in the process occurred when Britain felt under most direct threat, both domestically and overseas, during the 1790s and early 1800s. At the height of revolutionary threats from France and in the Caribbean, British abolitionism remained at an ebb. Thereafter, all of the major British steps toward slave trade abolition and colonial slave emancipation occurred in moments of triumph: Slave trade abolition (1806–7) followed Britain's decisive naval victory at Trafalgar (1805); successful internationalization of slave trade abolition came in the wake of the two defeats of Napoleon (1814 and 1815); colonial slave emancipation followed the peaceful parliamentary reform of 1832. All these overseas reforms occurred when *Pax Britannica* dominated the oceans of the world.[11]

From 1788 to 1838 abolition was driven by the most successful national abolitionist movement in history. The first national abolitionist mobilization set the pattern. A mass petition to Parliament triggered the first nationwide wave of imitators in 1787–88. The pattern repeated itself during the next half century, with upwards of a hundred thousand signatories in 1788, four hundred thousand in 1791–92, more than seven hundred and fifty thousand in 1814, and reaching a crescendo with more than one and a quarter million adult inhabitants successfully demanding emancipation in the 1830s. At peak moments the proportion of accumulated signatures amounted to a fifth to a quarter of eligible signers. In all these instances opposing petitions were either negligible or nonexistent.[12]

From the outset many groups outside the usual boundaries of political participation felt empowered to enter the public sphere. Working men lent their names and voices to abolitionist mobilizations from Manchester in 1787 to the petition and parliamentary election rallies in the 1830s. Nonconformists also joined the campaigns from the very start. Women were initially considered to be ineligible as signatories, but they outnumbered men in the signing of petitions and addresses to young Queen Victoria by the last great mass campaign in 1838. Early in the process whole families were recruited for another kind of mobilization. An innovative boycott movement, unrestricted by gender or age, was launched in an attempt to undermine the economic power of the slave interest. Families were asked to abstain from the consumption of slave-grown sugar.

Although they were relatively few on the ground in Britain, Africans too entered the fray from the very beginning, most famously with *The Interesting*

---

[11] For a brief description of the process, see Seymour Drescher, "Public Opinion and Parliament in the Abolition of the British Slave Trade," in *The British Slave Trade: Abolition, Parliament and People*, ed. Stephen Farell, Melanie Unwin, and James Walvin (Edinburgh, 2007), pp. 42–65; and Drescher, *Abolition*, pp. 205–66.

[12] For an analysis of the abolitionist and antislavery petitions, see Seymour Drescher, *Capitalism and Antislavery: British Mobilization in Comparative Perspective* (New York, 1987), pp. 66–88, 125–34; Seymour Drescher, "Public Opinion and the Destruction of British Colonial Slavery," in *Slavery and British Society, 1776–1846* (London, 1982), pp. 123–49; and Seymour Drescher, "Whose Abolition? Popular Pressure and the Ending of British Slave Trade," *Past and Present* 143 (1994):136–66.

Narrative of the Life of Olaudah Equiano, or Gustave Vassa, the African, Written by Himself (1789) (fig. 1).[13] Caribbean slaves entered into the British public sphere in a much larger way during the decade before British emancipation in 1833. As soon as British legislators, under popular pressure, began to debate slave emancipation in the 1820s, Caribbean slaves thrust themselves into the popular contention. Within a few months of the first parliamentary debate in favor of gradual emancipation in 1823, a massive slave uprising broke out in Demerara (present-day Guyana). Under well-organized leadership, the ten thousand to twelve thousand insurgent slaves demonstrated their intention not to kill or injure their captive masters. When they met the military force dispatched to suppress them, the slaves offered written testimonies from the captive masters attesting to their good treatment. Equally important, the insurgents aligned their demands with those of workers in Britain. They made an appeal for rights, fair wages, days off, and ultimate freedom. This enabled Britain abolitionists to transform the traditional image of a savage "servile insurrection" into a quasi-metropolitan laborers' "strike" against intolerable working conditions. The slaves' restraint contrasted dramatically with the summary shootings and executions of hundreds of black laborers in the suppression of the revolt. Within two years, Britain's parliamentary election of 1826 became the first occasion for the introduction of emancipation as an electoral issue on the hustings.

A second, more massive slave uprising in Jamaica eight years later had a similar impact. The disproportionate brutality of its suppression again served as a catalyst to metropolitan agitation for emancipation. The contrast with a contemporary American slave uprising is stark. As David Brion Davis aptly notes, Nat Turner's American slave revolt broke out in Virginia just before the Jamaica uprising. Nat Turner's men "murdered nearly sixty whites, most of them women and children." In all, Turner's rebels in Virginia "killed at least 3.5 times as many whites as the *combined* total who died in the infinitely larger Barbadian, Demeraran, and Jamaican insurrections." In short, the Caribbean slaves were fully aware that they were dealing with a very

---

[13]See J. R. Oldfield, *Popular Politics and British Antislavery: The Mobilization of Public Opinion against the Slave Trade, 1787–1807* (Manchester, 1997); Clare Midgley, *Women against Slavery: The British Campaign, 1780–1870* (London, 1995); Drescher, *From Slavery to Freedom*, pp. 35–56; and Vincent Carretta, *Equiano the African: Biography of a Self-Made Man* (Athens, Ga., 2005).

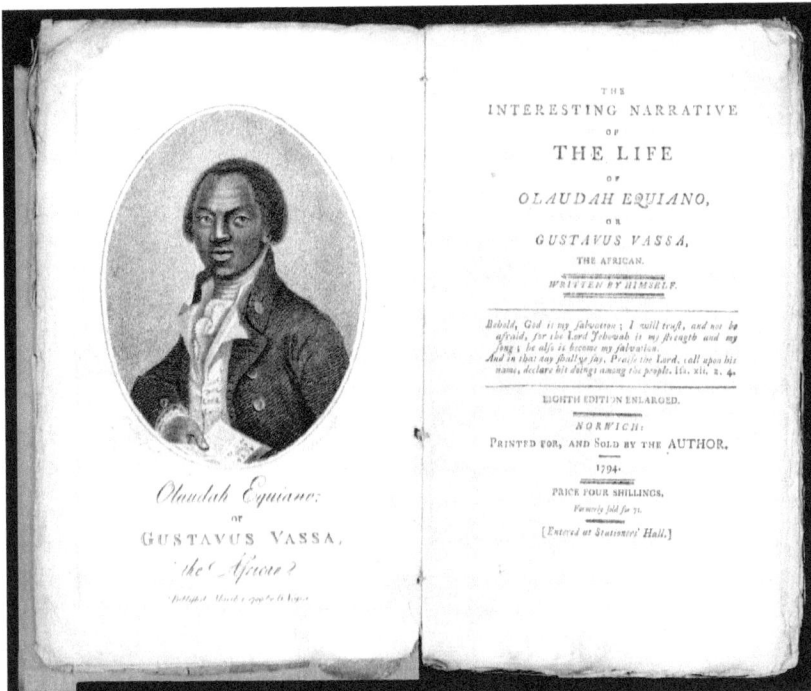

FIG. 1. The frontispiece and title page from the 1794 edition of *The Interesting Narrative of the Life of Olaudah Equiano*. (Prints and Photographs Division, Library of Congress)

different public sentiment and parliamentary possibilities than those confronting Nat Turner's insurgents.[14]

The parliamentary response to the British abolitionist mobilization was significant. Abolitionism's victory in Britain was no easy matter. We have already noted the formidable barrier to antislavery created by the economic importance of the British slave system. Its relative imperial significance only increased during the generation following the loss of Britain's continental colonies after 1783. The slave interest was able to postpone the ending of

---

[14]See Davis, *Inhuman Bondage*, pp. 208–21, quotes on pp. 208 and 220 (Davis's emphasis). On the Demerara uprising in particular, see Emilia Viotti da Costa, *Crowns of Glory, Tears of Blood: The Demerara Slave Rebellion of 1823* (New York, 1994). For a comparison of the impact of the Demeraran and Saint-Domingue uprisings on British abolitionism, see Seymour Drescher, "Civilizing Insurgency: Two Variants of Slave Revolts in the Age of Revolution," in *Who Abolished Slavery? Slave Revolts and Abolitionism* (New York, 2010), pp. 120–32.

the British transatlantic slave trade for two decades after the launching of popular abolitionism.

Nevertheless, British legislators immediately acknowledged the significance of the unprecedented popular mobilization. In response to the first wave of petitioning, Prime Minister William Pitt framed his motion to investigate abolition as a necessary response to "the great number and variety of petitions." He was powerfully seconded by the leaders of the opposition, Charles James Fox and Edmund Burke. The second popular mobilization in 1792 dramatically reversed the legislative defeat of William Wilberforce's first parliamentary attempt the year before. The House of Commons resolved in favor of the gradual abolition of the slave trade and set a date for its implementation. As noted above, the emergencies of the French and Caribbean wars postponed abolition for another fifteen years. Nevertheless, despite the temporary setback, motions for abolition were debated in Parliament year after year, with the personal support of the prime minister. In the final debates over the slave trade in 1807, die-hard opponents of abolition bitterly recognized the significance of an aroused public in securing the overwhelming final majority in favor of prohibition.[15]

In 1814 another British popular mobilization, now in favor of internationalizing slave trade abolition, was decisive in making the project a priority in British foreign policy until the transatlantic trade was finally brought to an end fifty years later. Parliament and the British government were again impelled to discuss slave emancipation by further mobilizations in the 1820s and 1830s. Without maximum electoral pressure in 1832 and record-setting petition campaigns in 1833 and 1838, parliamentarians would not have found it easy to facilitate the passage of emancipation by offering slave owners the then-astonishing sum of twenty million pounds in compensation.

In 1840, when the first "world conference" for ending world slavery convened in London, abolitionists both at home and abroad had reason to consider British slave emancipation a resounding success (fig. 2).[16] British emancipation had come about without any replay of the massive bloodlettings of the Haitian revolution and the wars of Spanish American independence. The dawn of freedom in the British slave colonies was celebrated

---

[15]Drescher, "Whose Abolition?" pp. 136–66.
[16]Seymour Drescher, *The Mighty Experiment: Free Labor versus Slavery in British Emancipation* (New York, 2002), pp. 144–57.

Fig. 2. *The Anti-Slavery Society Convention, 1840*, by Benjamin Robert Haydon (died 1846), given to the National Portrait Gallery, London, in 1880 by the British and Foreign Anti-Slavery Society, oil on canvas, 1841 (117 in. × 151 in.). *(National Portrait Gallery, London)*

without the loss of a single life. William Wilberforce, the iconic abolitionist Member of Parliament, was laid to rest in Westminster Abbey just as the Emancipation Act passed through Parliament in 1833. His funeral procession had many of the trappings of a royal funeral. By 1839 Wilberforce's statue was already installed atop a column at Hull, five years before Nelson was mounted on his own column in Trafalgar Square.[17]

Above all, in nationalist discourse, the long march to emancipation was considered to be the cause and consequence of an entire people in action. What began at Westminster Abbey in 1833 ended with the gathering of West Indian slaves assembling to greet the dawn of freedom on August 1,

---

[17] J. R. Oldfield, *"Chords of Freedom": Commemoration, Ritual and British Transatlantic Slavery* (Manchester, 2007), pp. 59–68.

1834. What most impressed abolitionists abroad was abolition as a peaceful parliamentary reform—"the act of the nation and not of its rulers."[18]

French Emancipation: Citizens and Slaves

Well before the end of the Napoleonic Wars, the historical paths of the French and British abolitionist processes had clearly diverged. The French path to abolition of the slave trade and slavery demonstrated a volatility and fragmentation almost completely at odds with the incremental pattern of British emancipation. The French leaped ahead in the attack, quickly reversed themselves, and thereafter moved forward reluctantly, ever-suspicious of their neighbor's efforts to dismantle the slave trade and the institution itself. During a sixty-year process French civil society remained relatively indifferent to the fate of its slave system. French antislavery never lapsed entirely, but for the nation as a whole it never rose to the level of a priority political problem.[19]

Inspired by London's example, a French abolitionist society was organized in Paris in 1788. With the collapse of the old regime, abolitionists on both sides of the Channel expected that the demand for root-and-branch reform might well accelerate international abolition beyond anything that British abolitionists alone could hope for. The initial program of the French abolitionists was potentially more radical than its British counterpart. The *Amis des Noirs* included the gradual abolition of slavery itself in their founding document. When the first two estates renounced their traditional privileges on the famous night of August 4, 1789, one representative proposed extending the emancipation of serfs to colonial slaves. The proposal never

---

[18]Alexis de Tocqueville, "On the Emancipation of Slaves (1843)," in *Tocqueville and Beaumont on Social Reform*, ed. and trans. Seymour Drescher (New York, 1968), quote on pp. 150–51. In 1835, when a French abolitionist deputy invoked the nonviolent British emancipation to request consideration of a similar policy for France, he condemned the first French emancipation (1794) as a source of "innumerable evils." See Frédérique Beauvois, "Indemnisé les planteurs pour abolir l'esclavage," Thèse de Doctorat, University of Lausanne, 2011, p. 98.

[19]See, *inter alia*, Yves Benot, *La Révolution Française et la fin des colonies* (Paris, 1998); Lawrence C. Jennings, *French Anti-Slavery: The Movement for the Abolition of Slavery in France* (New York, 2000); *Abolir l'esclavage: Unréformisme à l'epreuve, France, Portugal; Suisse xviii–xix siècles*, ed. Olivier Pétré-Grenouilleau (Rennes, 2008); and Drescher, "Two Variants of Antislavery."

reached the final printed summary of abolished abuses. Nor did any reference to slavery appear in the Declaration of the Rights of Man and Citizen published a few months later.[20]

Slavery's absence from these two founding documents was symptomatic of a line that was tacitly drawn between institutions and conditions in the metropole and those permitted in the overseas colonies. The same exclusion continued in the French constitution of 1791. No abolitionists were elected to the Constituent Assembly's Colonial Committee, tasked with formulating an article on the colonies. The assembly sanctioned a constitutional decree which gave solemn assurance that the nation would protect "colonial property" and would not "innovate in any branch of colonial trade." Most newspapers supported the decision. The French colonies were not included in the constitution, and thereby were not bound by the "natural and civil liberties guaranteed to every citizen." Like states in the new American Constitution, and without mentioning the word slavery, the colonies retained internal autonomy with regard to "local customs." When the constitution was promulgated in 1791, even criticism of the colonial status quo was deemed unpatriotic. Any incitement to unrest overseas was made a crime. Slavery and the slave trade became taboo subjects.[21]

What caused the French Revolutionary legislators to reach such a position of determined silence, contrary to the continuous public and parliamentary debates occurring across the Channel? In Britain abolitionism was the beneficiary of the two great petition mobilizations in its favor (1788 and 1791–92). Even its opponents conceded that public opinion, however misled, had crystallized in favor of abolition as a priority national issue. In France the small Parisian abolitionist group found itself lost in a public tumultuously focused on metropolitan reform. The vast national "poll" of French grievances, the Third Estate's *cahiers de doléances* of 1789, called for action against a host of compulsory labor services, including serfdom and corvées. These calls were ten or twenty times as numerous as those seeking action against

---

[20]See Jean-Pierre Hirsch, *La nuit du 4 août* (Paris, 1978), pp. 180–81. John Markoff notes that the proposal for extending serf emancipation to include slaves was one of the few that aroused disapproval among the notables on the floor of the National Assembly. "It would take a slave revolt to match the peasant insurrection [in France] before the legislature really moved on slavery [and more than two years after the slave uprising]"; *The Abolition of Feudalism* (University Park, Pa., 1996), p. 431 n. 12.
[21]David P. Geggus, *Haitian Revolutionary Studies* (Bloomington, Ind., 2002), pp. 159–61.

slavery or the slave trade. The parish cahiers ignored the colonies and slaves altogether.[22]

It was not merely relative inattention, however, that prevented the National Assembly from discussing any abolitionist proposal. In response to the first antislavery initiatives, French colonial and mercantile interests dispatched a volume of antiabolitionist petitions and addresses to the National Assembly that could not be matched by the *Amis des Noirs*. When Thomas Clarkson was sent to France to stimulate the *Amis* to further action in 1789, he was shocked to hear that their only suggestion for generating public pressure was to ask Clarkson to get up a British petition to the French Assembly. Given that he was already accused of acting as a foreign agent in Paris, Clarkson replied that such interference could only be counterproductive. Later developments would affirm his instinctive response.

One must remember that during the first two years of the French Revolution the slave colonies were the most productive area of the French empire, both economically and fiscally. For a bankrupt national government facing mass peasant and urban uprisings and widespread refusal to pay taxes, the slave colonies seemed to be islands of tranquility, prosperity, and revenue in a sea of troubles.[23] Like American southern slaveholders sixty years later, members of that government openly speculated that the metropole, not the colonies, revealed the weakest links in the imperial edifice. Many colonies openly demanded greater autonomy as an incentive for remaining attached to France.

In contrast to Britain, the real pressure on the metropolitan legislature to break the compact of silence came from the colonies. The decisive event was the explosion of a horrific slave revolution in Saint-Domingue, the world's most dynamic and valuable slave colony. The slave uprising that began in August 1791 was enormous from the very outset. Within a month

---

[22] The parish *cahiers* virtually ignored the colonies and slavery altogether. Both categories ranked in the residual "tied for last place." Even in the "elite" *cahiers* of the third estate, slaves ranked below prisoners, serfs, and far below those subject to labor services or royal corvées. See Gilbert Shapiro and John Markoff, *Revolutionary Demands: A Content Analysis of the cahiers de doléances of 1789* (Stanford, 1998), pp. 438, 442 (appendix table 1.1), and Drescher, *Capitalism and Antislavery*, p. 54, table 3.1; and Seymour Drescher, "Women's Mobilization in the Era of Slave Emancipation: Some Anglo-French Comparisons," in *Women's Rights and Transatlantic Slavery in the Era of Emancipation*, ed. Kathryn Kish Sklar and James Brewer Stewart (New Haven, 2007), p. 103, table 5.1.

[23] On the extent of turmoil in France see Markoff, *Abolition of Feudalism*, chap. 7.

more than a thousand plantations had been burned and hundreds of whites killed. An even greater number of slaves were slaughtered indiscriminately in reprisal. The continuous brutality and pain inflicted in the conflict was a clear sign of the enormous social and psychological distance separating all sides in the struggle. Calls for revenge were the order of the day.

A large proportion of newly imported slaves invoked African religious and political traditions to mobilize recruits for the uprising. A few insurgents appealed to the rights of man, but far more often they invoked the authority of the French king against a French national legislature that had responded to their enslavement with indifference and now responded to their revolt with suppression. When the French king was executed and the French Convention declared war on Spain in 1793, many rebel leaders simply switched their allegiances to the Spanish monarchy, which continued to furnish them with arms.[24]

The distance between French civil society and the slave revolution is best illustrated by an event that occurred when British popular mobilization was reaching its peak in the winter of 1791–92. As a result of the Saint-Domingue upheaval, the price of sugar in Europe rose to levels unmatched for a century. At that same moment, Britain was in the midst of its campaign against slave-grown sugar. The reaction in France was quite different. In response to the soaring price of sugar, the women of a poor quarter of Paris began a *taxation populaire*. They seized commodities from a warehouse and sold it to gathered crowds at the traditional "just price." These sugar riots triggered legislative discussion in Paris, but their major concern was with increasing popular access to a product that contemporary British abolitionists were attempting to boycott. No widespread abstentionist movement developed in France in the wake of the colonial uprising. The sugar riots bespoke the relative remoteness of metropolitans from concern with the cause of the rebelling slaves.[25]

The following two years brought a dramatic reversal in the relative positions of British and French policies toward slavery. The catalyst for French

---

[24] See Geggus, *Haitian Revolutionary Studies*, pp. 12–13, and part 3; and Laurent Dubois, *Avengers of the New World: The Story of the Haitian Revolution* (Cambridge, Mass., 2004), chap. 4.
[25] See Drescher, "Women's Mobilization," pp. 98–120. In the wake of the events in Paris a small radical contingent raised their voices in favor of abstention. Several revolutionary societies in the provinces also abjured the use of the "luxuries" of coffee and sugar. See Drescher, *Capitalism and Antislavery*, p. 217 n. 46.

action again came as much from the external military situation as from any major impulse within, even at France's most radical revolutionary moment. By mid-1793 France was at war with all of its neighbors in Europe, and with the British, Dutch, and Spanish empires overseas. With its military resources fully engaged at home, the government could not supply sufficient troops to either suppress the slave revolt in the colonies or to guarantee them against the Anglo-Spanish invasion threat. The French government's Revolutionary agents in Saint-Domingue, led by Léger-Félicité Sonthonax, then made a crucial decision. They decreed emancipation for the colony's slaves and recruited them against both the colonial and enemy forces that clung to the status quo. In response, the radical French government hesitated for months about whether to treat their own colonial agents as traitors or heroes. Finally, in February 1794 the Convention opted to declare all of France's slaves free. The anti-British dimension of the French liberation decree was explicit. In Danton's famous words, French emancipation meant that "today the Englishman is dead."[26]

After Napoleon's seizure of power in 1799 and his conclusion of peace with Britain (1802), the roles of the two nations began to reverse again. France's new ruler restored both slavery and the slave trade in 1802. In three separate negotiations with Bonaparte between 1801 and 1814, the British government tried to conclude a joint abolition of the slave trade. On each occasion Napoleon refused to negotiate. Instead, in one final horrific conflict, Napoleon attempted to reconquer Saint-Domingue at a cost of tens of thousands of his soldiers. The victorious ex-slaves created Haiti, a nation of free citizens. In the rest of France's empire, Napoleon's military mobilization successfully reenslaved tens of thousands of his own citizens. The long bloody conflict between 1791 and 1804 probably cost the new nation 30 percent of its population and bequeathed a militarized society to the survivors. In France itself the volatile and violent episode impacted French antislavery right down to the final abolition of 1848.[27]

French civil society was never mobilized for abolition or emancipation on a scale or intensity similar to British society. Before 1848, there were no mass petitions confronting a reluctant or ambivalent legislature to take

---

[26] Jeremy D. Popkin, *You Are All Free: The Haitian Revolution and the Abolition of Slavery* (New York, 2010).

[27] Dubois, *Avengers*, pp. 251–301.

urgent action in favor of dramatic new legislative moves against the slave trade or slavery in the generations between Napoleon's restoration of slavery and the second emancipation. Although there were a few stirrings of abolitionism among some of the Catholic clergy, the Church remained officially neutral on the issue of emancipation. Neither the hierarchy nor the laity launched major antislavery initiatives. Women were also circumspect. When one small "Petition from the Women of Paris" accrued some signatures in 1847, abolitionist Victor Schoelcher sadly noted that French women still hesitated to rival their British sisters.[28]

What a mass mobilization on the British scale might have done is illustrated by the panic with which the slave interest reacted to the impact of the minor petition movement on the French legislators in 1847. The Chamber of Deputies refused to hear the French citizens who petitioned for emancipation. One Colonial Council hurriedly formulated an emancipation plan that would ensure both indemnity and government-guaranteed plantation labor.[29]

One response of the government was to consider declaring the emancipation of a small number of slaves in the new French colony of Algeria in 1847 as a symbolic response to the ten thousand petitioners for emancipation in 1847. This antislavery gesture would have liberated about as many slaves as there were petitioners. It also had the political advantage of applying only to non-French Muslim slaveholders. Marshall Bugeaud, the governor general of Algeria, dismissed the suggestion as potentially destabilizing to the newly conquered colony. With the British example obviously in mind, Bugeaud asked Paris: Where were the voices of millions of peasants in France supporting the abolitionist demands of the Parisian "liberal theorists" (*theóriciens*)?[30]

The colonial slaves, perhaps sensing the lack of active metropolitan civil society support, initiated no mass uprisings in the decades before their liberation. They may well have anticipated that, contrary to the situation in Britain, metropolitans would regard any slave revolt as an attempt to repeat the scenes of Saint-Domingue. Significantly, the largest French slave uprising occurred in 1848—*after* the arrival of the first news of the

---

[28] Drescher, "Women's Mobilization," pp. 108–9. Jennings, *French Antislavery*.
[29] See Drescher, *Public Opinion*, p. 28, fig. 2, for Anglo-French comparisons.
[30] Drescher, *From Slavery to Freedom*, pp. 172–73, and 178 (for quotation).

Revolution's intention to decree emancipation. They accelerated the promulgation of emancipation in the islands.

What of France's legislators? Following the restoration of the monarchy in France after Napoleon's fall, mention of Haiti's revolution for emancipation remained a completely taboo subject in the two legislative chambers. French representatives did not criticize the government for its ten-year delay in recognizing Haitian independence (1825). No deputy objected to the government's insistence that the Haitians become the only ex-slave population in the world who would have to pay a collective indemnity for their masters' property losses. In the French parliament, the Haitian Revolution was treated as "an event so savage as to need no discussion." An oblique reference to the past produced an outburst of allusions to "revolt," "massacre," and "ruins," adding another military humiliation to the final defeat of French armies in Europe in 1814. The story of French slave emancipation was simply too entwined with fresh memories of division, defeat, and death to warrant inclusion in French nationalist discourse.[31]

It must be emphasized that no French legislator would identify himself as an advocate of slavery. Instead, advocates of reform read France's connection with liberation back into the centuries before the traumatic events of the French and Haitian revolutions or British abolitionism. French adherence to (ultimate) emancipation was grounded in tradition. Christianity was credited with instituting the long-run medieval process that imperceptibly caused slavery to disappear from France itself. For French abolitionists it sufficed to say that the modern French nation had simply contributed to universalizing the theory of rights and the practice of liberty. France could now, like the British, abolish slavery through orderly change.[32]

French legislators, however, were hampered by Britain's antislavery development. By 1815 abolitionism was nationalistically celebrated by a triumphalist Britain. Its mobilized public claimed priority in the fight against slavery. Until Napoleon's abdication in 1814, his government had notoriously refused to even discuss British proposals to include a slave trade abolition in any treaty of peace. Such a prohibition could "never be tolerated by a

---

[31] See Elodie Le Garrec, "Le debat sur l'abolition de la traite des Noirs en France (1814–1831)," thesis, University of Bretagne Sud (2002–3), pp. 202–6.

[32] Olivier Pétré Grenouilleau, "Abolitionnisme et l'idee nationale: Divorces et compromise, France 1789–1831," in *Abolir l'esclavage*, pp. 185–208.

great people who are not yet in a situation to be insulted with impunity." The first colonial minister of the restored Bourbons was equally dismissive of British pressure for French slave trade abolition: "Do you English mean to bind the world?"[33] Only slowly, over the course of two decades, could French legislators bring themselves to insist on fully enforcing a prohibition that their monarch had only reluctantly agreed to after Waterloo. This memory of pressured prohibition made French deputies hesitant to even allude to any British initiative that implied a French "deficit" in its commitment to slave trade suppression. During the entire period of the Bourbon Restoration (1815–30) Britain's popular petitions were never once mentioned by French parliamentarians.[34]

When a French national mobilization over suppression of the slave trade did finally take place, it occurred against a British diplomatic initiative to mobilize the entire European community against the traffic. In 1838, riding the crest of British antislavery's last great popular mobilization, Britain proposed an international treaty to finally close down the transatlantic slave trade. Its most important clause provided for a mutual right-of-search. This allowed naval officers of one nation to board and capture any vessel found carrying slaves to the New World. By September 1840 diplomatic representatives of all the great powers—Britain, Austria, Prussia, Russia, and France—had signed on. Before the French legislature could ratify the treaty, however, another international crisis intervened. During a confrontation between the Pasha of Egypt and his nominal suzerain, the Ottoman Sultan, France aligned itself with the Pasha. The other powers supported the Sultan. They also signed a four-power agreement promising him their full military support in the event of a conflict. Isolated and humiliated, France backed down.

---

[33] See Paul Michael Kielstra, *The Politics of Slave Trade Suppression in Britain and France, 1814–1848* (London, 2000), p. 20; and Robin Blackburn, *The Overthrow of Colonial Slavery, 1776–1848* (London, 1988), p. 320. One of the few abolitionist pamphlets to appear during the diplomatic crisis commented on the correlation between "the apparent indifference of the nation towards the slaves and its lively preoccupation with international questions"; Felix Milliroux, *Demerary, Transition de l'esclavage à la liberté: Colonies françaises, future abolition* (Paris, 1843), p. 128.
[34] Garrec, "Le debat sur l'abolition," p. 110. For a sustained comparative analysis of parliamentary discourse on slavery in France and Britain, see also Frédérique Beauvois, "Indemnisé les planteure pour abolir l'esclavage?" doctoral thesis, University of Lausanne, 2011.

The French moment for revenge came when the anti–slave trade treaty was submitted for legislative ratification in 1842. For the first time in postrevolutionary French history, there was a popular national mobilization over an antislavery question. Inside the legislature and outside in the press there was a virtual consensus. No treaty would be ratified that allowed British warships to stop and board a ship flying the French national colors. Even most legislators belonging to the small French abolitionist society aligned themselves with colonial agents and port chambers of commerce. Amid intense cheering, all of the familiar conspiratorial arguments about British motives were revived. The few voices raised in defense of British good faith were greeted by sardonic laughter and sneering dismissal. The beleaguered French foreign minister, François Guizot, had to abandon consideration of the treaty. Privately, he noted, "I have often fought popular impressions but never a stronger impression."[35]

The collateral damage of the conflict also spilled over into the public discussion of French slave emancipation. The French abolitionist society had planned to hold its first public meeting in Paris, in 1842, with British abolitionists in attendance. The government, citing fears of potential public disorder, forced the abolitionists to abandon the meeting.

In 1848 a second French emancipation came in the wake of yet another revolution. It came in the form of a provisional governmental executive decree. Victor Schoelcher, the abolitionist whose presence in the government was decisive, initially argued for immediate emancipation by decree as a means of averting a slave uprising. After the fact, however, he acknowledged a different reason. It was the situation in the metropole, not the colonies, that precipitated his rush to immediate emancipation. He feared that the newly elected French Constituent Assembly might reflect the low priority of colonial emancipation among French society. An election fought over the great issue of protecting private property in France might have linked liberation to an indemnification of the slaveholders. The relative indifference of the French public to antislavery was again demonstrated. After emancipation was ensured, the Abolitionist Society simply ceased

---

[35]For the above incident see Kielstra, *Politics of Slave Trade Suppression*, pp. 211–17. Three years later, after the British government abandoned its demand for a mutual right of search, a new Anglo-French treaty was ratified for the suppression of the slave trade. For the rest of the century France continued to resist entering into any international treaty providing for the right of search against shipping sailing under the French flag.

to function. No further collective antislavery activity reappeared until the American Civil War.³⁶

The Lull and the Storm: U.S. Emancipation

In some respects antislavery came both early and late to America. The territory that became the United States was the first region in either hemisphere of the Atlantic world to initiate collective political activity against the slave trade. It was also one of the last to enact the national termination of the institution. Over the course of nine decades, from the 1770s to the 1860s, American antislavery developed in ways that both resembled and differed from its transatlantic counterparts. Like the British, late-eighteenth-century Anglo-Americans shared the most widely diffused and least censored communications network in the world. Early in the next century Americans developed an array of voluntary and religious associations that made them frontrunners in an emerging associational world. In terms of civil society their citizens were superbly positioned to emulate the British pattern of antislavery mobilization.

For governments in Britain and France, slavery was always a geographically segregated institution. On one side of the Atlantic lay settlements overwhelmingly dominated by commitment to slavery and the slave trade. On the other lay territories juridically committed to being places where the "air was too free for a slave to breathe," where chattels' status changed as soon as they set foot on the soil of France or England. North America's British colonies entered nationhood in a different situation.³⁷ They were New World colonies that ran a spectrum from miniscule direct dependence on slave labor to one in which the majority of the workforce was both black and enslaved.

Where the proportion of the U.S. slave population was lowest there was little need for large-scale or repeated extraparliamentary mobilizations. North of the Chesapeake the proportion of slaves in the population stood at

---

³⁶Drescher, *From Slavery to Freedom*, pp. 179–81.
³⁷On the juridical situation in prerevolutionary France and pre-abolitionist Britain, see Sue Peabody, *"There Are No Slaves in France": The Political Culture of Race and Slavery in the Ancien Regime* (New York, 1996); Drescher, *Capitalism and Antislavery*, pp. 25–49; and Drescher, *Abolition*, pp. 91–114.

10 percent or less. In these Northern states the abolition of the institution proceeded by slow, incremental steps. Where the proportion was higher there were more extended periods of political debate. The general legislative outcome was a policy of gradual emancipation. Children of slaves were legally freed at birth, with allowance to masters for an obligatory term of servitude in order to cover the cost of raising the children. Further south, slavery remained both a thriving and a rapidly expanding institution. In every colony from Maryland southward, from one-third up to 60 percent of the population was enslaved and vital to the economy. The acquisition of the Louisiana territory, where the institution was already embedded, further added to slavery's expansion.

This divergence of internal development and potential conflict had to be resolved at the national level. Initially, the American response was similar to France's at the beginning of its own national reconstitution. The resolution involved deference to local self-determination. In the early 1770s some American colonial legislatures vainly attempted to curtail or prohibit further importations of overseas slaves in the face of British imperial resistance. In 1776 Thomas Jefferson distilled these frustrated initiatives within a draft article of the Declaration of Independence. It condemned the British monarch for "waging cruel war against human nature itself violating its most sacred rights of life and liberty . . . [by] captivating and carrying a distant people into slavery in another hemisphere [and] leading them to death in their transportation." As with the French National Assembly's deletion of slavery from the intolerable abuses of the old regime, the Continental Congress dropped this accusation from the final version of the Declaration.[38]

That was an accurate harbinger of things to come. Between 1776 and the framing of the federal Constitution there is ample evidence that in the deliberations of the Continental Congress and the United States Confederation, antislavery sentiment was deliberately muted in the interest of national unity. Both the Congress and the Confederation touched upon slavery but never as a moral or political problem to be resolved at the national level.

In retrospect, the decisions of the Constitutional Convention and the French National Assembly seem like lost moments for national debates over

---

[38] Joseph J. Ellis, *American Sphinx: The Character of Thomas Jefferson* (New York, 1997), pp. 51–52.

slavery. Discussions of slavery impinged on many of the deliberations of the Convention, but apart from the slave trade debate, delegates made no concerted effort to affect the future of the institution itself. Unlike their French counterparts, the American delegates did open the door to legislatively ending the fresh importation of slaves from across the Atlantic—but only after a delay of twenty years. On the other hand, the French Constitution did not provide for the return of slaves who successfully escaped to France, as did the American Constitution. The fugitive slave clause passed without an opposing vote from any state at the Convention. In the American case, "all clauses directed specifically at slavery itself seemed to favor the institution."[39] The omission of the word "slave" from both the American and the French constitutions represented the only symbolic concession to antislavery sentiment on either side of the Atlantic.

The implicit American consensus, that forming a more perfect union required excluding antislavery, is evidenced by Benjamin Franklin's silence. The president of the Pennsylvania Abolition Society made no recorded intervention at the Convention in discussions of slavery. Nor did he present the society's memorial requesting the Convention to abolish the slave trade. The pattern was confirmed when the first U.S. Congress met in 1790. Two state Quaker societies petitioned for federal action to address the condition of persons "degraded into perpetual bondage." Southern representatives responded virulently. The House of Representatives affirmed that Congress had no authority "to interfere in the emancipation of slaves, or in the treatment of them within any of the states."[40]

For more than thirty years thereafter there was no manifestation of national antislavery popular opinion remotely resembling the social movement launched in Britain at the very moment when the American Constitution was being ratified. Even when the U.S. transatlantic slave trade was legally prohibited in 1807, there was no general public celebration of its passage. Clarkson's voluminous narrative of British abolition's twenty-year odyssey in the Parliament had no counterpart across the Atlantic. Congress accepted a donated copy of Clarkson only over the objection of sixteen representatives. Apart from some commemoration in northern

---

[39]Don E. Fehrenbacher, *The Slaveholding Republic: An Account of the United States Government's Relations to Slavery*, ed. Ward M. McAfee (New York, 2001), chap. 2: quotation on p. 36.
[40]Ibid., pp. 138–39.

African American communities, visible public reaction to the passage of the American prohibition was muted.[41]

As we have noted, the initial French legislative compact of silence regarding slavery lasted for little more than two years. It was broken by the intervention of Caribbean slaves. In the United States it took four decades before any major confrontation (Missouri statehood) occurred in the national legislative. Even that battle was fought more against the unlimited expansion of the institution than as a direct step toward its diminution. As late as 1830, Daniel Webster ended his most famous speech with the words—"Liberty *and* Union, now and forever, one and inseparable." In 1830, however, "Union" still precluded "liberty" for one kind of person. In that speech Webster repeated, word for word, the Congress's 1790 resolution renouncing any national authority over slaves of any state in the Union. For four full decades, he observed, no northern gentleman in either House of Congress had breached that resolution: "It is the original bargain—the compact—let it stand." Outside Congress no national mobilizations, civil or military, had produced any challenge to America's domestic institution.[42]

Even as Webster issued his reaffirmation of noninterference, American antislavery was poised to enter a new phase. The British model of victorious nonviolent militancy inspired the demand for a new policy. That determination brought the issue of slavery into the vortex of national congressional debate. The organization of the new antislavery movement closely followed the British pattern of civil mobilization, reaching a new intensity in the early 1830s. William Lloyd Garrison had witnessed the cortege of Wilberforce's burial in Westminster Abbey as a national saint. He considered the "instantaneous transformation of almost a million chattels into rational and immortal being" as "the greatest moral miracle of the age."[43]

Within months of the passage of the British Emancipation Act the American Antislavery Society was founded. It made up for lost time, calling for immediate emancipation; publications rolled off the press in the hundreds

---

[41]Howard Albert Ohline, "Politics and Slavery: The Issue of Slavery in National Politics, 1787–1815," Ph.D. dissertation, University of Missouri–Columbia, 1969, pp. 429–30; and Matthew E. Mason, "Slavery Overshadowed: Congress Debates Prohibiting the Atlantic Slave Trade to the United States, 1806–1807," *Journal of the Early Republic* 20 (2000):59–81.

[42]*The Webster-Hayne Debate on the Nature of the Union: Selected Documents*, ed. Herman Belz (Indianapolis, 2000), pp. 89–91.

[43]William Lloyd Garrison, in *The Liberator*, Aug. 20, 1840.

of thousands. Within five years of its national formation, there were 1,346 local branches in the northern United States, claiming a hundred thousand members. American antislavery telescoped other elements of British popular mobilization. Female participation, which had taken nearly four decades to develop in Britain, took less than four years to emerge as a formidable cohort.

None of the European antislavery societies had a large cohort of Afro-Europeans in their ranks. Even within the British empire, apart from individual abolitionist authors and speakers, blacks who mobilized against slavery were transatlantic slave insurgents, separated from Britain by thousands of miles of ocean. The United States offered a new dimension to antislavery agitation. Free African Americans mobilized against slavery in the North either in integrated or parallel antislavery organizations. Most noteworthy, perhaps, is the fact that most free African Americans stuck to the same civil society approach to abolition as did their white British and American counterparts. They neither called for, nor attempted to organize, large-scale slave insurgency in the U.S. South. For most black abolitionists the primary target audience was fellow abolitionists in the United States or Great Britain.[44]

Frederick Douglass is exemplary in this respect. In his speeches before the American Civil War, he did not refer to revolutionary Saint-Domingue/Haiti as a model for African American imitation. "We have discovered," he told both British and American abolitionist audiences, "that there is a power even stronger and more potent than the bullet box and cartridge-box." Even the Revolution of 1848, which produced the second French slave emancipation, did not cause Douglass to abandon his preference for the cumulative power of peaceful mobilization: "What is bloody revolution in France is peaceful reformation in England. The friends and enemies of freedom, meet not at the barricades thrown up in London, but on the broad platform of Exeter Hall. . . . Their Hotel de Ville is the House of Commons. Their fraternity is the unanimous sympathy of the oppressed and hungry millions."[45]

---

[44]See Leon F. Litwack, *North of Slavery: The Negro in the Free States* (Chicago, 1961), p. 219 n., and Richard Blackett, *Building an Antislavery Wall: Black Americans in the Atlantic Abolitionist Movement, 1830–1860* (Baton Rouge, 1983).

[45]Drescher, *Abolition*, p. 266.

With the first onrush of American abolitionist petitions in the 1830s, Southern legislators seemed to be haunted by the British example. They feared that the combined mobilizations of British and American antislavery movements marked a new danger to their domestic institution. "The moral power of the world is against us," Francis Pickens warned his fellow Southerners in Congress. In the Senate, John C. Calhoun pointed to the cumulative power of mass petitions already demonstrated on the other side of the Atlantic. Any contest in which slaveholders could be constantly arraigned before world public opinion would be beyond mortal endurance. "We must, in the end," he warned, "be humbled, degraded, broken down and worn out."[46]

Unfortunately for American abolitionists, neither the American public nor the U.S. Congress reenacted the British scenario of People and Parliament. In Britain, abolitionist activity never encountered the virulent reception that greeted abolitionist agitation. A wave of hostile mobs and riots greeted abolitionist lecturers even in the U.S. North. With the tacit approval of the executive branch, Southerners decisively prevented abolitionist printed matter from moving into their region. Each state was permitted to block the entrance of publications it deemed to be incitements to disorder.

The national legislature was equally accommodating to Southern demands to create a wall of silence against antislavery. By the late 1830s, hundreds of thousands of petitions poured into Washington requesting at least the abolition of the slave trade in the District of Columbia. For eight years Congress imposed a "gag rule" against the formal acknowledgment of antislavery petitions (fig. 3). Even when the gag rule was lifted, the impact of civil society petitioning was far outweighed by the political process. Whatever the power of the petition box over the bullet box, it could not overrule the power of the ballot box. The political and electoral outcomes of national elections in the 1830s and 1840s showed that the overwhelming majority of the enfranchised white majority remained profoundly hostile to any challenge to states' rights to determine the legal status of slavery within their own boundaries.

This consensus presented an almost insuperable barrier to legislating even gradual, much less immediate, emancipation in the short term. A pervasive racist consensus among most of the white citizenry fortified the

---

[46]Ibid., p. 299.

FIG. 3. "Abolition Frowned Down," 1839 lithograph cartoon satirizing the enforcement of the "gag rule" in the House of Representatives prohibiting the discussion or reference to any abolitionist petitions in the House of Representatives. *(Prints and Photographs Division, Library of Congress)*

unwillingness of the enfranchised majority to threaten the institution of slavery where it already existed. As late as the eve of Confederate secession, Americans could be as prone to virulent national unity against British seizures of slavers carrying the American flag as the French had been in the 1840s. In 1858 Abraham Lincoln still foresaw the "ultimate extinction" of slavery in not *"less* than a hundred years *at the least."* Even that forecast presumed that slavery would not be allowed any movement into the territories.[47]

Only Southern policies that threatened to nationalize the institution by encroaching on the autonomy of Northern civil society (e.g., the enforcement of the fugitive slave law) or encroached on the right of the majority to self-determination in organizing new states sufficiently motivated Northern

---

[47] Quoted in Stanley L. Engerman, *Slavery, Emancipation, and Freedom: Comparative Perspectives* (Baton Rouge, 2007), p. 11 (emphasis mine). See also Manisha Sinha, *The Counter-Revolution of Slavery: The Politics and Ideology of South Carolina* (Chapel Hill, 2000). On the American hostile reaction to British naval searches, see Fehrenbacher, *Slaveholding Republic*, pp. 184–87.

political society against Southern demands for ever-greater protection for their now "peculiar institution."

In the end it was not a Northern nonviolent civil mobilization but a Southern military mobilization—a revolution against the existing constitutional compact—that determined the fate of slavery. Like the first French Revolutionary emancipation, the ending of slavery came in the wake of a prolonged armed conflict. It was the war and military victory that transformed the possibilities for immediate emancipation. The American Civil War entailed the death of between 750,000 and 900,000 men under arms. It cost the American nation more than three times the value of slaves in the United States in 1860 and an enormous loss of other wealth. The number of African Americans recruited into the Union armies probably also exceeded that of their counterparts in the Haitian Revolution.

Despite the enormous destruction of American lives and wealth, however, the structure of U.S. civil society never broke down to the extent that it did in the course of the Haitian conflict.[48] In proportion to their respective populations, economies, and polities, the Haitian conflict was far more devastating than its counterpart in the United States. Liberated Haiti emerged from its wars of civil and political revolution far more militarized in structure than did the United States. African Americans were unable, however, to fully share in the political or civil equality apparently assured by America's Second Revolution. The difficulties experienced in passing the Thirteenth Amendment to the Constitution, even after four years of bitter warfare against the Confederate republic, were a harbinger of how difficult it would be to overcome the pervasive sentiment of racial hostility in American civil society that survived the American Civil War. For most African Americans, a segregated society replaced a slave society.

---

[48]See Davis, *Inhuman Bondage*, pp. 298–301; and Claudia Goldin, "The Economics of Emancipation," in *Without Consent or Contract: The Rise and Fall of American Slavery (Technical Papers)*, vol. 2: *Conditions of Slave Life and the Transition to Freedom*, ed. Robert W. Fogel and Stanley L. Engerman (New York, 1992), pp. 614–28. Claudia Goldin and Frank Lewis, "The Economic Costs of the American Civil War," *Journal of Economic History* 75 (1975):304–9. For the cost of slavery to the slaves prior to emancipation, see Jenny Bourne, "Double Take: Abolition and the Size of Property Rights," in this volume. It has recently been argued that we have overlooked the Civil War as history's most massive slave rebellion. See Steven Hahn, "Did We Miss the Greatest Slave Rebellion in Modern History?" in *The Political Worlds of Slavery and Freedom* (Cambridge, Mass., 2009), pp. 55–110.

The relative international impact of British emancipation, the American Civil War, and the Haitian Revolution on New World or global slavery has never been systematically assessed. Absent the Civil War, however, it is easy to imagine that both U.S. and world slavery would have been as robust during the last third of the nineteenth century as they had been for a century before. We might well imagine any number of counterfactual scenarios built on the survival of American slavery beyond the 1860s. What is certain is that in the short term its sudden destruction sent a deep tremor through those New World societies (Cuba, Puerto Rico, and Brazil) where slavery still remained intact. The mid-1860s signaled both the ending of the transatlantic slave trade and the intensification of pressure on the institution of slavery itself in its Ibero-American redoubts.[49]

We can hardly ignore the potential toll of an intact institution tolerated in late-nineteenth-century colonized Africa. Half a century's delay in the timing of New World slave emancipations might have produced even more devastating global consequences than the twentieth century actually experienced. Had the Southern confederacy in the United States succeeded in departing from the Union, the probable costs to its own chattels would have compounded the costs to those enslaved elsewhere. The perpetuation of the largest slaveholding polity in the world would certainly have lessened pressures for rapid emancipation beyond North America. Even without an expansionist slave Confederacy, the Latin American economies still based upon racial slavery might easily have endured until well into the next century.

Only three generations after the abolitions of the transatlantic slave trade and U.S. slavery, Europe itself was reorganized on the basis of an institutionalized racial hierarchy. The program of its rulers axiomatically included the elimination and enslavability of inferior races. As it was, Germany was able to make a strong bid for the dominion of Eurasia. What impact might two major New World slave powers have had on the history of the twentieth century after the rise and expansion of a European state institutionally organized for mass enslavement and annihilation?

Estimating the possible impact of robust New World slaveholding societies on a resurgent and racial slavery in the Old World may demand too

---

[49]Drescher, *Abolition*, pp. 332–71. On the impact of the earlier Haitian Revolution, see David P. Geggus, *The Impact of the Haitian Revolution in the Atlantic World* (Columbia, S.C., 2001).

many contingent outcomes to be counterfactually compelling. At the very least we can hypothesize that the existence of major twentieth-century slave societies in the Americas, and in the Afro-Asian world as well, would hardly have diminished the growth of European racism during the half century of "high imperialism" between the 1880s and the 1930s.[50] Any authoritarian hierarchical state that appeared in the twentieth-century Old World, whether in Europe, Africa, or the Far East, would certainly have attracted the attention and perhaps gained at least the benevolent neutrality of its counterparts in the Americas. There would have been far less of a free New World to redress the wrongs of the Old.

---

[50]I have in mind the world of 1940, with its institutionalized racialized state in the Union of South Africa, and with a rapidly expanding Japanese empire that embraced a racialized state ideology and a massive system of coerced labor production.

Amy S. Greenberg

The Ranchero Spotty

An 1848 Perspective on Abraham Lincoln's Congressional Term

WE ALL KNOW Honest Abe. Young children, the functionally illiterate, even college students who might struggle a bit to locate Mexico on a map can tell you that Honest Abe was America's greatest president.[1] But who remembers the Ranchero Spotty? The rail-splitter gained this sobriquet at the close of 1847 for the single significant position he took during the lone congressional term that most scholars consider a "failure."[2] That was his "Spot Resolutions" opposing the war that the United States was then fighting against Mexico.

La Invasión Norteamericana (as it was known in Mexico) began when President James K. Polk ordered U.S. troops under the command of General Zachary Taylor to a disputed area between Texas and Mexico with the intention of starting a war. Negotiations with Mexico over the fate of her northern territories (Texas, newly annexed as a U.S. state, New Mexico, and California) had failed. Polk wanted war and was planning on declaring war if the Mexican army didn't rise to the bait. On May 9, 1846, Polk and his cabinet agreed to send "a declaration of war against Mexico" to Congress the following Tuesday, but conveniently enough the president received

---

[1]My thanks to Mark E. Neely, a scholar who knows Honest Abe as well as anyone, for his assistance on this essay.
[2]Donald W. Riddle, *Congressman Abraham Lincoln* (Urbana, Ill., 1957), p. 4.

a message, mere hours later, that Mexican forces had killed several U.S. soldiers in a skirmish on April 25.[3]

So it was that on Monday, May 11, Polk appeared in front of Congress and reported that "Mexico has passed the boundary of the United States, has invaded our territory and shed American blood upon American soil.... War exists, and, notwithstanding all our efforts to avoid it, exists by the act of Mexico herself."[4]

Polk attached this declaration of war as a preamble to a bill authorizing funding for the troops. He placed the bill in front of Congress and demanded not only that they declare a war already in progress (for the first time in American history) but also publicly assent to his version of events. His supporters skillfully managed to stifle debate in both the House and the Senate. Although many representatives had serious doubts about Polk's claims, and more suspected that the president had provoked war by moving U.S. troops into an area rightfully claimed by Mexico, Congress overwhelmingly supported Polk's declaration. Only fourteen Whigs in the House of Representatives were brave enough to oppose it.

Abraham Lincoln was a candidate for Congress at the time these events took place. It was a full nineteen months later when he and the rest of the Thirtieth Congress were finally seated. But the war Polk had started in May of 1846 was not yet over, and American soldiers were still dying in Mexico. Congressman Lincoln (fig. 1), the lone Whig in the Illinois congressional delegation, had been seated less than three weeks when he rose to the podium and offered a series of resolutions that called Polk on what was, in his eyes, an obvious lie.

Lincoln demanded to know the exact "spot" upon which Mexicans troops shed "American blood on American soil." Acting every bit the lawyer he was, Lincoln made a series of legal arguments designed to show that American troops began the war by making an unprovoked attack on Mexico. The eight resolutions he offered that day noted that the land in question was Mexican, by historical fact and by occupancy at the time, and asked rhetorically if "the people of that settlement, or a majority of them, or any of them, have ever submitted themselves to the government or laws of Texas or

---

[3]Allan Nevins, ed., *Polk: The Diary of a President, 1845–1849* (New York, 1952), pp. 82–83.
[4]James D. Richardson, ed., *A Compilation of the Messages and Papers of the Presidents, 1789–1897*, 10 vols. (Washington, D.C., 1896–99), 6:2292.

FIG. 1. The only known portrait of Congressman-Elect Abraham Lincoln, this daguerreotype, attributed to Nicholas H. Shepherd, was taken in 1846 or 1847. *(Prints and Photographs Division, Library of Congress)*

of the United States, by consent or by compulsion, either by accepting office, or voting at elections, or paying tax, or serving on juries, or having process served upon them, or in any other way."

Lincoln went further. He reminded listeners that the residents of the "contested region" fled "from the approach of the United States army, leaving unprotected their homes and their growing crops." He also made clear that the "American blood" shed at the Rio Grande belonged to "armed officers and soldiers, sent into that settlement by the military orders of the President, through the Secretary of War."[5] Lincoln returned to the themes of his Spot Resolutions in coming weeks, and with increasing vehemence firmly aligned himself with antiwar forces in Congress.

There was little that was particularly novel about Lincoln's Spot Resolutions. His approach was unusually lawyerly, pointed, and eloquent, but the grounds of his attack were familiar, perhaps even tired by December of 1848. In May 1846, when President Polk initially stunned Congress with his war message, Kentucky Whig Garrett Davis protested that "It is our own President who began this war. He has been carrying it on for months."[6] Other Whigs offered similar complaints both in private and in public. Indeed, it seems unlikely that any but the fiercest Democratic stalwarts in Congress accepted Polk's claims about "American soil" at face value.

As the war progressed, congressional opponents became increasingly creative in their attacks on the president and on U.S. actions in Mexico. In February 1847, Ohio Senator Thomas Corwin (later appointed minister to Mexico by President Lincoln) offered that, "If I were a Mexican I would tell you, 'Have you not room enough in your own country to bury your dead men? If you come into mine we will greet you with bloody hands, and welcome you to hospitable graves.'"[7]

Nor was this strictly a party issue. Democratic proslavery firebrand John C. Calhoun, also in the Senate, argued from the start that the war could have been avoided. He became increasingly a thorn in Polk's side, warning that an invasion of central Mexico would lead to a "war between the races" that would "end in the complete subjugation of the weaker power." He also cautioned Polk that to annex large portions of Mexican territory to the United States would "subject our institutions [meaning slavery] to political death."[8]

---

[5] Abraham Lincoln, Dec. 22, 1847 (Printed Resolution and Preamble on Mexican War: "Spot Resolutions"), Abraham Lincoln Papers, Manuscript Division, Library of Congress (hereafter, ALP). Available online at http://memory.loc.gov/ammem/alhtml/alhome.html.
[6] *Congressional Globe*, 29th Cong., 1st sess., 1848, p. 794.
[7] Ibid., 29th Cong., 2d sess., 1849, app., pp. 216–17.
[8] Quoted in John H. Schroeder, *Mr. Polk's War, American Opposition and Dissent, 1846–1848* (Madison, 1973), pp. 69–70.

Given this context, it is perhaps not surprising that Lincoln's invective was largely ignored in Washington. President Polk mentioned neither Lincoln nor his attacks in his diary, although Polk kept a very detailed diary, full of accusations of disloyalty against politicians he believed to be traducing his administration and hampering the war effort.

The picture was different back in Illinois, where Lincoln's Spot Resolutions were big news. The Whig press was largely supportive of Lincoln, if not energetically so. It was the Democratic press that evinced true enthusiasm for the resolutions, which were precisely the evidence they needed to tar Lincoln as a new "Benedict Arnold." The *Illinois State Register* labeled him "the Ranchero Spotty," and the *Peoria Press* predicted "What an epitaph: 'Died of the *Spotted Fever*.' Poor Lincoln."[9] Illinois Democratic newspapers were unified in agreement that the "miserable man of 'spots'" was following a "traitorous course in Congress."[10] The Democratic press in neighboring states also joined the chorus of disapproval of the Ranchero Spotty.[11]

Lincoln's opposition to the war would prove the signature position of his congressional term. During his second year in office he delivered an uninspired address on federal aid for internal improvements that, he admitted, "no one will read," and a speech in favor of the Whig candidate for president in 1848.[12] He worked to write legislation to institute gradual emancipation in Washington, D.C., but when it became clear that said legislation had no chance of passing, he decided against submitting it. The Ranchero Spotty chose not to stand for reelection in 1848. A Democrat won his seat, previously considered the only "safe" Whig congressional seat in Illinois.

Charges of "spotted fever" followed Lincoln long after he left Congress. During their famed 1858 senatorial campaign debates, Stephen A. Douglas reminded the Illinois public that "Whilst in Congress," Lincoln "distinguished himself by his opposition to the Mexican War, taking the side of the common enemy against his own country; and when he returned home he found that the indignation of the people followed him everywhere, and

---

[9] "Benedict Arnold" and "Ranchero Spotty" in *Illinois State Register*, Mar. 10, 1848; "Died" in the *Peoria Press*, quoted in the *State Register*, Feb. 25, 1848.

[10] Quoted in David Herbert Donald, *Lincoln* (New York, 1995), p. 125.

[11] See Gabor S. Boritt, "A Question of Political Suicide?: Lincoln's Opposition to the Mexican War," *Journal of the Illinois State Historical Society* 67 (1974):87, for a complete list of citations.

[12] Lincoln to William Herndon, June 22, 1848, in Roy P. Basler, ed., *The Collected Works of Abraham Lincoln*, 9 vols. (New Brunswick, N.J., 1953–55), 1:492.

he was again submerged or obliged to retire into private life, forgotten by his former friends."[13] The editor of the *Chicago Tribune* wrote a confidential letter to Lincoln afterward, warning the candidate that Douglas's charges were "calculated to do mischief" among potential Republican voters. "Tens of thousands of our party are old Democrats, and you know their sentiments on this Mexican War supply question."[14]

Lincoln did know. In point of fact, Congressman Lincoln was always careful to distinguish between his support for the troops in the field and his opposition to Polk. He well understood, without having to be told by a newspaper editor, what happened to politicians who failed to vote funds to soldiers in the field, or to support their families at home. The immolation of the Federalist Party as a result of their opposition to the War of 1812 offered a cautionary tale to every dissident Whig in America. As one former Federalist turned Whig explained, when asked if he would oppose the war with Mexico in 1847, "No, by G-d, I opposed one war, and it ruined me, and hence forth I am for *War, Pestilence* and *Famine*."[15] Republican Abraham Lincoln, who had watched his beloved Whig Party collapse in the 1850s, was well aware of the necessity of evincing patriotism in 1858 in front of his fragile new political coalition.

But again in 1860, Lincoln's opponents revisited the legend of the Ranchero Spotty, accusing him of aiding and abetting the enemy in 1848. The charges did not fall on dull ears; questions about Lincoln's patriotism and actions at that time remained unresolved among voters of all education levels. One "undisided yet . . . honest man" wrote Republican candidate Lincoln in 1860 to ask two questions: "the first is this did you vote against sending provisions to the soldiers when they was in mexico . . . the second is this did you refuse to vote A bill of thanks to the soldiers that fought in mexico did you say that you would not vote A bill of thanks to the soldiers without they would add this amendment to it. that it was an injust war."[16]

A New York iron merchant also hoped for clarification before casting his vote in 1860. On business stationery featuring an attractive representation

---

[13] "First Joint Debate, Ottawa, August 21, 1858," Robert W. Johannsen, ed., *The Lincoln-Douglas Debates of 1858* (New York, 1965), p. 42.
[14] Joseph Medill to Abraham Lincoln, June 23, 1858, ALP.
[15] Justin Butterfield, quoted in Boritt, "A Question of Political Suicide?," p. 100.
[16] William Honselman to Abraham Lincoln, Oct. 21, 1860, ALP.

of his spacious iron dealership (fig. 2), William H. Wilson queried Lincoln, "Will you be kind enough to say if you *did* or *did not* while you were in congress vote against supplies to the american army while on the Battle fields of Mexico. The charge has been brought forward by your opponents and *I* have as often charged it to be a *falsehood* and although opposed to betting I as a last resort have agreed to back *my* opinion that such was not the fact."[17]

Lincoln scholars have never evinced much enthusiasm for the study of his single congressional term. There is exactly one full-length study of Lincoln in Congress, while volumes that focus on Lincoln's early years, most notably Don Fehrenbacher's *Prelude to Greatness*, have taken 1850 as the starting point for considering the evolution of Lincoln's political "greatness."[18]

Furthermore, as the brief introduction to Lincoln's Spot Resolutions I have just provided demonstrates, it is almost impossible to avoid slipping from Lincoln in 1848 to Lincoln in 1860. For the same reasons that the study of the U.S.–Mexico war has languished as a result of its interpretive status as a prelude to or cause of the Civil War, so too has the study of Lincoln's antiwar activity suffered from an all-consuming interest in Lincoln's presidency and leadership during the greater military struggle thirteen years later. The pull of the Civil War is such that it has proved difficult for scholars to take seriously either the 1847 war, or opposition to that war by Lincoln, on their own terms.[19]

Not surprisingly, then, those few scholars who have expressed interest in Lincoln's Spot Resolutions have done so by contextualizing the resolutions within the evolution of his political leadership. In particular, they have focused on two questions, both of which reflect on the development of Lincoln's political acumen. The most heated debate, although one hesitates to apply the term to a rather limited discussion, has focused on the assertion that the Spot Resolutions "cost" Lincoln his seat, and whether, as Fehrenbacher put it, the victory of a Democrat in the 1848 race for Lincoln's seat "could only be interpreted as a repudiation of 'Spotty' Lincoln's views on the Mexican War."[20]

---

[17]William H. Wilson to Abraham Lincoln, Oct. 29, 1860, ibid.
[18]Donald W. Riddle, *Congressman Abraham Lincoln* (Urbana, Ill., 1957); Don E. Fehrenbacher, *Prelude to Greatness: Lincoln in the 1850s* (Stanford, 1962).
[19]The premier statement of the U.S.–Mexico war as prelude is offered in James M. McPherson, *Battle Cry of Freedom: The Civil War Era* (New York, 1988). This paradigm may be shifting. Daniel Walker Howe's *What Hath God Wrought: The Transformation of America, 1815–1848* (New York, 2007) places imperialism and the war at the heart of his narrative of the history of Jacksonian America.
[20]Fehrenbacher, *Prelude to Greatness*, p. 1.

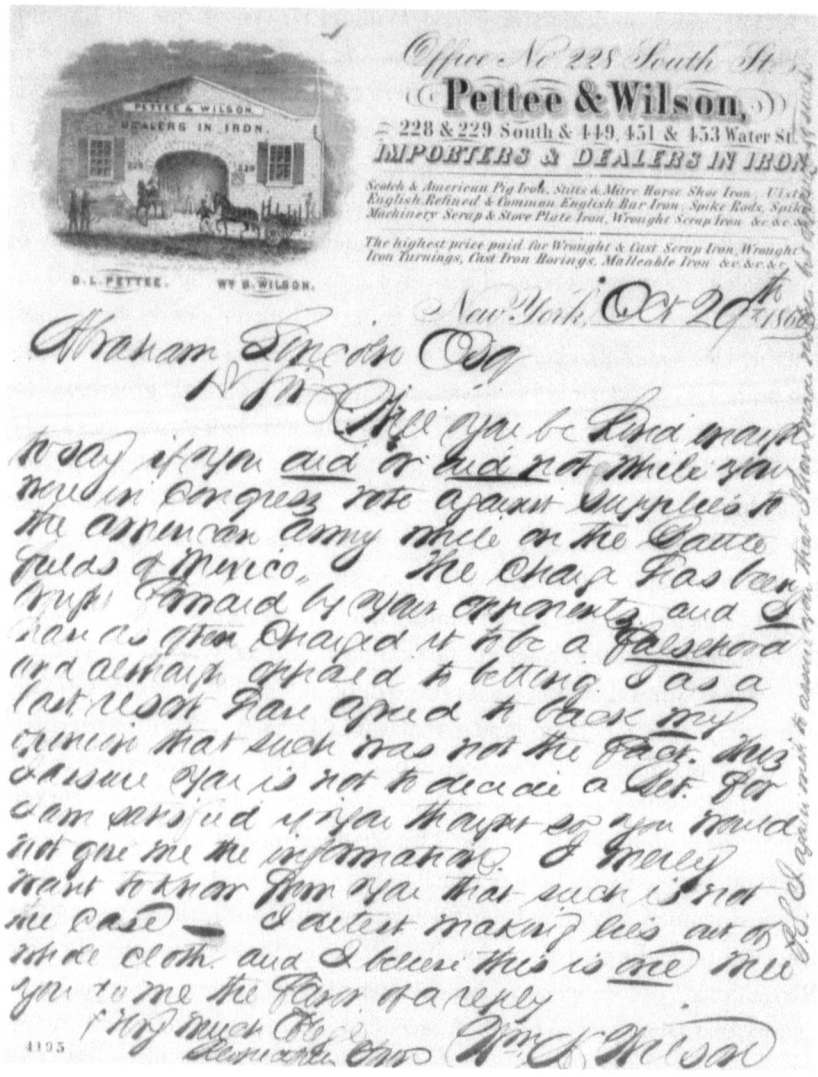

FIG. 2. In 1860 even some wealthy and well-educated voters harbored doubts about Lincoln's war record as a congressman. *(Letter from William H. Wilson to Abraham Lincoln, Monday, Oct. 29, 1860, the Abraham Lincoln Papers at the Library of Congress)*

For about half a century after the 1928 publication of Albert Beveridge's brilliant two-volume study, *Abraham Lincoln 1808–1858*, a near unanimity existed among scholars that Lincoln's position poisoned him among Illinois voters and forced him out of Congress, despite the fact that, as his law partner William Herndon claimed, he would certainly have run for reelection if he hadn't committed "political suicide" by opposing the war.[21]

But in an exhaustively researched "argument by analogy" in 1978, Mark E. Neely persuasively argued that Lincoln's stance against the war (but always supporting the troops) was perfectly palatable to Illinois Whig voters, and if the example of Indiana is relevant, was far from radical among congressmen from that region in similarly "safe" Whig seats. Neely suggests that Lincoln chose not to run for a second term in Congress in 1848 because he didn't enjoy living in Washington.[22]

The second argument has focused on the sincerity of Lincoln's opposition to the war. Again, Beveridge was the source of an argument that for decades virtually all scholars found persuasive: that Lincoln adopted his position opposing the U.S.–Mexico war in the hopes of currying favor with the East Coast power brokers of his party. His attack on Polk and his war was a political gamble that either went horribly wrong (if one believes that the Ranchero Spotty was essentially forced out of office as a result) or illuminates his political savvy (if one accepts Neely's argument), but was by no means heartfelt.

In 1974, Gabor Boritt offered a revisionist reading proposing that, rather than view Lincoln's opposition to the war as opportunistic, we recognize it as an early example of the "politics of morality" that would become his signature as president. "Lincoln's opposition to the Mexican War had as firm an ethical foundation as did his antislavery beliefs," Boritt concluded.[23]

What has yet to be reevaluated is the extent to which Lincoln's sole congressional term was a failure. Even if Lincoln left after his single term, by choice, having done virtually nothing beyond presenting the Spot Resolutions (which were not adopted by Congress), can we consider his first sojourn in Washington in any way a success?

This essay proposes that in order to answer this question we need to forget about the president Lincoln was later to become, and instead adopt an

---

[21] Albert Beveridge, *Abraham Lincoln, 1809–1858*, 2 vols. (Boston, 1928); William H. Herndon and Jesse W. Weik, *Abraham Lincoln: The True Story of a Great Life*, 2 vols. (New York, 1901), 2:270.

[22] Mark E. Neely Jr., "Lincoln and the Mexican War: An Argument by Analogy," *Civil War History* 24 (March 1978):5–24.

[23] Boritt, "A Question of Political Suicide?," pp. 79–100, quote on p. 100.

1848 perspective. From the viewpoint of January 1848, the most important issue in America was the war still ongoing with Mexico. When would it end? How would it end? How much of Mexico would be ceded to the United States? How many more Americans would die?

From this vantage point it makes sense to consider Congressman Lincoln and his actions in relation to the U.S.–Mexico war, or, to adopt the language of the day, to think about him as an actor in the drama of the war, not as the Honest Abe he would later become, but as the Ranchero Spotty.

Why Ranchero? The term would have had clear meaning to readers, perhaps more then than it does today, thanks to popular fiction produced in response to the war. Mexican ranchers were stock characters in many fictional works produced after the start of hostilities with Mexico, and in particular in two popular 1847 dime novels, Charles Averill's *The Mexican Ranchero; or, The Maid of the Chapparal* and Newton Curtis's *The Hunted Chief: or Female Ranchero*.[24]

These two novels were written by well-known authors, and are among the best of a healthy genre of sensationalistic war fiction. Both were set in Mexico, both placed fictional characters in real battles, and both featured plenty of sex, violence, and racial stereotyping. Both highlighted romance between white American soldiers and light-skinned Mexican women that helped U.S. readers imagine the ultimate resolution of a violent war not as theft, misery, and the forced displacement of Mexican citizens, but as international race romance.[25]

The journalist who imagined Lincoln as a ranchero meant nothing flattering by the comparison. So virulent and widespread was racism against Mexicans that it was universally understood by readers that bestowing a Spanish sobriquet on an American politician, even a somewhat positive title like ranchero (as opposed to, say, peon), was damming at any point in the era, let alone during a time of war. By tarring Lincoln as the Ranchero Spotty, the

---

[24]Charles Averill, *The Mexican Ranchero; or, The Maid of the Chapparal* (Boston, 1847); Newton Curtis, *The Hunted Chief: or Female Ranchero* (New York, 1847); Sacvan Bercovitch, ed., *The Cambridge History of American Literature*, 8 vols. (Cambridge, 1994–2005), 2:162.

[25]On the literature of sensation see Shelley Streeby, *American Sensations: Class, Empire and the Production of Popular Culture* (Berkeley, Calif., 2002); on the relationship between territorial annexation and interracial romance, see Amy S. Greenberg, *Manifest Manhood and the Antebellum American Empire* (Cambridge, 2005), pp. 88–134.

Illinois State Register suggested not just that Lincoln was siding with Mexico, but that he was himself tarred, or racialized, Mexican, that he was an evil figure drawn from popular melodrama about the war with Mexico.[26]

Nor was he just any evil Mexican figure. The rancheros in both Averill's and Curtis's dime novels are skilled guerrillas who terrorize American troops by "picking off every one who ventured alone at any distance from the camp," and in Averill's book, attempt to prevent peace by kidnapping Nicholas Trist, the American diplomat, as he is in the process of bringing a treaty to Guadalupe Hidalgo. In reality, dealing with guerrilla activity was an intractable problem for U.S. troops, and one that had been widely commented on by the time Lincoln delivered his Spot Resolutions. It would hardly have been a stretch to place congressional critics of the war in the same category as these Mexican partisans, who were endangering the troops with what were considered to be cowardly, vicious, and unmanly attacks. President Polk had made a similar comparison early in the conflict when he charged that criticism of the war gave "aid and comfort" to the enemy.[27]

By suggesting that we focus on the Ranchero Spotty when thinking about the Spot Resolutions, I am not suggesting that Lincoln was actually a pro-Mexican partisan, or that anyone believed that Lincoln was either Mexican or literally a villain out of a dime novel. But I will suggest that by considering his actions from the perspective of a particular moment, when the war with Mexico was unresolved and seemingly unresolvable, we can gain a new appreciation for Lincoln's actions, one which vindicates not only the Spot Resolutions, but Lincoln's congressional term as a whole.

To understand Abraham Lincoln's signature position in the Thirtieth Congress, one needs to understand the U.S.–Mexico war. The war with Mexico had the highest casualty rate of any American war: almost 17 percent of the 79,000 American soldiers who served died, mainly from disease. It also had the highest desertion rate of any U.S. conflict, about 8 percent. This

---

[26]For two different and compelling views of the mutability of race in America, and the ability of Americans to "race" those they considered foreign, see Noel Ignatiev, *How the Irish Became White* (New York, 1996); Kristin Tegtmeier Oertel, *Bleeding Borders: Race, Gender, and Violence in Pre-Civil War Kansas* (Baton Rouge, 2009).

[27]Curtis, *The Hunted Chief*, p. 3; Polk quote, Richardson, *Messages and Papers of the Presidents*, 6:2323. On the impact of guerrilla activity on U.S. forces, see Irving W. Levinson, *Wars within War: Mexican Guerrillas, Domestic Elites, and the United States of America, 1846–1848* (Fort Worth, Tex., 2005).

was the first war fought by America for reasons other than self-defense, it set a precedent for military action in Latin America in the name of American interests, and it permanently damaged relations with Mexico.[28]

It also set the United States on the road to empire. At the close of the war, Mexico transferred 500,000 square miles of her territory to the United States in exchange for fifteen million dollars. The U.S. states of California, New Mexico, Nevada, and Utah, as well as parts of Arizona, Colorado, and Wyoming, are all products of the Mexican cession ratified in the 1848 Treaty of Guadalupe Hidalgo.

The American public, schooled in the ideology of Manifest Destiny, and firmly convinced of the racial and cultural inferiority of Mexicans, largely embraced this war. But a vigorous antiwar movement, centered in New England and led by abolitionists, offered sharp critiques of the morality of the war. Antiwar activists argued that the war was unjust, that might did not make right, and that the conflict was evidence of a "slave power" manipulating the government in order to expand slavery.[29]

Polk's initial call for troops resulted in an outpouring of volunteer enthusiasm. There was great support for the war among northern Democrats who believed expansion was healthy for democracy, desired California's ports in order to commercially expand into Asia, and saw the annexation of Texas and California as the best means of preventing British encroachment in North America. But when Polk made it clear that he expected Mexico to cede a large portion of her territory at the close of the war, many in the North began to question whether Polk was waging war in the interest of southern slaveholders. When Pennsylvania Democrat David Wilmot offered a rider to a war appropriations bill in August of 1846 on the floor of Congress that banned slavery from any territory won from Mexico, he revealed the increasing sectional rift and growing power of free-soil ideology in the North.

At the outset of the war most European observers predicted that Mexico, fighting at home with her large standing army, would easily defeat the

---

[28]For background information on the war, see Amy S. Greenberg, "Mexican-American War," *The Princeton Encyclopedia of American Political History*, ed. Michael Kazin, 2 vols. (Princeton, N.J., 2009), 2:493–97.

[29]On the antiwar movement, see Schroeder, *Mr. Polk's War*; Frederick Merk, "Dissent in the Mexican War," *Proceedings of the Massachusetts Historical Society*, 3d ser., 81 (1969):120–36.

invaders from the north. But the war was actually a string of victories for the United States. The U.S. cause was greatly aided by ongoing wars between Mexican settlers and independent Indians in the Southwest, by political instability in Mexico City, and by the inept military leadership of General Antonio López de Santa Anna.

General Stephen W. Kearny's troops easily conquered New Mexico, and an initial revolt of Anglo settlers under the command of Captain John C. Frémont in California (known as the Bear Flag Revolt) culminated in the surrender of Mexican *Californios* to American forces in January of 1847. Zachary Taylor had secured the northern half of Mexico by the end of February 1847 after a series of stunning victories culminating in the battle of Buena Vista, where fewer than 5,000 U.S. soldiers defeated a Mexican army of 20,000. But the incensed Mexican government refused to negotiate.

As a result, Polk sent General Winfield Scott to Mexico's heartland. Scott's troops completed an amphibious assault on the port of Vera Cruz in Mexico's south, and marched west. At Cerro Gordo U.S. forces flanked and drove a much larger Mexican army out of a defensive position, clearing the way for a march on the capital, where they successfully stormed Chapúltepec Castle guarding Mexico City. Still, the Mexican government refused to negotiate, and after Scott's forces captured Mexico City in September 1847, the army was thrust into a tedious occupation of the nation's capital and tormented by guerrilla warfare. With no end to the war in sight, antiwar sentiment began to mount in the summer and fall of 1847.

Antiwar agitation in Congress also became increasingly animated in the second half of 1847. Dozens of antiwar petitions were sent to Congress from the Northeast and upper Midwest. In the midterm elections, Whigs took control of the House of Representatives, and when the Thirtieth Congress was seated, Polk found himself on the defensive about a war that most Americans agreed had gone on much too long.

Let us now place the Ranchero Spotty in this picture. Lincoln was nominated for Congress in May of 1846, just as the war began. His interest in foreign policy was low. The issues that mattered to him were economic: tariffs, internal improvements, and banking. In 1845, before his nomination, he wrote to a friend, "I never was much interested in the Texas question. I never could see much good to come of annexation; inasmuch, as they were already a free republican people on our own model; on the other hand, I never could very clearly see how the annexation would augment the evil of slavery. It always seems to me that slaves would be taken there in about equal numbers, with or without annexation."[30]

Lincoln did the best he could to avoid talking about the war while campaigning, although at a war rally in Springfield on May 30 he reportedly spoke "on the necessity of prompt and united action to support" the war, and called for volunteers. Seventy men signed up, in part, no doubt, due to Lincoln's "warm, thrilling, and effective" speech.[31] There is no evidence that he spoke about the war again during his campaign.

Lincoln and the rest of the Thirtieth Congress weren't seated until December 1847. In November he and his family set off on a rather circuitous route from Illinois to Washington, stopping along the way in Lexington, home of his in-laws, the Todd family. Scholars have suggested this was an important visit for Lincoln, his first extended exposure to slavery, and his first face-to-face encounter with his "beau ideal of a statesman," Henry Clay (fig. 3).

Henry Clay had been in seclusion at his Kentucky home since his devastating loss to Polk in the presidential race of 1844, and between 1845 and 1847 Clay suffered a series of personal traumas. He almost lost his house after cosigning a debt with his son, one grandson was killed, one son institutionalized, and worst of all, his favorite son, Henry Clay Jr., was killed in action during the signature battle of the war with Mexico, the February 1847 Battle of Buena Vista.[32]

The Whig party had for some time been imploring Clay, the titular head of their party, to speak out publicly against the war. In November 1847, after mourning his son, and being baptized into the Episcopal Church, Clay agreed to do so, and he decided to do so in Lexington. On November 14, 1847, at age seventy, and after a two-year political absence, Henry Clay delivered a monumental speech, and Abraham Lincoln was almost certainly in the audience.

Clay called the war with Mexico "unnecessary" and a war of "offensive aggression" that resulted in "a waste of human treasure ... mangled bodies ... death, and ... desolation." In images as gloomy as the weather, Clay told his audience that the United States had lost her "unsullied

---

[30]Basler, *Collected Works*, 1:347–48.

[31]*Sangamo Journal*, June 4, 1846, quoted in Riddle, *Congressman Abraham Lincoln*, p. 11.

[32]On Henry Clay see Robert V. Remini, *Henry Clay: Statesman for the Union* (New York, 1993).

FIG. 3. Daguerreotype of Henry Clay, taken by Matthew Brady's studio between 1850 and 1852. *(Prints and Photographs Division, Library of Congress)*

character" internationally and declared that the only end to this disgraceful and immoral war was the immediate withdrawal of all American troops from Mexico. He also declared that "slavery was a great evil" and directly connected the war with Mexico and the evils of slavery. Thanks to the newly developed telegraph, Clay's speech was reprinted within the week around the country.³³

One politician in particular was convinced by Clay's rousing condemnation of the war, and that was Lincoln. He wrote his law partner, William Herndon, that "as you are all so anxious for me to distinguish myself, I have concluded to do so before long."³⁴ Under ordinary circumstances Abraham Lincoln would have devoted his first congressional speech to the subject of internal improvements, particularly given that he had attended a convention on rivers and harbors in Chicago the summer before.³⁵ But these were not ordinary circumstances. Lincoln now saw clearly that his issue in Congress would not be rivers, harbors, or tariffs. It was a time of national crisis. If Henry Clay could attack the war, the president, and the spread of slavery, so could he.

When Lincoln arrived in Washington two weeks later, he found the political scene in tumult. Many congressional Whigs had finally moved to reject the war, and the level of their invective on the House floor was high and getting higher. A national war-weariness was now evident even to politicians previously intimidated by Polk. Yet the president and his Democrats were still strong, especially in the South and the West. There were Democrats demanding that Polk bully Mexico harder—that he take all of Mexico as spoils of war.

And three weeks after being seated, Lincoln introduced the Spot Resolutions. The extent to which he was influenced by Clay's speech is evident in the phrases and ideas that Lincoln borrowed directly from Clay, that the "spot" in question was "within the very disputed district," that the war resulted from Polk's order that Taylor move his troops to the Rio Grande, and that Polk had never made the purpose of the war clear.³⁶

One long-time "sincere friend" of Lincoln's, the *Tazewell* (Illinois) *Whig* editor Anson G. Henry, had been less impressed than Lincoln by Clay's Lexington speech, and, like Herndon, was not at all sure that the antiwar direction many Midwestern Whigs were taking was a wise one. It wasn't that Henry supported the war against Mexico, but that Clay's position

---

³³James F. Hopkins and Robert Seager, eds., *The Papers of Henry Clay*, 11 vols. (Lexington, Ky., 1959–92), vol. 10 (ed. Melba Porter Hay), pp. 361–76.
³⁴Herndon and Weik, *Abraham Lincoln*, p. 261.
³⁵Thanks to Mark E. Neely for pointing this out.
³⁶Riddle, *Congressman Abraham Lincoln*, p. 9

opposing any territorial indemnity from Mexico would cost the Whigs an opportunity to gain vast new domains of free territory via the Wilmot Proviso, which was making an unsteady way through Congress. "The South would have Texas with slavery, & now I will try to get Free Territory as an offset, & this is fair, & nothing more. . . . The Whigs now have the power" with the Wilmot Proviso to force the Democrats "to swallow the same kind of a pill they forced down our throats in May '46," when they manufactured a war for territory.

It is unclear if Henry had heard about Lincoln's Spot Resolutions of the week before, which, however stark, said nothing about the territorial issue that Henry believed to be potentially fatal to the party. Henry admitted feeling "a very great anxiety to know what course you design taking in relation to the Mexican War. I hope you will not feel disposed to go with Mr. Clay against all Territory." He predicted that "that speech of Mr Clay will beat us as a party for years to come, unless we can unite upon 'Old Zach.'"

The difficulty that many Midwestern Whigs had with Clay's position is indicated by the fact that Henry was no longer sure if he could continue editing a Whig newspaper under the circumstances. When Lincoln's friend Edward Baker lined up behind Clay and opposed any Mexican territory, Henry couldn't even report it. He admitted to Lincoln that "I did not like the ground he took, and I did not report him as taking as strong ground against Territory *as he really did* for I did not think it would do our party or him any good."[37]

At least one friend, William Herndon, begged Lincoln to stop attacking Polk, and warned that his censure of Polk would end his political career. After Lincoln cast a vote in favor of the Ashmun Amendment, which affirmed that "the war was unnecessarily and unconstitutionally commenced by the president," Herndon became further incensed. Lincoln responded that "if you had been in my place you would have voted just as I did. Would you have voted what you felt and knew was a lie? I know you would not. . . . You are compelled to speak; and your only alternative is to tell the truth or tell a lie. I can not doubt which you would do."[38]

---

[37]Anson G. Henry to Abraham Lincoln, Dec. 29, 1847, ALP. On Henry, see Paul M. Zall, "Dr. Anson G. Henry (1804–65): Lincoln's Junkyard Dog," in *Lincoln Looks West: From the Mississippi to the Pacific*, ed. Richard W. Etulain (Carbondale, Ill., 2010), pp. 174–88.
[38]Herndon and Weik, *Abraham Lincoln*, p. 267.

Here, again, it is easy to find one's attention slipping from 1848 to the timeless Honest Abe of national myth, and to assume that Lincoln was just speaking the truth and doing the right thing. But the truth is more complicated. In fact, Anson Henry's concern about the electability of antiwar Whigs was shared by Lincoln. While Henry Clay might be Lincoln's beau ideal of a politician, Lincoln seems to have agreed with Henry that Clay's courageous Lexington speech had doomed him as a candidate. Lincoln might be opposed in principle to taking land from Mexico, but he recognized that this position was untenable from a national perspective. He voted against a "no territory" resolution in early January when one appeared before Congress.[39]

Lincoln also began to work for Zachary Taylor's election, even while attacking Polk in Congress. As the lone Whig from Illinois in Congress, and as an early supporter of Taylor's presidential aspirations, he was in a unique position to shape Taylor's candidacy. In notes he prepared in January 1848 for a speech to be delivered by the presidential candidate and war hero, Lincoln suggested that Taylor tell his audience: "As to the Mexican war, I still think the defensive line policy the best to terminate it—In a final treaty of peace, we shall probably be under a sort of necessity of taking some teritory; but it is my desire that we shall not acquire any extending so far South as to enlarge and agrivate the distracting question of slavery—Should I come into the presidency before these questions shall be settled, I should act in relation to them in accordance with the views here expressed."[40]

Yet in spite of whatever misgivings he might have had about the political ramifications of his position, the Ranchero Spotty continued to raise the heat of his rhetoric against Polk. On January 11, he made his first full-length congressional speech, an elaborate attack on Polk. As Lincoln later wrote out the speech for publication, he savaged the president.

> He is deeply conscious of being in the wrong—that he feels the blood of this war, like the blood of Abel, is crying to Heaven against him. That originally having some strong motive—what, I will not stop now to give my opinion concerning—to involve the two countries in a war, and trusting to escape scrutiny, by fixing the public gaze upon the exceeding brightness of military

---

[39]Mark E. Neely, "War and Partisanship: What Lincoln Learned from James K. Polk," *Journal of the Illinois State Historical Society* 74 (1981):199–216.

[40]Abraham Lincoln, [Jan.?] 1848 (Notes on What Zachary Taylor Should Say), ALP.

glory—that attractive rainbow, that rises in showers of blood, that serpent's eye, that charms to destroy—he plunged into it, and has swept, *on* and *on*, till, disappointed in his calculation of the ease with which Mexico might be subdued, he now finds himself, he knows not where—How like the half insane mumbling of a fever-dream, is the whole war part of his late message![41]

It is possible that the speech Lincoln actually delivered was even more passionate than the version he recorded for posterity. According to one hostile report, reprinted in the *Illinois State Register*, the Ranchero Spotty asked his audience if "God of Heaven has forgotten to defend the weak and innocent, and permitted the strong band of murderers and demons from hell to kill men, women, and children, and lay waste and pillage the land of the just."[42] Both versions of the speech suggest that he was deeply committed to attacking Polk and his war, even while his private writings suggest that he was aware of the political implications of his attack. He emulated Henry Clay, but campaigned for Taylor. Perhaps there was something of the guerrilla about our hero after all?

Little did the Ranchero Spotty know, but the president had suddenly found himself "he knows not where," utterly confounded by the chain of events. Back in the summer of 1847, Polk had dispatched diplomat Nicholas Trist to negotiate a treaty with Mexico, authorizing him to set a boundary between the two nations more or less where it ultimately was set. But as the occupation of Mexico City wore on, a movement to take all of Mexico as spoils of war suggested to the president that his original offer might have been shortsighted. General Taylor had earlier suggested to Polk that a boundary at either the Río Grande or the "the Sierra Madre Line," giving the United States the cities of Matamoros and Monterrey, and the states of Chihuahua and Sonora, "was the best course that can be adopted." He told Polk that the Sierra Madre line would be easily defensible with small garrisons at Monterrey, Saltillo, Monclova, Linares, Victoria, and Tampico, and Polk grew hungry for more territory.[43]

By January 1848, Polk was siding with the aggressive expansionists in his cabinet, believing that the ideal location for a boundary would fall

---

[41]Abraham Lincoln to Congress, Jan. 12, 1848 (revised draft prepared for publication), ALP.
[42]Quoted in Beveridge, *Abraham Lincoln*, 1:430.
[43]John Frost, *Pictorial History of Mexico and the Mexican War* (Philadelphia, 1871), p. 339.

somewhere along the twenty-sixth parallel, running directly west from Matamoros, below the southern tip of Texas at the Río Grande, including at least a portion of Baja California. This would have given the United States another 187,000 square miles, or about a third of Mexico's territory below the current international boundary.

In the meantime, Polk recalled Trist, but as the president learned in early January, the diplomat refused to come home and began negotiating without authorization on behalf of the United States. Trist had come to the conclusion that the war should be ended with as little territorial loss to Mexico as possible. With his recall known to all, along with the certain increased territorial demand from any future negotiator, Trist and his Mexican counterparts met in the town of Guadalupe Hidalgo and hammered out a treaty. Polk received the treaty on February 29.

Placing Lincoln's Spot Resolutions, and his January attack on Polk, in the context of these ongoing negotiations provides an alternative perspective on the success of Lincoln's congressional term, as opposed to a retrospective evaluation grounded in his presidential career. Lincoln offered his Spot Resolutions just before Christmas. On January 2 Polk informed his cabinet that at the very least, "We might accede to a cession of New Mexico, the two Californias, and the passage across the Isthmus of Tehuantepec, paying for them a much less sum than Mr. Trist had been authorized to offer, and that we should in addition secure the port of Tampico" (fig. 4).[44]

Several days later, Polk learned that Trist had ignored his orders, and was now negotiating on his own. Within two weeks of this shocking realization, Lincoln attacked Polk directly. About a month later, on February 19, the Treaty of Guadalupe Hidalgo arrived in Washington. Entirely against his will, Polk concluded that he had to accept the treaty, in part because of congressional agitation against the war, including, as he wrote in his diary, attacks on how he had started the war. "If the treaty was now to be made," he fumed, "I should demand more territory, perhaps to make the Sierra Madre the line." But what would be the "consequences" of rejecting the treaty Trist had negotiated? "A majority of one branch of Congress is opposed to my administration; they have falsely charged that the war was brought on and is continued by me with a view to the conquest of Mexico," Polk wrote. "If I were now to reject a treaty made upon my own terms . . .

---

[44]Nevins, ed., *Polk Diary*, pp. 290–91.

The Ranchero Spotty 59

ARRANGING THE PRELIMINARIES OF A TREATY BETWEEN THE UNITED STATES AND MEXICO.
Mr. Trist—(Very firmly)—MY GOVERNMENT, GENTLEMEN, WILL TAKE "NOTHIN' SHORTER."

FIG. 4. "Arranging the Preliminaries of a Treaty between the United States and Mexico," *Yankee Doodle* (New York), Aug. 28, 1847. This cartoon incorrectly assumed that Trist shared Polk's territorial ambitions, and represents the diplomat demanding a boundary line below Mexico City at the Isthmus of Tehuantepec, leaving Mexico little more than the Yucatan peninsula. *(American Periodical Series Online)*

the probability is that Congress would not grant either men or money to prosecute the war ... and I might ... lose the two Provinces of New Mexico and Upper California, which were ceded to the United States by this treaty."[45]

So while Polk never mentioned the Ranchero Spotty or his attacks directly, the cumulative effect of congressional antiwar agitation was to limit both the duration of the war and Polk's demands for Mexican territory. Had Lincoln chosen to focus on something else during his congressional term, say tariffs, would Polk have felt the same degree of assault from Congress? It is impossible to know for sure, but at the very least we can conclude that the Ranchero Spotty's stance against the war contributed to Polk's decision

---

[45] Ibid., pp. 306–7.

to accept the Treaty of Guadalupe Hidalgo. Charles Averill's fictional Mexican Ranchero attempted to kidnap Trist in order to prevent an ignominious peace for Mexico, but the Ranchero Spotty may well have helped Trist accomplish his mission.

Whatever the Spot Resolutions might or might not reveal about Lincoln's political development, or whether they cost him his seat in Congress, considering the Ranchero Spotty from the perspective of 1848, and not 1860, suggests that Lincoln's single congressional term was no failure. On the contrary, Congressman Lincoln deserves commendation for the role he played in helping to bring the bloody and contested U.S.–Mexico war to a conclusion.

James Oakes

"Disunion . . . Is Abolition"

IT WAS LATE December 1860, just before Christmas and only a few days after South Carolina seceded. The Union was beginning to fall apart, and a Republican newspaper in Massachusetts took a few moments to consider what it all meant. The crisis would be "decisive as to the supremacy of slavery," the editors predicted. If the South stays within the Union, slavery "will live longer and die more gradually and quietly." But if the southern states persist in their effort to leave the Union, slavery's "life will be one of constant peril and strife, and, like all great criminals, it will be pretty certain to come to a violent and bloody end."[1] Whichever way events turned, slavery was finished. That, at least, is what Republican newspapers were saying.

Before the secession crisis, it was uncommon for antislavery radicals and politicians to predict "a violent and bloody end" for slavery. Except for one small fraction of the abolitionist movement, virtually all opponents of slavery—from William Lloyd Garrison to Abraham Lincoln—accepted that the Constitution did not allow the federal government to "interfere" with slavery in the states where it already existed. Radical calls for the "immediate" abolition of slavery were sincere, but they were also rhetorical. *Immediatism* was a stance rather than a policy. A handful of radicals openly supported revolutionary insurrection by the slaves themselves, but in practical terms

---

[1] *Springfield* (Mass.) *Daily Republican*, Dec. 22, 1860, in *Northern Editorials on Secession*, ed. Howard C. Perkins, 2 vols. (New York, 1942),1:483 (hereafter *NES*).

the federal policies most abolitionists supported were designed to bring about the gradual, peaceful abolition of slavery. They would surround the slave states with a "cordon of freedom"—suppressing slavery on the high seas, freeing the northern states from any obligation to sustain slavery, banning slavery from the western territories, and denying any new slave states admission to the Union.[2]

In this program lay the great success of the abolitionist movement. Beginning in the 1830s antislavery radicals formulated the first coherent *national* antislavery policy. They would use the power of the federal government to force the slave states to abolish slavery on their own. Abolitionists first succeeded in getting the Liberty Party to endorse this platform in 1840 and 1844, then the Free Soil Party in 1848, and ultimately the Republican Party in the 1850s. All across the North, from New England to the West Coast, local and state Republican Party organizations endorsed the same set of federal antislavery policies, withdrawing all federal support for slavery on the high seas, in the northern states, and in the western territories. "Like a scorpion girt by fire," antislavery leaders declared, slavery would eventually sting itself to death.[3] The imagery was violent, but it did not imply war.

And yet, as soon as the slave states seceded from the Union the Republican press erupted with threats of immediate, violent emancipation. The reasoning was simple: Secession meant war, and war had always meant military emancipation. For millennia, slave societies at war used emancipation as a weapon designed to defeat enemies or suppress insurrections. In colonial America British colonists often promised freedom to slaves who helped put down uprisings by Native Americans. During the American Revolution, both the British and the Americans offered freedom to slaves in return for military service. The British freed thousands of American slaves during the War of 1812, and the Americans themselves freed hundreds of slaves during the Second Seminole War of the 1830s. Military emancipation was a thoroughly mainstream policy, endorsed by nearly all American statesmen. Its purpose was not to destroy slavery but to win wars.[4]

---

[2]James Oakes, *Freedom National: The Destruction of Slavery in the United States, 1861–1865* (New York, 2013).

[3]James Oakes, *The Scorpion's Sting: Antislavery and the Coming of the Civil War* (New York, 2014).

[4]Ibid., chap. 4.

Not until the 1840s did antislavery radicals, taking their cue from John Quincy Adams, begin to imagine using military emancipation as a means of abolishing slavery. But even then, abolitionists were not counting on war. Most often they pointed to the likelihood of military emancipation as a reason the South would never provoke a war by seceding from the Union. When the southern states did begin seceding in the wake of Lincoln's election, it was because his Republican Party was committed to putting slavery on a course of "ultimate extinction" by means of the "cordon of freedom."

Secessionists waved aside all Republican promises not to "interfere" directly in the states where slavery already existed. "Where they cannot attack it in the States they will attack it at every other point they can reach," a Louisiana secessionist paper argued. "They will set fire to all the surrounding buildings in the hope that some spark may catch, and everything be destroyed in a general conflagration. They will undermine the pillars of the institution, and then wait quietly for the whole edifice to tumble." Lincoln's election would bring with it "no direct act of violence against negro property," the *Richmond Enquirer* pointed out. Instead, the Republicans would go after slavery indirectly. "[U]nder the fostering hand of federal power," abolitionism would insidiously plant itself in the border states, "converting them into free States, then into 'cities of refuge' for runaway negroes from the gulf States." The Republicans could accomplish all of this while technically adhering to their promises not to interfere directly with slavery in the southern states. "No act of violence may ever be committed, no servile war waged, and yet the ruin and degradation of Virginia will be as fully and as fatally accomplished as though bloodshed and rapine ravished the land."[5] The *Charleston Mercury*, the leading editorial voice of the South Carolina secession movement, predicted that once Republicans were "enthroned at Washington, in the Executive and Legislative departments of Government," the process of abolition would commence. First slavery would be systematically weakened in the Border States, so that Kentucky, Virginia, and Missouri would soon "enter on the policy of making themselves Free States." Surrounded by hostile free states, the *Mercury* warned,

---

[5] *New Orleans Daily Crescent*, Dec. 14, 1860; *Richmond Enquirer*, July 10, 1860, in *Southern Editorials on Secession*, ed. Dwight L. Dumond (1931; reprint ed., Gloucester, Mass., 1964), pp. 141, 333 (hereafter *SES*); *Congressional Globe*, 36th Cong., 1st sess., Mar. 14, 1860, p. 1162.

the "timid" in the cotton states would begin selling off their own slaves, but there would be no purchasers. The value of slave property would sink to nothing.[6]

The secession movement began in South Carolina within weeks of Lincoln's election, and by Christmas 1860 the Palmetto State had declared its independence from the Union (fig. 1). But the remaining states of the Deep South hardly needed South Carolina's coaxing. Beginning in early January and continuing into February all the cotton states—Florida, Georgia, Alabama, Mississippi, Louisiana, and Texas—seceded from the Union. By February 1861 they had come together to form a new government, the Confederate States of America, under an explicitly proslavery constitution, with an interim president, Jefferson Davis, a wealthy cotton planter from Mississippi. As they made their departures from the Union, each of the seceded states made it unmistakably clear that their action was prompted by the urgent need to protect the right of property in slaves from the impending assault of the Republicans who were about to take control of the federal government.[7]

The conflict over slavery had become irreconcilable. Secessionists argued that it was both naïve and dangerous for any slaveholder to think that slavery could remain secure under the rule of Republicans who denied that there was such a thing as a right of property in slaves. Disunion was the only way to protect slavery from the assaults that Republicans themselves were promising to deliver. What secessionists did not expect was the way disunion itself would fundamentally alter the terms of the debate over slavery's fate. With remarkable speed Republicans shifted the focus of their antislavery policy from the "cordon of freedom" to military emancipation.

For nearly two months after Lincoln's election Republicans had maintained a deliberate silence on the secession crisis, hoping to dampen support for disunion by saying nothing to provoke the fire-eaters. By mid-January it was clear that policy was not working, and it was William

---

[6]*Charleston Mercury*, Oct. 11, 1860, and Nov. 3, 1860, in *SES*, pp. 179, 185–86, 204.
[7]In some ways the best brief narrative of secession remains Dwight Lowell Dumond, *The Secession Movement, 1860–1861* (New York, 1931). See also David M. Potter, *The Impending Crisis, 1848–1861*, completed and ed. Don E. Fehrenbacher (New York, 1976), and William W. Freehling, *The Road to Disunion*, vol. 2: *Secessionists Triumphant, 1854–1861* (New York, 2008).

"Disunion ... Is Abolition" 65

FIG. 1. *The "Secession Movement,"* by Currier and Ives, ca. 1861, depicts several Southern states as men riding donkeys following the lead of South Carolina, who rides a pig chasing a "Secession Humbug" butterfly off a cliff. *(Prints and Photographs Division, Library of Congress)*

Seward (fig. 2) who broke the Republican silence. Long viewed as an ideological spokesman for his party, one of those who worked hardest to formulate and popularize its positions on slavery, Seward had been a favorite to win the Republican presidential nomination in 1860. Yet, despite his loss to Lincoln, Seward was still recognized as one of the party's most important leaders. Lincoln's recent nomination of Seward to be his secretary of state did nothing to diminish Seward's stature. Many assumed that his was the public voice of the incoming administration. As a result, everyone waited expectantly for the major statement Seward was set to make in the Senate on January 12, 1861. It was a critical moment. Alabama and Florida had seceded the day before, Mississippi two days before that. It was clear that Louisiana, Georgia, and Texas would soon secede as well. What would Seward have to say about this? Would he, like most of his fellow Republicans, stand his ground and refuse to compromise with the secessionists? Or would Seward offer the South concessions that would save the Union?

Fig. 2. William H. Seward, in a photograph taken between 1860 and 1865 by Mathew Brady's studio. *(Prints and Photographs Division, Library of Congress)*

Seward conceded nothing. The tone of his January 12 speech was conciliatory, his prose was obscure, but his substance was unyielding. There was nothing to distinguish it from the speeches that had marked him as a radical ten years earlier. He would not concede that slaves were "property" under the Constitution, he would modify the Fugitive Slave Act of 1850, and he would suppress the Southern rebellion by force. Secession was illegal and the Union indissoluble.[8] In short, Seward held fast to the standard Republican positions. But he also said more than that.

If it comes to war—if the North has to invade the South to enforce the law—the result, said Seward, would be slave rebellion. For although this was ostensibly a dispute over the disposition of the territories, it was at bottom a more fundamental conflict over "the relation of African slaves to the domestic population of the country." It was a struggle over slavery, and the slaves knew it, Seward warned. "Freedom is to them, as to all mankind, the chief object of desire." With a "flagrant civil war" raging all about them, can anyone expect that the slaves "will remain stupid and idle spectators?" Of course not, Seward argued. All of human history teaches us what the slaves will do in the midst of civil war. An "uprising" and a "ferocious African slave population," numbering in the millions, would overwhelm the South and the entire slave system would come crashing down.[9]

There were only two ways to abolish slavery, Seward explained. The "American" way achieves abolition gradually by means of federal containment: Close off access to the African slave trade, restrict slavery to those states where it already exists, and let it die a natural death. As slavery weakens, the slave states themselves will eventually realize that they must abolish slavery on their own. This was the path he and the Republicans hoped to pursue. But there was a second, "European" path, by which "direct abolition" would be "effected, if need be, by compulsion." Seward was likely referring to those cases in which European nations had imposed abolition on their Caribbean colonies. In the United States the Constitution did not allow the federal government to emancipate slaves in the states—except in wartime when, as virtually all American authorities had long acknowledged, the federal government could legally free slaves in an effort to suppress a rebellion. So long as the slave states remained within the Union, the United States would follow the American path. But if the South secedes, "if dissolution prevail," Seward asked, "what guarantee shall there be against the full development here

---

[8] *Congressional Globe*, 36th Cong., 2d sess., pp. 343–44.
[9] Ibid., p. 342.

of the fearful and uncompromising hostility to slavery which elsewhere pervades the world?"[10] Secession meant war, Seward warned, and war promised swift, violent military emancipation.

Such were the alternatives Seward and the Republicans were offering to the slave states: Abandon any claim to a constitutional right of property in slaves and submit to a containment policy that would put slavery on the course of ultimate extinction, or leave the Union and face the prospect of immediate military emancipation.

Secession will "hasten the downfall of American slavery at least one hundred years," the *Indianapolis Daily Journal* explained. Far from resolving the sectional crisis, an Iowa Republican declared in January 1861, secession ensured that the "irrepressible conflict" would "gather fierceness and energy, and will continue until the last chain forged for the enslavement of men on this continent, will fall from the limbs of the bondman." The secessionists, the editor argued, are working "for the extinction of slavery" just as surely as they are "for the dismemberment of the Government." Secession will not protect slavery, Republicans warned. "Disunion, rather, is abolition," Salmon Chase explained, "and abolition through civil and servile war, which God forbid!" Secessionists left the Union to insulate the South from a policy aimed at slavery's "ultimate extinction." Republicans responded by declaring that secession itself made the swift destruction of slavery inevitable.[11]

Northern threats of military emancipation rose in tandem with secessionism in the lower South. The very idea of secession is "utterly preposterous," one Lincoln paper in Boston declared shortly after his victory was announced. "The only results to the rebellious States would be a bloody strife confined entirely to their own territory, [and] the immediate and violent abolition of slavery." In December, days before South Carolina seceded, the *Indianapolis Daily Journal* found some cause for "satisfaction" among those who hated slavery: "The dissolution of the American Union seals the doom of American slavery." Secession will fail, a Republican editor in Springfield, Illinois,

---

[10]Ibid. On the influence the British abolition of slavery had on the antislavery movement in the United States, see Edward Bartlett Rugemer, *The Problem of Emancipation: The Caribbean Roots of the American Civil War* (Baton Rouge, 2009).

[11]*Indianapolis Daily Journal*, Dec. 14, 1860, and Des Moines *Iowa State Register*, Jan. 23, 1861, in *NES*, 1:117, 439–41; Chase to Ruhama Ludlow Hunt, Nov. 30, 1860, in John Niven, ed., *The Salmon P. Chase Papers*, 5 vols. (Kent, Ohio, 1993–98), 3:38.

declared. "Universal Liberty is to be the eventual law of this land. Slaveholding traitors are only hastening the day when that law shall take effect." If the Union is destroyed, the Bloomington, Illinois, *Pantagraph* warned, "one may foresee that American slavery is destined to die a bloody death, and to come sooner and more suddenly to a tragical termination. It will not be in the power of man to avert it."[12] With secession, Republicans promised a military emancipation that would abolish slavery more quickly—and more violently—than peaceful containment.

Republicans everywhere were issuing similar threats, only more overtly. "Suppose the southern states go out of the Union to escape northern aversion to slavery." That would only "free" the North "from all the constitutional restraints that now limit its action." Until now the North has always been "willing to allow to slavery all the protection that the Constitution even by implication requires," the *Iowa State Register* argued. But "when the severance comes" the northern states "will see to it, that the curse of human bondage shall not pass beyond its present limits." An Indiana paper was even more emphatic that the North was constitutionally freed from slavery thanks to secession. "No more protection then," it declared, "no more fugitive slave laws, no more right of transit, no more suppressing of slave insurrections by Federal troops."[13] In warning that the federal government would no longer suppress slave insurrections, Republicans revealed one of the crucial premises of military emancipation: It depended on the slaves themselves.

Slaves so hated their bondage, Republicans argued, that it required the apparatus of a police state to maintain order in the South. An invading Union army would destroy that apparatus, giving free rein to the pent-up insurrectionary instincts of four million slaves. As soon as the secession crisis erupted, Republicans began forecasting slave rebellion in the South as the inescapable consequence of war. The slave states, even joined together in a confederacy, "have not the means within themselves of keeping their negroes in subjection in such a contest." Secessionists must consider "the *negro element*," the *Worcester Palladium* warned. "God only knows what that element would

---

[12] *Indianapolis Daily Journal*, Dec. 14, 1860, *Boston Daily Atlas and Bee*, Nov. 12, 1860, and Springfield *Daily Illinois State Journal*, Mar. 6, 1861, in *NES*, 1:117, 90, 2:640; *The Weekly Pantagraph* (Bloomington, Ill.), Jan. 9, 1861, in Don Munson, ed., *It is Begun! The Pantagraph Reports the Civil War* (Bloomington, Ill., 2001), p. 2.

[13] Springfield (Mass.) *Daily Republican*, Dec. 22, 1860, and Des Moines *Iowa State Register*, Jan. 23, 1861, in *NES*, 1:482, 440, 118.

accomplish, should it sweep over the land in the form of an ungovernable insurrection." It may be true that the slaves were "loyal and obsequious" to their masters under "ordinary circumstances," a pro-Lincoln paper in Kansas argued, but "we cannot escape the great facts which the history of this race reveals—that the black race perceive and deeply feel their wrongs, and when a fitting opportunity affords, will revenge them in the most implacable manner." It would be a sanguine business. Republicans warned that if Southerners did not abandon their "treasonable operations," slavery would "go out in blood." If the South refuses to accept the results of a proper presidential election, "then indeed any one may foresee that American slavery is destined to die a bloody death." The Union invasion of the South would become the catalyst for slavery's internal collapse, opening the door to the possibility of slave rebellion.[14]

Predictions of slave rebellion were not limited to the radicals within the Republican Party. Edward Bates, Lincoln's conservative attorney general, was "convinced that flagrant Civil war in the southern states would soon become a social war, and that could hardly fail to bring on a servile war." Days after the attack on Fort Sumter, George Templeton Strong, a conservative New Yorker, mused over the revolutionary potential of the slave population. "Very well," he wrote in his diary as he fumed over Jefferson Davis's declaration that privateers would be licensed to attack Northern ships. "Then we shall have no scruples about retaliating on Southern property, which is peculiar for possessing a capacity for being invited to go away, and legs to take itself off, and arms wherewith to use such implements as may aid it in so doing."[15]

Echoing the Republicans, southern opponents of secession—"cooperationists"—warned that any state leaving the Union would forfeit all the protection the Constitution guaranteed to slavery. "The Constitution of the United States recognizes and protects slavery," a Louisville editor explained; it was the Constitution that had always kept the abolitionists

---

[14]Indianapolis *Indiana American*, Nov. 21, 1860, *Worcester Palladium*, Jan. 16, 1861, and Manhattan City *Western Kansas Express*, May 11, 1861, in *NES*, 1:97, 222; 2:834; Kenneth M. Stampp, *And the War Came: The North and the Secession Crisis, 1860–1861* (Baton Rouge, 1970), pp. 250–52; *The Weekly Pantagraph* (Bloomington, Ill.), Jan. 6, 1861, in Munson, *It is Begun!*, p. 2.

[15]Diary entry, Mar. 16, 1861, *The Diary of Edward Bates, 1859–1866*, ed. Howard Kennedy Beale (Washington, D.C., 1933), p. 179; diary entry, Apr. 18, 1861, *Diary of George Templeton Strong*, vol. 3: *1860–1865*, ed. Allan Nevins (New York, 1952), p. 124.

at bay. "Take slavery out of the Constitution of the United States," and the entire South would find itself surrounded by "abolitionized" state and federal governments. On the other hand, if the Border States remain within the Union, "slavery will still be part of the Constitution" and thus "under its protection." The *Republican Banner* in Nashville agreed. Slavery "has depended mainly for its existence on the protection afforded by the Constitution. . . . But how will it be after the present government is dissolved, and the Northern States are absolved from their Constitutional obligations, and instead of being parties to the maintenance of slavery, as they are under the Constitution, become its open and avowed enemies? It is clear to be seen that the South will be greatly and fatally weakened" by secession, the editors concluded, "and the doom of slavery is irrevocably fixed."[16]

The Inaugural Address and the End of Compromise

Through the secession winter Lincoln stood firmly with his fellow Republicans in refusing to compromise on the fundamental issues—in particular the constitutional right of property in slaves on which every specific sectional dispute rested. Because it failed to address this fundamental question, the series of constitutional amendments proposed by Kentucky Senator John J. Crittenden in late 1860 went down to defeat. The Crittenden Compromise, as it has come to be known, would have recognized a constitutional right to slave property in the territories south of the old Missouri Compromise line, guaranteed the admission of new slave states organized south of the line, prevented Congress from abolishing slavery in Washington, D.C., and banned federal regulation of the domestic slave trade. Additional resolutions called for vigorous federal enforcement of the Fugitive Slave Act and the repeal of northern personal liberty laws. Far from representing a viable solution to the sectional crisis, the Crittenden Compromise endorsed nearly every item on the agenda of those who would make slavery national. Every element of the proposal presupposed the very thing Republicans most forcefully denied—that there was a constitutionally protected right of property in slaves. In effect, the Crittenden Compromise called for the

---

[16]*Louisville Daily Journal*, Jan. 26, 1861, and Nashville *Republican Banner*, Jan. 26, 1861, in *SES*, pp. 422–23, 425–26.

repudiation of Freedom National, and with it the rejection of every policy Republicans planned to implement in order to undermine slavery.

Most of the remaining compromise proposals were no more promising, and many were essentially meaningless. This was certainly true of the amendment to the Constitution, proposed by Ohio Republican Congressman Thomas Corwin in March 1861, that would have banned federal interference with slavery in the states where it already existed. Everyone already agreed that the Constitution contained such a ban. The amendment did nothing more than reassert the familiar federal consensus. Indeed the 1860 Republican Party platform explicitly affirmed the "inviolate" right of every state "to order and control its own domestic institutions according to its own judgment exclusively." An amendment saying what everyone already believed would have been superfluous. A number of congressional Republicans, recoiling against what felt like blackmail, voted against the Corwin amendment even though their own party platform endorsed it. Indeed, there is some evidence suggesting that Republicans endorsed the amendment knowing it was pointless but hoping to deflect charges that they were unwilling to compromise. Yet, even in the unlikely event that the Corwin amendment had been ratified, it would have done nothing to thwart Republican policies designed to quarantine slavery, squeezing it to death indirectly. For that very reason, neither the secessionists nor the cooperationists saw the Corwin amendment as a viable compromise proposal. It would not have forestalled the Civil War, and in any case a war would render it meaningless. Any states that seceded from the Union would still forfeit whatever protection the Corwin amendment might otherwise have afforded them, leaving them as vulnerable as ever to military emancipation. In short, the Corwin amendment changed nothing. Lincoln's lukewarm endorsement of it in his inaugural address was an empty gesture in a speech that stoutly reaffirmed the basic Republican positions.

What Lincoln's inaugural address actually revealed was how deeply the precepts of antislavery constitutionalism had penetrated into the political mainstream. He repeated the promise made by generations of antislavery activists—that he would not "interfere" with slavery in the states where it already existed, but he did not repudiate Republican plans to undermine slavery by means of containment. He would respect whatever "rights" the Constitution guaranteed to every state, knowing full well that a major source of conflict was the Republican claim that there was no such thing as a constitutional right of property in slaves. But the clearest indication of where Lincoln stood came in his extended remarks on the issue of fugitive slaves.[17]

Lincoln's first reference to the fugitive slave issue struck an eminently conservative tone. He quoted the entire fugitive slave clause of the Constitution and then noted that he, along with every member of Congress, was sworn to uphold the Constitution—"this provision as much as any other." Had he stopped there he might have eased the concerns of many a slaveholder. Instead, Lincoln went on to point out that there was "some difference of opinion whether this clause should be enforced by national or state authority." To say the least: Southern leaders insisted that the federal government had to enforce the fugitive slave clause within the northern states. But most Republicans, starting from the premise that freedom was national, argued that the federal government had no business enforcing the fugitive slave clause, that slaveholders seeking to recapture fugitives should be obliged to press their case in state courts. By this reasoning the federal enforcement provisions of the Fugitive Slave Act of 1850 were illegitimate.[18]

Lincoln's position on federal versus state enforcement was slightly unorthodox among antislavery politicians. Unlike most antislavery politicians, Lincoln was willing to concede that the fugitive slave clause might be enforced by the federal government, but in return for that concession he demanded a federal personal liberty law guaranteeing accused blacks "the usual safeguards of liberty, securing free men against being surrendered as slaves." In addition, Lincoln wanted northern civilians exempted from any obligation to participate in the enforcement of the fugitive slave clause. These proposals, both of which would require a substantial revision of the Fugitive Slave Act of 1850, were the only substantive compromise Lincoln offered during the secession crisis. Having been warned when he first made the proposal that most Republicans were "unwilling to give up their old opinion that the duty of executing the constitutional provisions concerning fugitives belongs to the States," Lincoln nevertheless revived it

---

[17]On the first inaugural address, see Harry V. Jaffa, *A New Birth of Freedom: Abraham Lincoln and the Coming of the Civil War* (Lanham, Md., 2000), pp. 237–355; Ronald C. White Jr., *The Eloquent President: A Portrait of Lincoln Through His Words* (New York, 2005), pp. 62–97; Douglas L. Wilson, *Lincoln's Sword: The Presidency and the Power of Words* (New York, 2006), pp. 42–70; Michael Burlingame, *Abraham Lincoln: A Life*, 2 vols. (Baltimore, 2008), 2:45–68, 333.
[18]Roy P. Basler, ed., *The Collected Works of Abraham Lincoln*, 9 vols. (New Brunswick, N.J., 1953–55), 4:263–64.

in his inaugural address. Once again he proposed a new fugitive slave law that would recognize the citizenship rights of free blacks. In "any law upon this subject," Lincoln said, "ought not all the safeguards of liberty known in civilized and humane jurisprudence be introduced," in particular the "privileges and immunities of citizens" to which free blacks were entitled. Lincoln's proposal flatly contradicted the Supreme Court's ruling in *Dred Scott*, which denied that blacks were citizens. It could hardly have mollified the slaveholders that Lincoln urged everyone to obey the fugitive slave law, like all the other laws "which stand unrepealed," until such time as Congress acted to repeal it.[19]

In an obvious play on the wording of the *Dred Scott* decision—made all the more extraordinary by the fact that its author, Chief Justice Roger Taney, was sitting there listening—Lincoln distinguished between those rights everyone agreed to respect because they were "plainly written in the Constitution" and those over which there was serious disagreement because they were not plainly specified. Taney had ruled against Dred Scott's suit for freedom partly on the ground that the Constitution "expressly" recognized a right of property in slaves, something Lincoln had repeatedly disputed. Now, in his inaugural address, Lincoln argued that much of the political disagreement about slavery arose precisely from those questions on which the Constitution was silent. "Shall fugitives from labor be surrendered by national or by State authority?" Lincoln asked. "The Constitution does not expressly say. *May* Congress prohibit slavery in the territories? The Constitution," Lincoln answered, "does not expressly say." All of "our constitutional controversies," Lincoln explained, arise from disagreements over what the Constitution "does not expressly say" regarding the enforcement of the fugitive slave clause and slavery in the territories. Whenever such disagreements arise, "we divide upon them into majorities and minorities" and disputes over what the Constitution says are settled by means of democratic elections. Thereafter the minority must "acquiesce," or else "the government must cease." Secession thus amounted to a minority's refusal to acquiesce in the democratic legitimacy of majority rule. In this case the specific issues prompting the minority's rejection of democratic decision making were the majority's views on the proper enforcement of the fugitive slave clause and

---

[19]Ibid., 4:156–57, 264.

the exclusion of slavery from the territories. These were the "real" ills that Lincoln freely admitted Southerners faced by remaining within the Union.[20]

But there were even "greater" ills that Lincoln was "certain" would arise if the slave states left the Union. Continuing his attack on the *Dred Scott* decision, Lincoln doubled back yet again to the matter of fugitive slaves. In ordinary cases the people could rely on the Supreme Court to settle constitutional questions, Lincoln explained. But the Supreme Court cannot resolve "vital questions, affecting the whole people"; otherwise "the people will have ceased, to be their own rulers." In the current crisis the vital question was clear: "One section of our country believes slavery is *right*, and ought to be extended, while the other believes it *wrong*, and ought not to be extended." Under the circumstances the laws regulating slavery could never be "perfectly" enforced because the supporters and opponents of slavery would never be able to agree on which laws should or should not be strictly applied. Lincoln cited two particular laws, the "fugitive slave clause of the Constitution, and the law for the suppression of the foreign slave trade." Both were about "as well enforced, perhaps, as any law can ever be in a community where the moral sense of the people imperfectly supports the law itself." So long as large numbers of Southerners were willing to violate the ban on slave trading, the ban could only be imperfectly enforced. And so long as Northerners were offended by the spectacle of slave-catchers in their midst, the fugitive slave clause would likewise be enforced "imperfectly." But what would happen if the South tried to secede from the Union? Lincoln asked. Then the circumstances of law enforcement would be changed. The South, he predicted, would reopen the Atlantic slave trade and the commerce, "now imperfectly suppressed, would be ultimately revived without restriction." Meanwhile in the North, Lincoln added, "fugitive slaves, now only partially surrendered, *would not be surrendered at all*." Having opened his discussion of fugitive slaves with a respectably conservative promise to abide by his oath of office and uphold the law, Lincoln steadily gravitated toward the somewhat more radical conclusion that if the South "separated" from the Union, neither the federal government nor the northern states would enforce the fugitive slave clause of the Constitution.[21]

---

[20]Ibid., 4:267.
[21]Ibid., 4:268–69 (emphasis added). Lincoln seems to have accepted the premises of William Jay, Samuel May, and other abolitionists who argued—most famously in the *Amistad* case—that the U.S. government should not capture and return fugitive slaves from foreign

In a speech often condemned for avoiding the issue of slavery, Lincoln actually referred to slavery repeatedly—citing it as the only cause of the sectional crisis, questioning the federal government's obligation to enforce the fugitive slave clause, reasserting the government's constitutional right to exclude slavery from the federal territories, and affirming the conviction that slavery was a moral wrong. If the inaugural address was Lincoln's attempt to avoid the subject of slavery, it was a miserable failure.

"An Active War of Emancipation"

Perhaps because it reflected the familiar constitutional premises of the Republican Party, Lincoln's first inaugural address changed nothing. It brought none of the seceded states back into the Union and it provoked no new wave of secessions in the Upper South. As an affirmation of Republican dogma, the speech provoked cries of outrage among northern Democrats. "There can no longer be any doubt that anti-slavery is the *corpus*, the strength, the visible life of the party which has now assumed the reins of government," the *Philadelphia Evening Journal* declared the next day.[22] If the new president carries out the "provisions and recommendations" of his speech, a Wisconsin Democrat declared, "blood will stain soil and color the waters of the entire continent." Nevertheless, the national argument over slavery's fate remained where it had stood for several months.

The attack on Fort Sumter (fig. 3) had a more discernible effect. On April 12, 1861, heavily fortified Confederate batteries surrounding Charleston harbor opened fire on the U.S. military installation at Fort Sumter in the middle of the bay. There was no way the Union troops inside the fort could withstand the assault. With their inevitable surrender to the South, the war that everyone expected finally began. Lincoln immediately called up 75,000 volunteers to suppress the rebellion. His action provoked four more slave states—Virginia, North Carolina, Tennessee, and Arkansas—to join the Confederacy, and with that the antislavery mood among

---

countries. Once the slave states declared their independence, Lincoln seemed to be arguing, the federal government would no longer be obliged to enforce the fugitive slave clause. As we shall see, this was precisely the same logic General Benjamin Butler would use two months later to justify his refusal to return slaves to their owners at Fortress Monroe.

[22] *Philadelphia Evening Journal*, Mar. 5, 1861, in *NES*, 2:635.

"Disunion ... Is Abolition" 77

Fig. 3. Bombardment of Fort Sumter by the Batteries of the Confederate States, April 13, 1861. (Harper's Weekly, *Apr. 27, 1861. Courtesy of Donald R. Kennon)*

Northerners grew more defiant than ever. For the first time a small but vocal minority of northern Democrats joined the Republican chorus in declaring that slavery was doomed. For many Northerners, the secession of the Upper South, especially Virginia, was the final act of treachery, prompting more threats of slave rebellion and renewed demands for emancipation. Many of these demands were now aimed at the new Republican president.

Lincoln could hardly have missed all the prophesying about slavery's doom among his fellow Republicans. His own cabinet members were predicting that secession would lead to slave rebellion and emancipation. And Lincoln's mailbox was rapidly filling up with letters from politicians and pundits across the Republican spectrum, all of them telling the new president the same thing. In late April the radical William Channing wrote to Lincoln "advising [the] abolition of Slavery by martial law as the surest way to conquer rebellious States & preserve the border ones." Similar letters to Lincoln arrived from other states, and not only from radicals. "Had I the power," George Field wrote from Brooklyn in early May, "I would march an army forthwith to Richmond proclaiming every where *immunity*

& protection to all *of any color* who would desert the Rebel standard." "The war must be carried into Africa," a Republican politician from New York wrote in May of 1861. "Take the occasion by the hand," one Pennsylvanian wrote, "*and make The bound of freedom wider yet.*" Lincoln's mercurial Illinois friend Orville Browning predicted that the time would come when the president would have to push the war "to the uttermost extremity," when "it will be necessary for you to march an army into the South, and proclaim freedom to the slaves." Browning's letters expressed the views of many Northerners at the time. Slavery had caused the rebellion; suppressing the rebellion would therefore require the destruction of slavery.[23]

The "contest sounds the death-knell of slavery," an Indiana journal explained a few days after Fort Sumter was captured. And who "will mourn its loss?" Slavery has divided the country and hindered its progress for so long that "it would be truly a God's blessing to be rid of it. So every patriot feels in his heart of hearts." An independent newspaper in Paris, Maine, echoed the thought. We are in the midst of a revolution caused by the institution of slavery, the *Oxford Democrat* explained. Whatever happens, "the final abolition of slavery will be hastened by the movement." Slave insurrections will erupt across the South, "touched off by any John Brown or Nat Turner that has the courage to apply the fuse." The federal government has long been "the great protection of slavery in this country," but with the slave states gone from the Union, that same government "will be the greatest agency that can be brought into existence to extinguish slavery in the United States." Southerners must understand, another paper in Roxbury, Massachusetts, explained, that "[t]he rule of the Slave power in America is at length ended." Slavery's "besotted arrogance has proved its ruin." It was April 1861, the war had just begun, and already there was nothing remarkable about Republican declarations that the conflict could only result in the complete destruction of slavery.[24]

---

[23] Diary entry, Apr. 27, 1861, *Inside Lincoln's White House: The Complete Civil War Diary of John Hay*, ed. Michael Burlingame and John R. Turner Ettlinger (Carbondale, Ill., 1997), pp. 12–13. George Field to Abraham Lincoln, May 9, 1861; Burt Van Horn to Abraham Lincoln, May 1861; "Pennsylvanicus" to Abraham Lincoln, May 8, 1861; and Orville H. Browning to Abraham Lincoln, Apr. 30, 1861, Abraham Lincoln Papers, Manuscript Division, Library of Congress, Washington, D.C.

[24] *Evansville* (Ind.) *Daily Journal* [Lincoln], Apr. 20, 1861; Paris, Me., *Oxford Democrat* [Independent], Apr. 26, 1861; and Roxbury, Mass., *Norfolk County Journal*, May 4, 1861, in *NES*, 1:463–64, 2:812–13, 821.

Over the next several years Republicans would disagree among themselves about many things—the confiscation of rebel property, the power of the president versus Congress, and above all Reconstruction policy—but they did not disagree about slavery and abolition. Even before the war started William Howard Russell, the perceptive reporter for the London *Times*, could not find any Republicans in Washington, D.C., who doubted that the war would end in the complete destruction of slavery. The reporter showed up at a state dinner held at the White House on March 28—halfway between the inauguration and the attack on Fort Sumter. The affair was hosted by the president and the First Lady; Lincoln's cabinet members and leading Republican politicians were in attendance. As Russell worked the room, chatting with them and listening in on their conversations, he noticed a "uniform tendency" in the way they spoke. "They seemed to think," Russell reported, "that England was bound by her anti-slavery antecedents to discourage to the utmost any attempt of the South to establish its independence on a basis of slavery, and to assume that they were the representatives of an active war of emancipation."[25]

Russell viewed such talk among Republicans as arrogant bluster, and no doubt much of it was. The war had not yet begun. Until then all the Republicans could do was make predictions, issue warnings, and hurl threats. It was easy enough for Republicans to wrap themselves in the mantle of emancipation, threaten the South with slave rebellion, and predict the downfall of slavery. But scenarios were not the same as policies. It remained to be seen whether Republicans were prepared to act on their promises. Yet surely it matters that Republicans were contemplating slavery's destruction from the beginning. If it is too much to say that they went to war with clearly formulated plans about how to go about abolishing slavery, it is a more serious mistake to claim that Republicans were not talking openly about the destruction of slavery.

On the contrary, by the time Lincoln was inaugurated, Republicans had inherited two broad scenarios for a federal attack on slavery—a peacetime policy that would "cordon" off the slave states and gradually force them to abolish slavery on their own, and a wartime policy of immediate

---

[25]Diary entry for Mar. 28, 1861, William Howard Russell, *My Diary North and South* (New York, 1863), quote on pp. 44–45.

emancipation as a military necessity—both of which they repeatedly affirmed during the secession winter of 1860–61.

Yet the path to slavery's final destruction turned out to be crooked—full of unexpected twists and turns. What nobody could have imagined was the way the Civil War became a social revolution and in the process radicalized both Republican policies and led eventually to a third. Military emancipation initially followed the pattern familiar to earlier wars as the federal government began offering freedom to slaves who "came within" Union lines in the rebellious states. But by the middle of 1862, radicalized by the war, Republican policymakers adopted an unprecedented policy of *universal* military emancipation. Similarly, the war enabled Lincoln to put unprecedented pressure on the states to begin abolishing slavery on their own. At first he offered the states incentives—compensation, a gradual timetable, and subsidies for former slaves who chose to emigrate. By early 1862, however, Lincoln was warning the states that slavery would be undermined by the prolonged effects of military emancipation. In 1863 Lincoln began actively recruiting slaves from the Border States into the Union army, and by the end of the year he made emancipation a condition for readmission to the Union by any seceded states. By 1864 Lincoln was actively engaged in a series of struggles to get several states—Arkansas, Missouri, Maryland, Tennessee, and Louisiana—to abolish slavery on their own.

If the steady radicalization of both federal antislavery policies had been largely unforeseen, no one had come close to imagining what happened in 1864, when the Republican Party committed itself to a constitutional amendment abolishing slavery everywhere in the United States. In retrospect this can be made to look like the logical conclusion of all that had come before, but in fact there was no straight line to the Thirteenth Amendment from either military emancipation or state abolition.

Orville Vernon Burton

Lincoln, Secession, and Emancipation

EVERY FOUR YEARS, on the first Tuesday of November, Americans elect or reelect a president. If it is the first term, the newly elected president must wait two months before officially taking office. The two months' wait can be maddening when crises abound. When in 2008 Americans looked to President-Elect Barack Obama as the new leader of the country, he was compelled to wait. After all, as he said, America has only one president at a time. From his election on November 4, 2008, until his inauguration on January 20, 2009, he could prepare, and did so, but for one and one-half months he could not act as the president because George W. Bush was still in charge. This interlude had been in effect since the Twentieth Amendment in 1933. Prior to 1933 the interlude was four months, with the new president taking office on March 4 following the November election. The change from four months to two was the result of the long delay before President-Elect Franklin D. Roosevelt could take any action to address the Great Depression. In 1860–61 the situation faced by Abraham Lincoln was direr than that faced by Franklin Roosevelt, or by any other president. During those four months, secessionist states formed a confederacy, wrote a new constitution, and elected their own president. And what could Abraham Lincoln, who had not yet taken office as president, do about this secession movement?[1]

---

[1]There are a number of books that deal with Lincoln and secession. Two recent works come at it from different perspectives and complement one another; see especially Harold

* * *

On December 20, 1860, church bells rang and cannons boomed out across Charleston harbor. South Carolinians packed into the city's largest hall to watch delegates from all over the state add their names to an Ordinance of Secession, declaring the creation of the Independent Republic of South Carolina. As throngs of white citizens cheered the signing of the ordinance, they had no idea they were celebrating the suicide of the world they loved so dearly. Sadly, South Carolina was not alone in its suicidal tendencies. The *New York Times* reported that cities across the South celebrated South Carolina's honor, "and some states re-convened their state conventions to discuss their own secession from the Union."[2] By early March, Mississippi, Alabama, Georgia, Florida, Louisiana, and Texas also passed secession ordinances.[3]

Secession does not necessarily lead to war. Could the country be brought back together again? Could peace, albeit uneasy, prevail? That would depend on the rationale for secession.

Abraham Lincoln (as president-elect for three months and president for one month) did everything he possibly could, short of sacrificing principle, to forestall bloodshed. Among the many items of business on Lincoln's agenda during those four long months was an analysis of secession itself. He offered the country a calm, reasoned logic. He offered the South reasons to reconsider secession. He offered the North and the South the necessity of a reliance on the rule of law.

Did states have a legal right to withdraw from the Union? On what pretext? With what consequences? The Declaration of Independence asserted that government derives its just powers "from the consent of the governed," that when it failed to protect citizens' rights, "it is the Right of the People to alter or to abolish it." What was the meaning of this right to make and unmake government if the South was not allowed to assert it? What, on the

---

Holzer, *Lincoln President-Elect: Abraham Lincoln and the Great Secession Winter, 1860–1861* (New York, 2008), and Russell McClintock, *Lincoln and the Decision for War: The Northern Response to Secession* (Chapel Hill, 2008).

[2]"How Secession Is Regarded," *New York Times*, Dec. 22, 1860, p. 1.

[3]The percentage of enslaved workers may have affected the order of secession. In South Carolina, 57 percent of the population was enslaved; in Mississippi, 55 percent; in Alabama, 45 percent. See Orville Vernon Burton, *The Age of Lincoln* (New York, 2007) for further information, and a table of the order of secession and proportion of African American population, at the book's website, ageoflincoln.com.

other hand, did the American people's sovereignty amount to, if it could be nullified in a moment by the whim of a disgruntled few?

The rule of law was the basis for Lincoln's political philosophy—more important than slavery, more important than emancipation. Early in his political career as a member of the Illinois House of Representatives, on January 27, 1838, Lincoln delivered a speech at the Young Men's Lyceum in Springfield that staked the nation's future on *"a reverence for the Constitution and law"* (Lincoln's emphasis). Lincoln called on Americans to renew their patriotic attachment to sober reason, law and order, and the political edifice of liberty and equal rights bequeathed them by their forebearers. Here was boundless commitment to, if not necessarily blind faith in, general intelligence, sound morality, and reverence for the rule of law. And on its strengths, the twenty-eight-year-old Lincoln was prepared to assert that even "the gates of hell shall not prevail against it."[4] Throughout his life, his belief in the rule of law as outlined in this Lyceum speech, and his belief that only by adherence to the laws and processes of government could the United States persist, would be the bedrock of Lincoln's philosophy.

The rule of law meant that the president of the United States could not interfere with slavery where it existed. The U.S. Constitution in 1860 allowed slavery. The Supreme Court ruled in favor of slavery in territories and in free states (*Dred Scott v. Sandford*, 1857, not overturned until the Thirteenth and Fourteenth Amendments). The Constitution even allowed greater southern representation in Congress to reflect their enslaved population. Despite endless complaints to the contrary, the Constitution benefited the South politically and financially, granting no power to emancipate slaves. The election of a Republican president would not change that.

In his inaugural address on March 4, 1861, two weeks after Jefferson Davis was sworn in as the Confederacy's leader, Lincoln painstakingly explained why secession was not legal. Using the Constitution and the Declaration of Independence as evidence, Lincoln spoke plainly about the illegality of disunion. With the language of a contract lawyer, he asked, "If the United States be not a government proper, but an association of States in the nature of contract merely, can it, as a contract, be peaceably unmade

---

[4]Lincoln, Jan. 27, 1838, in *The Collected Works of Abraham Lincoln*, ed. Roy P. Basler, 9 vols. (New Brunswick, N.J., 1953–55), 1:108–15 (hereafter *CW*).

by less than all the parties who made it?" Clearly not: "[o]ne party to a contract may violate it—break it, so to speak—but does it not require all to lawfully rescind it?"[5]

Only "a majority held in restraint by constitutional checks and limitations," Lincoln counseled, "and always changing easily with deliberate changes of popular opinions and sentiments" could offer the "true sovereign of a free people." Underlying his reliance on the rule of law was an abhorrence of disorder. Echoing his 1828 Lyceum speech, he stated, "Plainly, the central idea of secession is the essence of anarchy."[6] In his message to Congress in July of 1861, he said, "The principle [of secession] itself is one of disintegration, and upon which no government can possibly endure."[7]

Nine years later the Supreme Court would agree with Lincoln's analysis in denying the right of secession. In 1869 in *Texas v. White*, a case involving federal bonds, Chief Justice Salmon P. Chase wrote the majority opinion that the federal Constitution "in all its provisions looks to an indestructible Union, composed of indestructible States." In 1865 Lincoln had appointed Chase, a man who had been a thorn in his side politically, to the highest court in the land. Lincoln admitted to friends that he "would rather have swallowed his buckhorn chair than to have nominated Chase." But Lincoln knew that "To have done otherwise I should have been recreant to my convictions of my duty to the Republican Party and to the country."[8] And indeed, Chase's appointment was successful on several fronts, as he echoed Lincoln on rights for freed African Americans as well as on the illegality of secession.

In 1861, seceded states were very sure of their own legal grounding. In regard to a lawful contract, the Confederate states felt that the North as a whole had already abrogated that contract by not sufficiently protecting slavery. And with the northern half not meeting its contractual obligations,

---

[5]First Inaugural Address, Mar. 4, 1861, *CW*, 4:262–71, quote on p. 265.
[6]Ibid., quote on p. 268.
[7]Message to Congress in Special Session, July 4, 1861, *CW*, 4:421–41, quote on p. 436.
[8]*Texas v. White*, 74 US 700 (1869), quote p. 725. See also Peter Radan, "Lincoln, the Constitution and Secession," in *Secession as an International Phenomenon: From America's Civil War to Contemporary Separatist Movements*, ed. Don H. Doyle (Athens, Ga., 2010), p. 70. Doyle's book and Radan's article show pointedly the relevance of U.S. secessionism to separatist movements in the world today; diary entry, Dec. 15, 1864, Gideon Welles, *Diary of Gideon Welles, Secretary of the Navy under Lincoln and Johnson*, 3 vols. (Boston, 1911), 2:196; Burton, *Age of Lincoln*, pp. 238–39; Doris Kearns Goodwin, *Team of Rivals: The Political Genius of Abraham Lincoln* (New York, 2005), p. 680.

it was then legal for the South to negate its part. In its declaration of December 24, 1860, South Carolina asserted the right of secession because "We maintain that in every compact between two or more parties, the obligation is mutual; that the failure of one of the contracting parties to perform a material part of the agreement, entirely releases the obligation of the other."[9] The Texas ordinance of secession referred to a compact of union. That state found it had the legal right to secede because "the Federal Government has failed to accomplish the purposes of the compact of union between these States."[10]

Quoting language in the Declaration of Independence, which announced why the original thirteen colonies felt the need to secede from Great Britain in 1776, the seceding states declared their preference for a new government "on such principles and organizing its powers in such form, as to them shall seem most likely to effect their safety and happiness." The rationale for this point of view relied on the work of South Carolina's dominant political leader and political theorist, John C. Calhoun. Ironically, according to Lincoln's closest friend, Joshua Speed, Lincoln "was a great admirer of the style of John C. Calhoun." Lincoln, always interested in learning to write well and wanting to use rhetoric effectively to persuade others, studied Calhoun's writing, even preferring the Carolinian's style over that of his hero, Henry Clay. Calhoun had struggled with the problem of sectional conflict for most of his political life, even up to his death in 1850. He had subscribed to South Carolina's right to abolish federal laws during the Nullification Crisis in 1830, when Democratic President Andrew Jackson put Calhoun on notice at a dinner celebrating Jefferson Day (April 13, 1830). He toasted, "Our Union: It must be preserved." Calhoun responded to Jackson's challenge and offered the next toast: "The Union, next to our liberty, most dear." Tariffs notwithstanding, Calhoun's "liberty" meant the liberty to own slaves. Privately, Jackson threatened to hang Calhoun. When Jackson dispatched a fleet of eight ships and a shipment of five thousand muskets to

---

[9]"Declaration of the Immediate Causes which Induce and Justify the Secession of South Carolina from the Federal Union Declaration," Dec. 24, 1860, http://yale.edu/awweb/avalon/csa/scarsec.htm (accessed Aug. 29, 2010); see also Radan, "Lincoln, the Constitution, and Secession," p. 64.

[10]"An Ordinance: To Dissolve the Union between the State of Texas and the Other States, United under the Compact Styled 'The Constitution of the United States of America,' Adopted in Convention, at Austin City, the First Day of February, A.D. 1861,"www.tsl.state.tx.us/ref/abouttx/secession/1feb1861.html (accessed Sept. 13, 2013).

South Carolina, the state responded by organizing militia regiments across the state. Calhoun's brinksmanship paid off when Henry Clay, the "great compromiser," worked out a lower tariff. No other state supported South Carolina's dare at that time.[11]

In 1849 Calhoun hammered out his view of the state–federal government relationship in his *Disquisition on Government*: "it is federal and not national, because it is the government of a community of States, and not the government of a single State or nation." Accordingly, "That a State, as a party to the constitutional compact, has the right to secede—acting in the same capacity in which it ratified the constitution—cannot, with any show of reason, be denied by any one who regards the constitution as a compact."[12]

Ultimately, secession was a matter of power, and the election of Abraham Lincoln signaled that a minority of people from a sectional political party could decide the presidency. Could that minority then decide on the issue of emancipation? In declaring secession, Alabama, among others, raised just this issue—that the election of Abraham Lincoln could affect that state's "domestic institution" of slavery. Victory

> by a sectional party, avowedly hostile to the domestic institutions and to the peace and security of the people of the State of Alabama, preceded by many and dangerous infractions of the constitution of the United States by many of the States and people of the Northern section, is a political wrong of so insulting and menacing a character as to justify the people of the State of Alabama in the adoption of prompt and decided measures for their future peace and security.[13]

---

[11] Joshua F. Speed to William H. Herndon, Dec. 6, 1866, in Douglas L. Wilson and Rodney O. Davis, ed., *Herndon's Informants: Letters, Interviews, and Statements about Abraham Lincoln* (Urbana, Ill., 1988), p. 31; Douglas L. Wilson, *Lincoln's Sword: The Presidency and the Power of Words* (New York, 2006), p. 31; http://xroads.virginia.edu/~cap/CALHOUN/jcc1.html (last accessed Sept. 16, 2013); Edward Pessen, *Jacksonian America: Society, Personality, and Politics* (Homewood, Ill., 1969), p. 342.

[12] John C. Calhoun, "A Discourse on the Constitution and Government of the United States," 1850 (published posthumously, 1851) in *Union and Liberty: The Political Philosophy of John C. Calhoun*, ed. Ross M. Lence (Indianapolis, Ind., 1992), pp. 116, 212; www.constitution.org/jcc/dcgus.htm (accessed Aug. 29, 2010). See also Radan, "Lincoln, the Constitution, and Secession," p. 59; http://www.constitution.org/jcc/jcc.htm (accessed Aug. 29, 2010).

[13] "An Ordinance to Dissolve the Union between the State of Alabama and the Other States United under the Compact Styled 'The Constitution of the United States of America,'" Jan. 11, 1861; www.sonofthesouth.net/leefoundation/Alabama_secession_Ordinance.htm (accessed Sept. 16, 2013).

In Lincoln's first official speech, his inaugural address of March 4, 1861, he avoided any discussion of emancipation. Lincoln tried to convince southern secessionists that their actions were illegal. Lincoln also tried to assure secessionists that the Union deserved their support because of all they shared: one nation with a common history and culture. He tried to bring their focus to "a view and a hope of a peaceful solution of the national troubles and the restoration of fraternal sympathies and affections." Lincoln offered pride in the legacy of the Founding Fathers. He offered satisfaction that America was the land of opportunity. It was only in the Union that a Lincoln could rise from poverty to the middle class by working hard. His emotional appeal bordered on begging them to come to their senses and not "risk the commission of so fearful a mistake." He asked, "Before entering upon so grave a matter as the destruction of our national fabric, with all its benefits, its memories, and its hopes, would it not be wise to ascertain precisely why we do it?"[14]

In asserting nationhood, Lincoln spoke not of slavery and cultural differences, but of friendship and shared history: "We are not enemies, but friends. We must not be enemies. Though passion may have strained it must not break our bonds of affection. The mystic chords of memory, stretching from every battlefield and patriot grave to every living heart and hearthstone all over this broad land, will yet swell the chorus of the Union, when again touched, as surely they will be, by the better angels of our nature."[15]

Secessionists had been sharpening their reply over the years of sectional conflict. South Carolinian fire-eater Robert Barnwell Rhett asserted, in contrast, that "the people of England and Ireland, Russia and Poland, Austria and Italy, are not more distinct and antagonistic in their characters, pursuits, and institutions, their sympathies and views, than the people of our Northern and Southern States." Although the Unites States did have a shared language and history, as opposed to Rhett's examples, Rhett's assertion was a common point of view among some southern intellectuals who contrasted northern factories with southern agrarian life. Secessionists believed the northern and southern sections of the country had moved too far

---

[14]First Inaugural Address, Mar. 4, 1861, *CW*, 4:262–71, quote on p. 266.
[15]Ibid., quote on p. 271.

apart to claim a common culture. Slavery had kept the South pure while the North was a hotbed of radicalism.[16]

Pushing against any rapprochement between North and South were also irrational fears, and indeed fear-mongering burgeoned. One week after Lincoln's election, on November 13, 1860, the son of John C. Calhoun articulated a central fear of many southern slaveholders. Speaking to the South Carolina Agricultural Society, Andrew Pickens Calhoun predicted that the antislavery rhetoric of Lincoln and his cronies would incite slave rebellions. He blamed the foreign radical ideas of "liberty, equality and fraternity" as helping to instigate the slave revolt in Haiti, and he warned of a similar disaster in the American South. A secessionist press stirred animosity. One small-town Georgia newspaper was typical: "Can we suppose, for a moment, that the South will submit to a Black ruler of our Government?" The article vowed that the South would never recognize a "Negro President" and branded Lincoln a "notorious nigger thief"; the paper offered a reward of ten thousand dollars for "Hannibal's [Vice President–elect Hannibal Hamlin] and Abe's heads without their bodies."[17]

Earlier, John Brown's raid had played a crucial role in southern slaveholders' fear of emancipation. Like an Old Testament prophet leading the way to a new freedom in America, Brown was determined to cut through the moral temporizing and constitutional chess games which abolitionism had fallen into. On October 16, 1859, Brown's small group, armed with Sharps rifles, marched on the federal arsenal at Harpers Ferry, Virginia, though what Brown intended to do once he had captured it remains profoundly unclear. Broadly, the plan had been to secure arms inside and hand them out to slaves and local nonslaveholding whites, who he believed were eager to rise in rebellion.

In the immediate aftermath of the failed raid, Southerners conjoined outrage with panic and paranoia. While the Harpers Ferry raid focused

---

[16]Robert Barnwell Rhett, *The Political Life and Services of the Hon. R. Barnwell Rhett, of South Carolina, by a Contemporary (the Late Hon. Daniel Wallace)* (n.p., n.d.), p. 42; Paul Quigley, "Secessionists in an Age of Secession: The Slave South in Transatlantic Perspective," in *Secession as an International Phenomenon*, pp. 151–52; see Burton, *Age of Lincoln*, esp. chap. 2.

[17]Columbia *Daily South Carolinian*, Nov. 14, 1860; Charles B. Dew, *Apostles of Disunion: Southern Secession Commissioners and the Causes of the Civil War* (Charlottesville, 2001), pp. 40–41; *Waynesboro* (Georgia) *Gopher*, n.d., clipping ca. Nov. 1860, Abraham Lincoln Presidential Library and Museum, Springfield, Ill. (Lincoln kept a copy of this newspaper clipping); Holzer, *Lincoln President-Elect*, p. 55.

southern rage on northern agitation, it should have assuaged southern fears in three ways. First, given the opportunity and the means to rebel, enslaved people did not rise up, either in Virginia or further afield. Indeed, the only southern African American involved in the affair had proven loyal to southern society unto death; as for Brown's five northern African American accomplices, Southerners saw them as deluded by an excess of liberty and the clever words of their captain. Second, local white nonslaveholders had also proven their fidelity. Virginians of all classes and colors had turned their backs on Brown's blow for freedom. And third, Harpers Ferry affirmed for the South that, when slavery was threatened—as pitifully as Brown's raid may be said to have done so—the power of the federal government had been exerted in its defense. The swords and bayonets of U.S. Marines had defended slavery.[18]

Abraham Lincoln was no fan of John Brown. While admitting that "he agreed with us in thinking slavery wrong," nevertheless Lincoln severely faulted Brown for lawlessness. Motives "cannot excuse the violence, bloodshed, and treason."[19] Slavery was legal, and Lincoln disavowed extremists of every stripe who threatened governance by rule of law. Lincoln distanced his party from the actions of Brown. In his speech at Cooper Union in February 1860, he pointed out that the congressional investigation, under southern leadership, "failed to implicate a single Republican in his Harpers Ferry enterprise." He was sure "John Brown was no Republican."[20] Brown furnished slaveholders not merely with a symbol but with an opportunity to turn their aggressions outward on the meddling Yankee.

Determined to keep the focus on fear of emancipation, Robert Barnwell Rhett drew up an emotional and melodramatic bill of grievances for South Carolina's secession. The North, he charged, had "encouraged and assisted thousands of our slaves to leave their homes; and those who remain, have been incited by emissaries, books and pictures to servile insurrection."[21] Even moderate Carolinians seemed to have lost all sense of proportion. Congressman John Ashmore, from the upcountry Anderson District of yeoman

---

[18]See Burton, *Age of Lincoln*, pp. 92–100; Robert E. McGlone, *John Brown's War against Slavery* (Cambridge, 2009), pp. 244–328.
[19]Speech at Leavenworth, Kansas, Dec. 3, 1859, *CW*, 3:497–502, quote on p. 502.
[20]Address at Cooper Union, Feb. 27, 1860, *CW*, 3:522–50, quote on p. 538.
[21]*Journal of the Convention of the People of South Carolina, Held in 1860–1861: Together with the Reports, Resolutions, &c.* (Charleston, 1861), pp. 330–31; Dew, *Apostles of Disunion*, p. 12.

farmers of small and medium-sized farms, won his seat because of his moderate views. He declared his "firm conviction throughout my whole life that Disunion is the direst calamity that can befall the people (both North and South)." He believed in the right to secession "in the abstract," but in 1858 he opposed calling for it.[22] And yet this moderate changed when he came to believe the nonexistent threat that the North wanted "to turn loose a hungry horde of free negroes" who would jeopardize "the honor of his wife and daughter."[23] Another moderate, James L. Orr, who came frustratingly close to being Stephen Douglas's Democratic vice presidential running mate in 1860, warned upcountry farmers of their peril after Lincoln's election. He embraced secession's cause, but not from irrational fear. His prediction was more prophetic: Republican aggressions would never cease, he argued, until they had instituted "equality at the ballot box and jury box, and at the witness stand."[24] At that time, however, these were not Republican goals.

Lincoln pleaded for rationality and calm to prevail. He strove repeatedly to allay fears that his party aimed at dismantling slavery. "I have no purpose, directly or indirectly," he promised, "to interfere with the institution of slavery in the States where it exists." The presidency conveyed no such power, he asserted, and the Constitution permitted no such meddling. "I believe I have no lawful right to do so," he allowed, adding "and I have no inclination to do so." The rule of law constrained him no less than he expected it to constrain his fellow Americans. In only another four years, he pointed out, those dissatisfied might elect a president more to their liking. The country needed time and prudence, but those virtues were in short supply in the volatile atmosphere of paranoia over possible emancipation.[25]

Lincoln was very careful in his selection of words, and did not mention emancipation at all during the crisis. In the eight volumes of Roy P. Basler,

---

[22]Thomas Ashmore to Benjamin F. Perry, Jan. 30, 1858, in the Papers of Benjamin F. Perry, Alabama Department of Archives and History, Montgomery, Ala.; Charles B. Dew, "Lincoln, the Collapse of Deep South Moderation, and the Triumph of Secession: A South Carolina Congressman's Moment of Truth," in *Secession as an International Phenomenon*, p. 100.

[23]Ashmore, quoted in *Congressional Globe*, 36th Cong., 1st sess., Mar. 1–2, 1860, pp. 959–62; Dew, "Lincoln, the Collapse of Deep South Moderation, and the Triumph of Secession," p. 104.

[24]*Keowee Courier* (Walhalla, S.C.), Dec. 1, 1860; Roger P. Leemhuis, *James L. Orr and the Sectional Conflict* (Washington, D.C., 1979), p. 73; Burton, *Age of Lincoln*, pp. 120–21; Dew, *Apostles of Disunion*, p. 46.

[25]First Inaugural Address, Mar. 4, 1861, *CW*, 4:262–71, quotes on p. 263.

ed., *The Collected Works of Abraham Lincoln,* the word *emancipation/emancipate* appears 230 times, thirty-nine of which are editors' annotations. In the actual collected correspondence, Lincoln used the word 191 times. In the first four volumes, until April 30, 1861, including the secession crisis, *emancipation* appears forty-four times, three of those by the editors in annotations. Lincoln's first use of the word *emancipation* was in his July 6, 1852, eulogy for his beau ideal, Senator Henry Clay. There, Lincoln quoted one of the most quintessential Southerners, Thomas Jefferson, and spoke of gradual emancipation. He advocated Clay's idea of colonization: "There is a moral fitness in the idea of returning to Africa her children, whose ancestors have been torn from her by the ruthless hand of fraud and violence. Transplanted in a foreign land, they will carry back to their native soil the rich fruits of religion, civilization, law and liberty. May it not be one of the great designs of the Ruler of the universe, (whose ways are often inscrutable by shortsighted mortals,) thus to transform an original crime, into a signal blessing to that most unfortunate portion of the globe?"[26]

It was not until two years later, in 1854, in what some historian dub the "first Lincoln-Douglas debate," that Lincoln again uses the word *emancipation,* again advocating colonization: "My first impulse would be to free the slaves, and send them to Liberia—to their own native land." Lincoln considered several alternatives to slavery. For colonization there was not enough money or resources to accomplish it, even if people wanted to emigrate. For emancipation with the establishment of racial hierarchy ("Free them all, and keep them among us as underlings?"), he felt would not better the slaves' conditions. For full emancipation and equality ("Free them, and make them politically and socially, our equals?"), Lincoln wondered if equality of white and black were possible, and he acknowledged that many of his peers would deny any such idea: "My own feelings will not admit of this; and if mine would, we well know that those of the great mass of white people will not."[27]

Lincoln's conclusion was to entrust Southerners with the task of emancipation. "It does seem to me that systems of gradual emancipation might be adopted; but for their tardiness in this, I will not undertake to judge our

---

[26]Eulogy on Henry Clay, July 6, 1852, *CW,* 2:121–32, quote p. 132.
[27]Speech at Peoria, Illinois, Oct. 16, 1854, *CW,* 2:247–82, quotes p. 255. See, for example, John A. Corry, *The First Lincoln-Douglas Debates, October 1854* (Philadelphia, 2008); Lewis E. Lehrman, *Lincoln at Peoria: The Turning Point* (Mechanicsburg, Pa., 2008).

brethren of the south."[28] He maintained this stance throughout the Lincoln-Douglas debates of 1858 as well. But two years later, during his campaign for the presidency, there is a slight change of tone in Lincoln on emancipation, a note of frustration with southern voters. Francis Blair in Missouri had been defeated in his reelection bid to the U.S. House of Representatives (Blair contested the election and eventually won the seat), and in 1860 Lincoln in Hartford, Connecticut, expounded, "If those democrats really think slavery wrong they will be much pleased when earnest men in the slave states take up a plan of gradual emancipation and go to work energetically and very kindly to get rid of the evil. Now let us test them. Frank Blair tried it; and he ran for Congress in '58, and got beaten. Did the democracy feel bad about it? I reckon not—I guess you all flung up your hats and shouted 'Hurrah for the Democracy!'"[29] This was Lincoln's last use of the word *emancipation* until well after the presidential election and the secession of the southern states. (In May, Tennessee was the last southern state to secede, but it became official on June 18, 1861.) Lincoln only used the word in private correspondence with his Illinois friend Orville Browning on September 22, 1861.[30] He did not use the word publicly until well into the Civil War, he proposed gradual emancipation to Delaware in November 1861; on December 3, 1861, in his annual message to Congress, he suggested compensated emancipation and colonization; and on March 6, 1862, he asked Congress for aid to any state that adopted plans of compensated and gradual emancipation.[31]

In this digital age, new methods can be brought to bear on how words are used. The eight volumes of *The Collected Works of Abraham Lincoln* are all digitized, a remarkable resource for scholars and public alike, a resource that would have seemed miraculous a score of years ago. One new digital tool is a word cloud. Although a word cloud cannot measure poetry and grandeur, it shows, in my opinion, in an interesting and artistic way, the number of times certain words are used: the more times a word is used, the larger its

---

[28]Speech at Peoria, Illinois, Oct. 16, 1854, *CW*, 2:256.
[29]Speech at Hartford, Connecticut, Mar. 5, 1860 (*Evening Press* version), *CW*, 4:8–13, quote on p. 11.
[30]Lincoln to Orville Browning (marked "Private and confidential"), Sept. 22, 1861, *CW*, 4:532.
[31]Eric Foner, *The Fiery Trial: Abraham Lincoln and Slavery* (New York, 2010) is a superb account of the development of the Emancipation Proclamation. He has a chronology on pp. 339–45; see esp. p. 342 on emancipation.

FIG. 1. The three hundred words used most frequently by Lincoln from his nomination, May 18, 1860, to his inauguration on March 4, 1861. *(The author)*

size and prominence in the word cloud. This tool basically counts words. But, of course, words hold meaning, and so a counting can highlight the concepts emphasized in a speech or letter.[32] I studied a series of word clouds for Lincoln over time. Figure 1 represents an analysis of the three hundred words used most frequently by Lincoln from his nomination, May 18, 1860, to his inauguration on March 4, 1861. As explained above, emancipation does not appear. Lincoln's focus is on the rule of law: the most common words used—constitution, states, union, law, friends—are overwhelmingly positive; law, people, union, friends, constitution, government, good and great connote a good feeling. Slave(ry) appears as a less commonly used word, along with some other "smaller" words that are used: necessary/necessity, contrary, force, federal, fugitive, trouble, anxiety, impossible. Lincoln had to address slavery because slavery is why the Confederate states seceded. But Lincoln never threatened emancipation. Instead, he focused on preserving the Union. Only when the Union was torn apart could Lincoln use emancipation as a wartime measure to *preserve* (a word that shows in the cloud, top-left) the Union.

---

[32] The nine volumes (one is an index) of *The Collected Works of Abraham Lincoln* can be accessed at http://quod.lib.umich.edu/l/lincoln/. We have cleaned out the html markups and limited the texts to those by Lincoln, and only one copy. Please contact Vernon Burton for methodology.

During the secession crisis of December 1860 and early 1861, Lincoln strove to reassure secessionists that they need not fear any proclamations on emancipation; emancipation was not an option in 1861. He made every effort to reassure them in other ways. He refused to demonize slaveholders. Lincoln compassionately tried to understand other points of view. He wrote, "If I lived in the South, I would think as you do, I would act as you do." He appointed Southerners to his cabinet, even considering eventual Confederate Vice President Alexander Stephens, a fellow Whig congressman in the one term Lincoln served in the U.S. House of Representatives. The *New York Times* reported on December 27, 1860, that "during this season of sensations and alarms," many "old associates and friends throughout the South" were relieved over the appointment of Missourian Edward Bates. The paper suggested that such appointments showed that "nothing aggressive or ultra will characterize the policy of the next Administration."[33]

Lincoln believed that calm words and patient waiting would cause disunion to collapse. I believe scholars need to carefully investigate how Lincoln's family relations influenced how he dealt with others in the public sphere.[34] I have heard lawyers connect the home life of a judge, the feelings of well-being or irritation, the good breakfast or the bad coffee, to that day's judicial rulings. A case in point may be Lincoln's relationship with his wife, Mary. Lincoln loved Mary and he tolerated her temper tantrums in a simple way. He ignored them. He hoisted the boys on his shoulders and went for a little walk to give her time to calm down and be sensible. In a speech at Cincinnati in 1861, Lincoln suggested this same strategy in dealing with secession: "I think there is no occasion for any excitement. The crisis, as it is called, is altogether an artificial crisis. . . . Let it alone and it will go down of itself."[35] Unfortunately, the South proved much "madder" than Mary!

---

[33] *New York Times*, Dec. 27, 1860, p. 1.

[34] In an interview with Brian Lamb, Doris Kearns Goodwin discussed Edward Bates's seventeen children and his devotion to his wife, so much so that he could not stand to be separated from her in Missouri. She explained, "This shows how family life can affect public life." And I would suggest that with all the fabulous work on gender and family in the last forty years we have only scratched the surface. Doris Kearns Goodwin, "Winning and Governing," in *Abraham Lincoln: Great American Historians on Our Sixteenth President*, ed. Brian Lamb and Susan Swain (New York, 2008), p. 67.

[35] Lincoln, Feb. 15, 1861, *CW*, 4:215–16. For examples of Mary Todd Lincoln's temper, see David Herbert Donald, *Lincoln* (New York, 1995), pp. 107–8, 158, 312; Jean H. Baker, *Mary Todd Lincoln: A Biography* (New York, 1987), pp. xiii, xiv, 106, 122, 205, 239; Ruth Painter Randall, *Mary Lincoln: Biography of a Marriage* (Boston, 1953), pp. 119–24, 372–73.

While fire-eaters throughout the South advocated secession, some in Congress were not particularly worried, recalling the many times that such threats had been used. In 1856 Lincoln himself had scoffed at such threats. "Humbug, nothing but folly," Lincoln had declared at that time.[36] Senator Carl Schurz of Missouri recalled that in 1859 some members of the House seceded over the election of William Pennington, a Republican from New Jersey, as the new speaker of the House of Representatives. According to Schurz, "they seceded from Congress, went out, took a drink, and then came back." Schurz predicted that in their anger over Lincoln's election, "they would secede again and this time would take two drinks but come back again."[37]

Lincoln wanted to believe the irrationality of secession would stop. Most scholars hold that Lincoln misjudged the strength of secessionist feelings because he had not spent much time in the South, but this assessment does not take into account Lincoln's relationship with the South. While Lincoln and other Republicans dared not campaign in the South, and Lincoln had not really visited the Deep South except for one excursion to New Orleans early in his life, he had faced southern leadership in the halls of Congress and listened to southern boasts, complaints, and apologies during his time in Washington. More than this, the region in which he was born and lived—the Upper South and southern areas of Ohio, Indiana, and Illinois—were broadly populated by Southerners. Lincoln counted many Southerners as clients and friends, and his hometown of Springfield, Illinois, had many white Southerners. Before taking the name of Springfield, the early settlers had named the town Calhoun after John C. Calhoun. And it was these Southerners, as well as his wife and friends from Kentucky, who led Lincoln to believe that most Southerners wholeheartedly supported the Union while their support of the institution of slavery was more ambivalent.[38]

Lincoln himself, born in Kentucky, had southern roots. Both his father and his mother were Virginians. Growing up poor, with homesteading as a

---

[36]Speech at Galena, Illinois, July 23, 1856, *CW*, 2:355.
[37]Phillip Shaw Paludan, *The Presidency of Abraham Lincoln* (Lawrence, Kans., 1994), p. 5.
[38]David Moltke-Hansen, "Intellectual and Cultural History of the Old South," in *A Companion to the American South*, ed. John B. Boles (Malden, Mass., 2002), p. 213. See also Moltke-Hansen's essay "Regional Frameworks and Networks: Changing Identities in the Southeastern United States," in *Regional Images and Regional Realities*, ed. Lothar Hoennighausen (Tübingen, 2000), pp. 153–54; Burton, *Age of Lincoln*, esp. pp. 127–30; www.usacitiesonline.com/ilcountyspringfield.htm#history (accessed Aug. 26, 2010).

way of life, he respected hardworking, less wealthy but self-reliant southern men and women. He knew that many southern whites opposed slavery even as they also opposed abolitionism. More to the point, he knew that most southern whites did not want to see the Union torn apart. He thought that the majority of southern yeomen would not be persuaded by the fiery rhetoric of their leaders. In the end, after all, the master class had little to offer the South's common people. He, and many like him, connected the prosperity of the country with its promise of "Liberty for All." Lincoln calculated that most white Southerners, yeomen like his own family, would reject extremism. "The people of the South have too much of good sense, and good temper," he reasoned, "to attempt the ruin of the government."[39]

In his address to Congress on July 4, 1861, Lincoln again focused on the issue of secession and not the issue of slavery or emancipation: "It may well be questioned whether there is, today, a majority of the legally-qualified voters of any State, except perhaps South Carolina, in favor of disunion. There is much reason to believe that the Union men are the majority in many, if not every other one, of the so-called seceded States."[40] Perhaps Lincoln's assessment of his fellow Southerners was not far off the mark. No one knows how many white Southerners favored secession in those first days; leading secessionists did not trust the people to support such a move and did not put the issue up for a vote.

The newly sovereign Southerners, instead of taking practical measures to secure southern independence, working out a viable policy toward the upper South, and establishing a satisfactory foreign policy, set speedily about writing a new constitution. The argument that this reflects the immature enthusiasms gripping the South misreads the central purposes of the moderate men who controlled the new nation. The new constitution served primarily as a list of ransom demands Southerners intended to gain from the Union as a condition for reunification.[41]

The U.S. Constitution was a pure and good document, Confederates declared, but it had been betrayed and sullied by the "Black Republicans" of

---

[39] Abraham Lincoln to John B. Fry, Aug. 15, 1860, *CW*, 4:95; Stephen Oates, *With Malice Toward None: The Life of Abraham Lincoln* (New York, 1978), p. 180; Burton, *Age of Lincoln*, pp. 128–30.

[40] Message to Congress, July 4, 1861, *CW*, 4:437.

[41] Foundational document for their newly formed nation in February 1861 (the provisional constitution) and then in March (the permanent constitution, which was adopted on March 11). See Burton, *Age of Lincoln*, pp. 123–24.

the North. The differences between the two constitutions represent the terms of the new bargain slaveholders hoped to drive with Washington. The Montgomery document was achieved by "each State acting in its sovereign and independent character," its preamble notes; any rewriting of the American Constitution would have to proceed on the same basis. They argued that their freedom—or, for those who read closely, the price of reunification—meant that property, enslaved or otherwise, would be protected, states' rights would be paramount, and the southern "way of life" would not be under siege. The Constitution of the United States dealt with the slavery issue but did not specify slavery. The Confederate Constitution included a provision in Article IV, "the institution of negro slavery, as it now exists in the Confederate States, shall be recognized and protected by Congress and by the Territorial government; and the inhabitants of the several Confederate States and Territories shall have the right to take to such Territory any slaves lawfully held by them in any of the States or Territories of the Confederate States."[42] This was essentially the language of the constitutional amendment Congress had so recently passed, except that it included the indispensable territorial protection. Confederates included it in their document both to indicate their central demand and to suggest how simple and minor such a broad change could be made to seem.

Beyond that, the Constitution of the Confederate States of America was broadly similar to the Constitution of the United States. Both seek "to establish justice, insure domestic tranquility, and secure the blessings of liberty to ourselves and our posterity." On one particular point the two differed. Regarding the issue of secession, the U.S. Constitution says nothing about permanence. The Confederate States of America preamble, however, specified "in order to form a permanent federal government," thereby supposedly precluding other future secessions. Yet what would happen the first time Dixie's legislators disagreed among themselves? If a minority secedes, Lincoln reasoned, "they make a precedent which in turn will divide and ruin them, for a minority of their own will secede from them whenever a majority refuses to be controlled by such minority." If secession were legal, then "why may not any portion of a new confederacy a year or two hence arbitrarily secede again, precisely as portions of the present Union now claim to secede from it? All who cherish disunion sentiments are now being

---

[42]http://www.usconstitution.net/csa.html.

educated to the exact temper of doing this."[43] On what basis could Confederates prevent seceders from seceding once more? Indeed, the Confederacy did have to confront their own seceders, including Jones County, Mississippi, and the new state of West Virginia.[44]

On the whole, differences were minor. Indeed, the Confederate Constitution is noteworthy for its attempt to mirror the American Constitution and the restraint with which it seeks to alter it. They carefully wrote it with the intent that it would become the basis for a reconciliation, that it would not be asking too much for the northern states to accept the Confederate Constitution. However much they hungered for more, rebels omitted mention of such deal-breakers as reopening the transatlantic slave trade for fear of upsetting the bargain they hoped to strike.[45]

Lincoln could have eliminated secessionist fever if he had been willing to give in to southern demands that slavery be extended to the territories. Some southern moderates continued to hope their defiance would bring concessions from the North and thereby forestall any breaking up of the Union. While a few held secession up as the good and final end, many believed that once the South marched out of the Union, a chastened North, economically dependent on southern cotton, would come to its senses and beg forgiveness. In this scenario, disunion became simply the means to create a more perfect Union while precluding any chance of emancipation and by securing slavery's benefits for all.

It is sadly ironic that Abraham Lincoln was the president during our most bloody war. He actually believed wholeheartedly in compromise and settling disputes, a rule that governed his entire life and his legal career. His beau ideal was the Whig Great Compromiser, Henry Clay. His vision for America was not of a house divided. Amazingly for those who think of Lincoln as "The Great Emancipator," Lincoln actually accepted the proposed constitutional amendment supporting slavery where it existed. "I understand a proposed amendment to the Constitution—which amendment, however, I have not seen—has passed Congress, to the effect that the Federal Government shall never interfere with the domestic institutions of the States, including that of persons held to service." Because Lincoln

---

[43]First Inaugural Address, *CW*, 4:262–71, quotes on pp. 267–68.
[44]Victoria E. Bynum, *The Free Sate of Jones: Mississippi's Longest Civil War* (Chapel Hill, 2001); Sally Jenkins and John Stauffer, *The State of Jones* (New York, 2009).
[45]Burton, *Age of Lincoln*, pp. 123–24.

acknowledged that the Constitution already allowed slavery, "holding such a provision to now be implied constitutional law," he would offer "no objection to its being made express and irrevocable."[46]

Ultimately, Lincoln would not concede principle. Lincoln's antislavery sentiments were fervent and real, and go far toward explaining why southern slaveholders saw Lincoln's elevation to the presidency as a dangerous revolutionary step. Although Lincoln pledged that he would not interfere with the institution of slavery where it existed, what he refused to renounce—as all Southerners noted—was the Republican commitment resolutely to oppose slavery's advance in the territories. Many Southerners believed it was only a matter of time before their world was crowded into oblivion. The rule of law could promise a thoroughgoing if incrementalist revolution. The Republican president would appoint Republican judges, marshals, customs collectors, post office clerks, and more in every corner of the South. Around each man, they knew, a web of patronage and status would soon grow up, until antislavery evils, currently held at bay, would come to be whispered in their midst. The day would come, southern Democrats knew, when a southern Republican party would flare up among them, pandering to the interests of white nonslaveholders and splitting communities between rich and poor. What then would prevent political conflict from passing over into class war—and eventually race war besides? North Carolinian Hinton Helper had already scared plantation owners when he forecast such a catastrophe in his book *The Impending Crisis* (1857).[47]

Traveling by train to Washington, D.C., after the presidential election, Lincoln gave short speeches along the route, including one at Independence Hall in Philadelphia. He announced, "I have never had a feeling politically that did not spring from the Declaration of Independence . . . that which gave promise that in due time the weights should be lifted from the shoulders of all men, and that all should have an equal chance. . . . Now, my friends, can this country be saved upon that basis? . . . If it can't be saved upon that principle . . . if this country cannot be saved without giving up on that principle . . . I would rather be assassinated on this spot than to surrender it."[48]

---

[46]First Inaugural Address, *CW*, 4:262–71, quote on p. 270.
[47]Burton, *Age of Lincoln*, pp. 90–92; Republican association with Helper's book had been the impetus for southern congressmen withdrawing from the House in 1859.
[48]"Speech in Independence Hall, Philadelphia, Pennsylvania, Feb. 22, 1861, *CW*, 4:240.

Before taking office Lincoln was not passive as Congress dealt with the secession crisis. He kept his party in line about where not to compromise—not acceptable was any expansion of slavery. He was not yet president when, through correspondence, he thrust himself into the congressional debate. While he never proposed widespread emancipation, Lincoln wrote to Republican Senator Lyman Trumbull, "Let there be no compromise on the question of extending slavery.... Have none of it. Stand firm. The tug has to come, & better now, than any time hereafter."[49] To Elihu Washburne, he wrote: "Hold firm, as with a chain of steel."[50] Lincoln rejected outright any claim "that slavery has equal rights with liberty."[51]

Short of giving in and allowing slavery in the territories, Lincoln could have averted war by allowing the secession of the seven southern states. Initially, some abolitionists, including Christian pacifist William Lloyd Garrison, advocated letting the South "go in peace." Horace Greeley, editor of the *New York Tribune* and a major Republican Party supporter, also favored the idea of letting the rascals go. "We hope never to live in a republic whereof one section is pinned to the residue by bayonets."[52] Other presidential candidates at the time would have let the southern states go without a fight. The London *Times* would later claim to find it difficult to understand how "a people fighting ... to force their fellow citizens to remain in a confederacy which they repudiated, can be called the champions of liberty and nationalism."[53] There was considerable concern about how European powers like England and France, which worried whether southern cotton would continue flowing to their mills, might react if Lincoln tried to coerce the Confederacy. Lame duck President James Buchanan, though opposed to secession, questioned bluntly whether the federal government had the power to compel states to remain in the Union if they wished to withdraw. "After much serious reflection," he concluded

---

[49]Lincoln to Lyman A. Trumbull, "Private and Confidential, Dec. 10, 1860, *CW*, 4:149–50.
[50]Lincoln to Hon. E. B. Washburne, Dec. 13, 1860, *CW*, 4:151. Harold Holzer affirms that Lincoln's instructions helped to strengthen Republican resolve (Holzer, *Lincoln: President-Elect*, p. 159).
[51]See Lincoln to John D. Defrees, Dec. 18, 1860, *CW*, 4:155.
[52]*Chicago Tribune*, Oct. 11, 1860; *New York Tribune*, Nov. 9, 1860; Foner, *Fiery Trial*, p. 146; James M. McPherson, *Battle Cry of Freedom: The Civil War Era* (New York, 1988), pp. 251–52.
[53]Quoted in Norman Graebner, "Northern Diplomacy and European Neutrality," in *Why the North Won the Civil War*, ed. David Donald (Baton Rouge, 1960), p. 76; Holzer, *Lincoln: President-Elect*, p. 160.

unhelpfully, "I have arrived at the conclusion that no such power has been delegated."[54]

While the Pennsylvanian Buchanan dithered, the Southerner-turned-Illini Lincoln did not. Lincoln knew that the Civil War involved honor. Southerners were clear about it. On December 14, 1860, nearly half of the congressional representatives of southern states had announced that "we are satisfied that the honor, safety, and independence of the Southern people require the organization of a Southern Confederacy."[55] For either Lincoln or the secessionists to back down was to lose face with their communities North and South, to lose that esteem so essential to the men and culture of honor. In his first annual message to Congress, Lincoln emphasized that with regard to foreign powers America must maintain "our own rights and honor."[56] When a committee from Baltimore demanded that he let the South go in peace, Lincoln replied, "You would have me break my oath and surrender the Government without a blow. There is no Washington in that—no Jackson in that—no manhood nor honor in that."[57]

Still hoping for some reconciliation, even after hostilities had begun, Lincoln appealed to feelings of national pride on the world scene. In his address to Congress on July 4, 1861, Lincoln argued that the fundamental question, relevant "to the whole family of man," was "whether a constitutional republic, or a democracy—a government of the people, by the same people—can or cannot maintain its territorial integrity against its own domestic foes."[58]

The following year (December 1862) Lincoln called the American endeavor the hope of the world: "We hold the power, and bear the responsibility. We shall nobly save, or meanly lose, the last best hope of earth."[59] Liberty and freedom and the fate of democratic republics were precarious. Worldwide movements for freedom were not ending well, and democracy

---

[54]James Buchanan, "1860 State of the Union Address," Dec. 3, 1860, www.presidentialrhetoric.com/historicspeeches/buchanan/stateoftheunion1860.html (last accessed Sept. 16, 2013).
[55]John David Smith, "Discovering America: A Special Issue," *Journal of American History* 79 (1992):1176–78. Haskell M. Monroe Jr. et al., eds., *The Papers of Jefferson Davis*, 13 vols. to date (Baton Rouge, 1971–), Vol. 6: *1856–1860*, ed. Lynda L. Crist and Mary S. Dix (1989).
[56]First Annual Message to Congress, Dec. 3, 1861, *CW*, 5:35–53.
[57]Lincoln, "Reply to Baltimore Committee," Apr. 22, 1861, *CW*, 4:341.
[58]Message to Congress in Special Session, July 4, 1861, *CW*, 4:421–41, quote on p. 426.
[59]Annual Message to Congress, Dec. 1, 1862, *CW*, 5:537.

may have become an obsolete ideal. The French Revolution of 1789, based on the American Revolution of 1776, had plummeted downward into terror and dictatorship; the French Revolution of 1848 ended with the Second French Empire. Other European revolutions of 1848 were crushed by the old order; monarchies prevailed everywhere. The patriot of unification in Italy, Garibaldi was blocked by the power of the king and was not able to form a republic. Latin American attempts at republicanism were faltering, and attempts at democracy apparently brought only chaos.[60] And now the great experiment in democratic republicanism, the United States, appeared ready to topple. If people were not able to govern themselves, a government of the people, for the people, by the people, could not work. Lincoln hoped the secessionists would see that American government, a democratic republic, was a model of freedom and opportunity for the world and should not be destroyed.

Certainly Lincoln would not allow its destruction, and he had some confidence that if the South waited for a covert act of aggression from the North, they would have to wait forever. So far, the battle was fought with words. Lincoln's determination not to let the South go went hand-in-hand with his restraint. Across the South, armed militants seized U.S. arsenals, shipyards, and forts, asserting their sovereignty and daring Washington to react, but Lincoln refused to be goaded. Military confrontation was the last thing Lincoln wanted. If Northerners avoided calls for emancipation, time's passage might permit moderates to solve the impasse.

But the South dared not wait. As March turned to April, Confederate fever seemed to be waning across the South, as the tasks of spring cultivation beckoned once more. Men put down their muskets and picked up their hoes, ready to put politics aside for a season. In Montgomery, Confederate options seemed to have run out. There had been no meaningful negotiations with the North, and few prospects that Lincoln could be needled into some rash act which would drive the upper South out of the Union. Secession would peter out; disunion and war would be averted.

Radicals, however, would not accept that the rebel cause looked likely to fail. Their answer was the same one John Brown had understood at the hour of his own death. According to the radical Edmund Ruffin of Virginia, a

---

[60]Don H. Doyle, "Union and Secession in the Family of Nations," in *Secession as an International Phenomenon*.

man who had hurried across Virginia to see John Brown swing barely a year earlier, "The shedding of blood will serve to change many voters in the hesitating states from the submission or procrastinating ranks, to the zealous for immediate secession."[61]

And so it was that, at 4:30 A.M. on April 12, General Pierre Gustave Toutant Beauregard ordered South Carolina militia, now constituted as Confederate troops, to fire on Fort Sumter.

With the firing on Fort Sumter and Lincoln's subsequent call to arms, President Lincoln defined the war as one to preserve the Union. He was careful to characterize the war in terms of following the rule of law rather than ending slavery. Scholars still struggle with the complexities of Lincoln's insistence that the war was about the Union rather than about emancipation. Lincoln's call to preserve the Union rallied northern opinion to the cause, but it also let nonslaveholding Southerners off the hook. By bracketing slavery, Lincoln allowed white Southerners, when they took up arms against the Union, to tell themselves that they did so in defense of their families, households, and communities, and not in defense of slavery as such. Moreover, as war loomed, the international press was electrified by reports that Lincoln had invited Giuseppe Garibaldi, the international hero of Italian unification, to take a command in the Union army. Early in his negotiations with U.S. officials, Garibaldi posed the question of the hour: "Tell me also if this agitation is regarding the emancipation of the Negroes or not"? If not, he said, "the war would appear to be like any civil war in which the world at large could have little interest or sympathy." The Italian revolutionary hero Garibaldi was not interested in a simple domestic dispute.[62]

Garibaldi's question loomed large in the global context as puzzled foreigners waited for each side to explain whether this was something of real consequence to the larger world. By the time of the Emancipation Proclamation, effective January 1863, and perhaps more so by the time of the Gettysburg Address in November 1863, the war to prevent secession had

---

[61]McPherson, *Battle Cry of Freedom*, p. 273.
[62]John Parris, *The Lion of Caprera: A Biography of Giuseppe Garibaldi* (New York, 1962), p. 269; Jasper Ridley, *Garibaldi* (New York, 1974), p. 521; H. Nelson Gay, "Lincoln's Offer of a Command to Garibaldi," *Century Illustrated Monthly Magazine* 75 (1907):65, 72; H. Nelson Gay, "Garibaldi's American Contacts and His Claims to American Citizenship," *American Historical Review* 38 (1932):1–19; Don Doyle at http://opinionator.blogs.nytimes.com/author/don-h-doyle/.

changed. "Heir of the thought of Christ and of [John] Brown," Garibaldi celebrated Lincoln as the "Pilot of Liberty," and proclaimed "You will pass down to posterity under the name of *the Emancipator!*"[63] With the Gettysburg Address, Lincoln proclaimed the hopeful determination of the human spirit for freedom. The president spoke a language of love, patriotism, and piety to his listeners: honor, dedication, increased devotion, high resolution need to be brought to the labor. Human liberty and democracy themselves were at stake. What would victory in this awful war look like? Lincoln's vision was at once conservative and revolutionary. There would be overflowing cemeteries, vacant chairs at family tables, men broken bodily and spiritually, but "government of the people, by the people, for the people shall not perish from the earth." More than simply preserving the liberty of the fathers, the nation, Lincoln's new nation, "under God," would have "a new birth of freedom."[64] Lincoln's vision of America still resonates today, one of preserving and expanding freedom and liberty while remaining within the context of the rule of law.

---

[63]Garibaldi to Abraham Lincoln, Emancipator of the Slaves in the American Republic, Aug. 6, 1863, Giuseppe Garibaldi, *Scritti politici e militari*, ed. Domenico Ciàmpoli, (Rome, 1907), p. 330; the English translation can be found at http://www.reformation.org/garibaldi_lincoln.html, and as published in the *New York Times* at http://www.nytimes.com/1863/08/30/news/the-italian-liberals-to-president-lincoln-a-letter-written-by-garibaldi.html.

[64]Gettysburg Address, *CW*, 7:22–23.

Beverly Wilson Palmer

Stevens, Sumner, and the Journey to Full Emancipation

CONGRESSIONAL ENACTMENT OF the Thirteenth Amendment on January 31, 1865, did not occur overnight. Many forces contributed to the official abolition of slavery in the United States, notably Northern victories and President Abraham Lincoln's developing leadership on the issue. But two members of Congress (figs. 1 and 2), Senator Charles Sumner (1811–74) and Representative Thaddeus Stevens (1792–1868), also played a crucial role in the journey to full emancipation. By examining both their public utterances and their private letters, we can trace this journey through Congress. Similar in their commitment to ending slavery, these two Radical Republicans differed in their backgrounds and personalities. Both were lawyers, with undergraduate degrees from Harvard and Dartmouth, respectively. Sumner held an L.L.B. from Harvard, however, while Stevens read law with a Gettysburg attorney and traveled across the Pennsylvania state line to take a rudimentary bar exam in Maryland. Unlike Stevens, Sumner traveled internationally, gaining friendships with prominent leaders in both France and Great Britain, and upon his return to the United States kept up a steady correspondence with British liberals like John Bright and Richard Cobden. Stevens spent far more time practicing law than did Sumner, and gained recognition in Gettysburg and Lancaster, Pennsylvania, as a successful trial lawyer. The orations of Sumner were just that, true orations, with passages of scholarly references, historical precedents, and flowery rhetoric.

Fig. 1. Thaddeus Stevens in a photograph taken between 1860 and 1875. *(Brady-Handy Photograph Collection, Prints and Photographs Division, Library of Congress)*

Although Stevens also employed legal studies and classical allusions in his speeches, they tended to be sprinkled with humor and homespun language. Attentive to his reputation, Sumner carefully saved virtually all his incoming correspondence. He also worked diligently in the last years of his life to publish a complete set of his works that contains his copious notes,

FIG. 2. Photograph of Charles Sumner taken between 1861 and 1874, possibly taken by Mathew Brady. *(Prints and Photographs Division, Library of Congress)*

including press reactions to his speeches. "These speeches are my life," he claimed in an 1868 letter. They emphasized "the great battle with Slavery, & what I have done in it." By contrast, although Stevens spoke at times of the legacy he would leave, he apparently cared little for his papers, leaving behind only a small collection of his correspondence at the Library of Congress.¹

Despite their parallel objectives both before and during the Civil War, the two rarely referred to each other, moving in different social circles in the nation's capital. The known correspondence from Stevens to Sumner in this period comes to just one exchange in 1849, and one other 1863 letter, discussed below. Only after Andrew Johnson assumed the presidency did the two exchange letters in the summer of 1865 about their concern over Johnson's conciliatory policy toward the former Confederacy. When Stevens died in 1868, Sumner wrote that he differed with Stevens only on financial issues. "[I]n all else he was a great leader—to whom all gratitude and honor."²

Both men served in Congress for more than fifteen years. First a member of the Pennsylvania state legislature, Stevens was elected to Congress in 1848. Except for two terms in the 1850s, he represented the Lancaster district until his death. Sumner served as Massachusetts senator from 1851 to 1874; like Stevens, he died in office. During the Civil War, as chairmen of key congressional committees, Sumner of the Foreign Relations Committee in the Senate and Stevens of the House Ways and Means Committee, they exercised considerable power in prosecuting the war. But they exercised that power in different ways. Sumner was the moralistic philosopher, who employed his oratorical gifts to condemn slavery, while the practical and pragmatic Stevens often guided antislavery legislation through the House. Utilizing their singular strengths, these two men prodded and urged their congressional colleagues, President Lincoln, and the country to embrace full emancipation.

---

¹*Works of Charles Sumner*, 15 vols. (Boston, 1874; hereafter CS, *Works*); Sumner to Samuel Gridley Howe, Dec.7, 1868, *Selected Letters of Charles Sumner*, ed. Beverly Wilson Palmer (Boston, 1990), p. 447 (hereafter CS, *Letters*). The microfilm edition, *Papers of Charles Sumner*, ed. Beverly Wilson Palmer (Alexandria, Va., 1988) comes to 85 reels (of which approximately 75 percent are letters to Sumner that are housed at the Houghton Library, Harvard University, Cambridge, Mass.). The *Thaddeus Stevens Papers*, ed. Beverly Wilson Palmer and Holly Byers Ochoa (Wilmington, Del., 1994), comprising fourteen reels, contain Stevens's correspondence, speeches, congressional remarks and resolutions, and his legal arguments. In letterpress publications, letters from Sumner alone make up two volumes, while the *Selected Papers of Thaddeus Stevens*, ed. Beverly Wilson Palmer and Holly Byers Ochoa, 2 vols. (Pittsburgh, 1997–98) (hereafter TS, *Papers*), feature his significant letters (almost always brief), speeches, and incoming correspondence.

²CS, *Letters*, 2:307, 324; TS, *Papers*, 2:4, 6, 8, 9, 10, 31, 95. CS to John Bright, Aug. 13, 1868, CS, *Letters*, 2:439.

* * *

THE FIRST ISSUE to occupy them was the justification for the Civil War, a controversy that continues into the twenty-first century. Was the war fought to end slavery? Or to ensure states' rights? Or to bring the seceding states back into the Union? On July 24, 1861, Senator Andrew Johnson of Tennessee submitted a resolution on the war's aims, which addressed the third question. It read in part that the Civil War was not being fought "for any purpose of conquest or subjugation, nor for the purpose of overthrowing or interfering with the rights or established institution of those [seceding] States, but to defend and maintain the supremacy of the Constitution." All Republicans except Sumner and Lyman Trumbull of Illinois voted for the resolution, Sumner abstaining. In the characteristically elaborate note that Sumner added to this resolution in the edition of his *Works*, he wrote that he "saw in it an effort to commit Congress the wrong way, so that inaction on Slavery should be the policy of the war." But, because he was "unwilling to separate openly from political associates, anxious also with regard to the President . . . he was silent."[3] Thus did Sumner recognize that explicitly opposing Johnson's resolution and arguing that emancipation was the true goal of the war would, at that moment, be premature.

Like Sumner, Thaddeus Stevens chose to abstain from supporting a House resolution on July 22 limiting the war's aims to preserving the Union. But on August 2 he bluntly stated in the House that the aim of the war "is to subdue the rebels." He went on to say that he would rather "reduce them [the South] to a condition where their whole country is to be repeopled by a band of freemen than to see them perpetrate the destruction of this people through our agency," that is, Congress's complicity. But, he added, "I do not say that it is time to resort to such means." Stevens allowed that he had "spoken more freely, perhaps, than gentlemen within my hearing might think politic." He emphasized that the war would be long and bloody and result in a time when "every bondman in the South—belonging to a rebel, recollect; *I confine it to them*—shall be called upon to aid us in war against their masters, and to restore this Union."[4] We note that despite Stevens's admitted outspokenness, he still declined in the summer of 1861 to expand the war's aim to full emancipation of *all* slaves (rebel and Border

---

[3] CS, *Works*, 5:500–501.
[4] TS, *Papers*, 1:224–25, emphasis added.

States alike). He limited abolition to those slaves owned by slaveholders in the Confederacy.

Before the war, both men had in 1860 enthusiastically supported the Republican presidential candidate Abraham Lincoln, who they believed would bring an end to the expansion of slavery. At a Republican state convention in August 1860, Sumner declared, "[T]he country needs repose;—but it is the repose of Liberty, and not the repose of Despotism. . . . The first stage in securing for our country the repose which all covet will be the election of Abraham Lincoln as president." Voters must see that Lincoln's election meant "the Prohibition of Slavery in the Territories." And in a campaign speech at the Cooper Institute in New York City, Stevens characterized Lincoln as an "earnest anti-slavery man. . . . He will resist the extension of slavery into any territory now free." Stevens asked his audience to join the "triumphal throng who are about to escort a Republican President to the executive mansion of a Republican Nation."[5]

During the secession crisis, each had argued forcefully against any compromise with the South in order to avoid war. To Francis Bird, Sumner wrote on January 28, 1861, "I insist upon an inflexible 'No,' to every proposition. 'No'—'No'—'No'—; let the North cry out to every compromise & to every retreat. Then will be days of glory." In the House on January 29, 1861, Stevens stated, "Let there be no blood shed until the last moment, but let no cowardly counsels unnerve the people." Privately each expressed concern about Lincoln's inexperience and resolve. Worried about the future president, Stevens wrote secretary of the Treasury–designate Salmon P. Chase on February 3 that Lincoln "seeks to purchase peace by concession. . . . I shall give up the fight being too old for another seven (or thirty) years war." And Sumner wrote Henry Wadsworth Longfellow on March 16, "The Presdt. makes the great mistake of trying to deal with all possible cases, & this fritters away his valuable time."[6]

By July 1861, as Congress assembled for the first time since the firing on Fort Sumter, Stevens, Sumner, and other Radical Republicans saw the confiscation bill as an opportunity to start the country moving toward full

---

[5]CS, "Speech at State Convention of the Republican Party at Worcester," Aug. 29, 1860, CS, *Works*, 5: 264–65; TS, "The Presidential Question," Sept. 27, 1860, *Thaddeus Stevens Papers*, reel 9, fr. 93–97.

[6]CS, *Letters*, 2:49, 59; TS, *Papers*, 1:195, 200.

emancipation. That bill, proposed by Lyman Trumbull on July 15, would permit the federal government to seize any property used in furthering the rebellion; rebel slaveholders would forfeit ownership if and when their slaves were forced to take up arms against the United States. Despite the two men's refusal to accept the concept of slaves as "property," they were willing—at least on this occasion—to expand that definition in order to free slaves. The confiscation bill was supported by all Republican senators, and a strong majority in the House, 60–48, Stevens declaring, "[I]n time of war you have the right to confiscate the property of every rebel." Sumner noted that "there is no open mention of Slavery" in the two confiscation bills that he had introduced in early July, titled "For the Confiscation of Property of Persons in Rebellion against the Constitution and Laws of the United States" and "For the Punishment of Conspiracy and Kindred Offences against the United States and for the Confiscation of the Property of the Offenders." This bill was a modest step. As a reviewer in the *New York Times Book Review* observed, "Those who decried 'emancipation' as an unconstitutional attack on property rights found no objection when it was called 'confiscation.'"[7] Lincoln approved the bill on August 6.

Stevens believed the war would be prolonged; Sumner hoped it would be. The North's defeat in the Battle of Bull Run on July 21, which came as a shock to most, was not a surprise to Stevens, who stated in a speech on financing the war three days after that battle, "I believe that the battles which are to be fought are to be desperate and bloody battles; and that they are to be numerous." Sumner presciently wrote Wendell Phillips on August 3 that the battle had been "the worst event & the best event . . . the worst, as it was the greatest present calamity & shame,—the best, as it made the extinction of Slavery inevitable."[8] Indeed, Sumner believed that a quick resolution to the conflict would see the South return to the Union with slavery intact, an outcome he dreaded.

By the fall of 1861, both men became more open in their public pronouncements advocating emancipation. In an October speech in Worcester, Massachusetts, Sumner declared that "the overthrow of Slavery will

---

[7]TS, *Papers*, 1:225, 223; CS, *Works*, 6:31. Debby Applegate, "A Nation Stirs," review of *1861: The Civil War Awakening*, by Adam Goodheart, *New York Times Book Review*, Apr. 24, 2011, p. 9.
[8]"Speech on War Financing," July 24, 1861, TS, *Papers*, 1:218; CS, *Letters*, 2:74.

make an end of the War." He concluded that without emancipation there could be no Union nor any kind of peace. In a speech before the Cooper Institute in November, Sumner analyzed an October 14 order from Secretary of War Simon Cameron to a Union general that fugitive slaves could be employed in various kinds of military service. Cameron's order, declared Sumner, meant "all coming within the camp are to be treated as freemen. . . . All this falls little short of a Proclamation of Emancipation." Soon after, in his original report to the president in December 1861, Cameron devoted nine paragraphs to the status of fugitive slaves, declaring that the U.S. government had the right to "arm and equip them." However, in the final report these paragraphs were omitted, and Cameron was subsequently removed from his post and appointed ambassador to Russia. Although Stevens had previously thought little of his fellow Pennsylvanian's abilities and integrity, in a January 1862 speech he said, "No declaration of the great objects of Government, no glorious sound of universal liberty has gone forth from the capital." Only Cameron had "the sagacity to perceive and the courage to declare the true mode of ending this rebellion. . . . And now he has been driven from the Cabinet and exiled to Siberia."[9]

Seeking to prevent Britain's official recognition of the Confederacy, Sumner wrote regularly to his British friends, such as the Duchess of Argyll, John Bright, and Richard Cobden, sympathetic to abolition. To them Sumner repeatedly stated that the purpose of the war was to end slavery, even if the Lincoln administration had not officially said so. On October 29, 1861, he wrote British author, and another antislavery advocate, Harriet Martineau, "It is constantly said in England that this is not a war against Slavery. This is a mistake. It is a war to prevent the foundation of a slaveholding Confederacy, in which Slavery is to be soul & corner stone. . . . Surely in crushing such an attempt we are fighting for Freedom."[10]

In December 1861, Stevens, stating that, by the law of nations, it is "the right to liberate the slaves of an enemy to weaken his power," offered a resolution in the House: that the president be ordered to "declare free . . . all slaves who shall leave their masters, or who shall aid in quelling this rebellion." Stevens's resolution meant a move forward from the Confiscation Act, which limited emancipation to those slaves forced to fight for the

---

[9]CS, *Works*, 6:12, 28, 108–9; TS, "Subduing the Rebellion," TS, *Papers*, 1:230, 252, 297.
[10]CS, *Letters*, 2:81.

Confederacy. Stevens did not mention the more inclusive word *emancipation* here, but he used it in a letter to the abolitionist Gerrit Smith, who had praised Stevens for his act. Stevens wrote Smith that his resolution "emancipates all slaves whether of rebel or loyal master—I can see no other way to establish a firm Union." Speaking on his resolution, in a major speech in January 1862, Stevens initiated an argument he would return to in later months: the war could be shortened if slaves in the Confederacy, who were producing food and munitions for the rebels, were freed. He boldly declared, "Universal emancipation must be proclaimed to all," then qualified his stance somewhat later in the speech by stating, "Remember this is not a war begun by us for emancipation. But emancipation is a legitimate means to defend against a war forced upon us by bloody rebels." Why should white soldiers die for the Union when the important resource of freed slaves was available? Stevens demanded. To his colleagues and a wider audience of cautious Unionists he exclaimed, "You send forth your sons and brothers to shoot and saber and bayonet the insurgents, but you hesitate to break the bonds of their slaves to reach the same end. What puerile inconsistency!" Yet the House did not act on Stevens's resolution in this session.[11]

Throughout the war, both men paid keen attention to the treatment of slaves by Union generals. They supported General John C. Frémont's order in Missouri in August 1861, freeing all slaves of rebels, and criticized Lincoln's response in overruling that act and removing the general from his command. Stevens decried to a friend that "the hounds" had "run down" Frémont. In his letter to Martineau, Sumner also lamented Lincoln's response: "Had Fremont's Proclamation been maintained, & extended to other states, it would be equivalent to a decree of Emancipation."[12]

Later, in May 1862, Major General David Hunter, commander of the Department of the South, ordered that slaves be freed in Florida, Georgia, and North Carolina. When Lincoln once again countermanded the Union general, Sumner wrote Wendell Phillips, "I deplore what he has done." Hunter subsequently sent a letter to Secretary of War Edwin Stanton justifying his authority to enlist and arm fugitive slaves under his jurisdiction,

---

[11]TS, Resolution on Emancipation; TS to Smith, Dec. 14, 1861; TS, "Subduing the Rebellion," TS, *Papers*, 1:229, 232, 246.

[12]TS to Simon Stevens (no relative), Nov. 5, 1861, TS, *Papers*, 1:226; CS, *Letters*, 2:81.

prompting Stevens to "say a few words" in the House on July 2. Stevens worried that Lincoln was "too easy and amiable" and stated that his administration should "follow out the policy which has been inaugurated by that gallant sagacious soldier [Hunter] who now commands our army in South Carolina."[13]

Occasionally both Stevens and Sumner shifted their attacks from Lincoln to a Union general who did not follow Frémont's and Hunter's policies. For example, they publicly castigated Major General Henry W. Halleck, who had replaced Frémont as commander of the Department of the Missouri and in November 1861 ordered that fugitive slaves be returned to their masters. Speaking in favor of a motion on December 11, 1861, to request that Lincoln countermand Halleck's order, Stevens said that such fugitives "never desire to return . . . they are faithful to those who protect them." The House resolution should be approved, he continued, "for the purpose of affecting our generals everywhere else." Of Halleck, in a Senate speech of May 1, 1862, Sumner asked his colleagues, "What right, under the Constitution, has this General to set himself up as judge in cases of human freedom? . . . While professing to make war upon the Rebellion, he sustains its chief and most active power and degrades his gallant army to be the constables of Slavery."[14]

Many Republicans in Congress viewed Lincoln's plan, introduced on March 6, 1862, to compensate slave owners in the Border States who would gradually free their slaves as an important step toward eventual full emancipation. Although both Sumner and Stevens came to oppose Lincoln's measure, they generally refrained from voicing strong opposition in 1862. In fact, both men initially accepted the president's proposal. Anticipating Lincoln's compensation plan, Stevens even laid out specific amounts totaling $300,000 that would be paid to Border States, saying in January 1862, "We need not be alarmed about the cost." And, in a March 6 speech, Sumner reluctantly went along with Senator Henry Wilson's plan to pay one million dollars to District of Columbia slaveholders, stating, "I cannot hesitate at any appropriation within our means by which all these things of incalculable value [i.e., emancipation of slaves in the District] can be promptly

---

[13]CS, May 22, 1862, CS, *Letters*, 2:113; TS, "Attack on General Hunter," TS, *Papers*, 1:310, 313.

[14]TS, "Remarks on Fugitive Slaves," TS, *Papers*, 1:231; CS, "The Policy of Our Generals Towards Fugitive Slaves," CS, *Works*, 6:496, 498.

secured." He justified his support of compensation, however, with an elaborate rhetorical tactic: "I prefer the money we pay as in the nature of *ransom* rather than *compensation*, so that Freedom shall be *acquired* rather than *purchased.*" In contrast, Stevens abstained from voting on the resolution to support Lincoln's compensation plan. In a September campaign speech in Lancaster, Pennsylvania, he defended his decision: "I will not go with the President in paying for all the slaves—I did not vote for his resolution." Possibly for rhetorical effect, since Lincoln's plan was aimed only at slaveholding states in the Union, Stevens added, "*I will not* vote to pay for any slave of a *rebel!*" As months passed, Lincoln's plan gained little support in the Border States. By April 1864, referring to the "talk of compensation," Sumner could exclaim, "Thank God, that time has passed, never to return,—and simply because money is no longer needed for the purpose."[15]

During the first half of 1862, both lamented Lincoln's delay in emancipating the slaves and considered him weak and indecisive. To John Andrew on June 5, 1862, Sumner complained, "How long! Oh how long must we wait!" In April Stevens wrote a constituent that his hopes for the administration were poor as "Lincoln is nobody." Publicly Stevens showed his disappointment with Lincoln by comparing him to Andrew Jackson. For example, in a House speech in January 1862, he lamented, "Oh for six months' resurrection in the flesh of stern old Jackson! Give him power and he would handle this rebellion with iron gloves. He would abolish slavery as the cause and the support of the insurrection."[16] Stevens's rhetoric had obviously carried him away, for his audience surely knew that Jackson had owned slaves.

For Sumner and Stevens, the second Confiscation Act of July 17, 1862, which ended the second session of the Thirty-Seventh Congress, was another major step toward emancipation. This bill freed any slave of any person in insurrection against the United States, declared that no fugitive slaves could be returned to their masters, and stipulated that the president could employ "as many persons of African descent as he may deem

---

[15]TS, *Papers*, 1:245, 249, 246; CS, "Ransom of Slaves at the National Capital," CS, *Works*, 6:419; TS, *Papers*, 1:249; 322. See also, Eric Foner, *The Fiery Trial: Abraham Lincoln and American Slavery* (New York, 2010), pp. 195–96, 198–200. CS, "Universal Emancipation without Compensation," Apr. 8, 1864, CS, *Works*, 8:373.

[16]CS, *Letters*, 2:118; TS to Joseph Gibbons, Apr. 17, 1862, TS, "Subduing the Rebellion," Jan. 22, 1862, TS, *Papers*, 1:293, 247.

necessary and proper for the suppression of the rebellion." Sumner wrote John Bright about recent congressional legislation, "[T]here have been differences of opinion on questions of policy—especially on Slavery. . . . But the Bill of Confiscation & Liberation [Sumner's term] . . . is a practical Act of Emancipation." In a major speech in May 1862 on confiscation, Sumner declared, "The slaves of Rebels cannot be regarded as property, real or personal. . . . At home, beneath the lash and local law, they may be chattels; but they are known to our Constitution only as *men*." For the abolitionist senator from Massachusetts, slaves were always "men." When the confiscation bill came before the House on July 16, Stevens pressed for quick action and fought off attempts to dilute its provisions. In a September speech to his constituents in Lancaster, Stevens celebrated this sign of progress. The House had approved by a vote of 84 to 42 the July 1862 Confiscation Act, "where a year ago," he said, "not fifty could have been found."[17]

In the Lancaster speech Stevens insisted that the Lincoln administration must change its policy toward the slave: "I have protested against the present policy, not only to the people, but to the face of the President and his Cabinet, and on the floor of Congress . . . told them that they were exercising too much lenity at the request of border statesmen—not one of whom in my judgment, has loyalty in his heart." As this speech indicates, Stevens was more openly critical of Lincoln than Sumner. Indeed, Sumner, acknowledging the power of the presidency, was proud of his close association with Lincoln. His letters are scattered with references to conversations and meetings with the president, and his correspondence contains frequent letters from Mary Lincoln. As can be seen, Sumner confined his criticisms of Lincoln's administration to his private letters. In fact in June 1862, he published a letter in the *Boston Journal* praising the Lincoln administration: "[M]y constant and intimate intercourse with the President . . . not only binds me peculiarly to his Administration, but gives me a personal as well as a political interest in seeing that justice is done him." Stevens's personal connection to Lincoln, on the other hand, consisted mainly of requests for appointments or promotions of colleagues.[18]

---

[17]CS, *Letters*, 2:123, 122; CS, "Rights of Sovereignty and Rights of War," CS, *Works*, 7:75; TS, *Papers*, 1:322–23.

[18]TS, *Papers*, 1:322. CS, *Works*, 7:118. For example, see TS to Abraham Lincoln, Feb. 19, 1863, TS, *Papers*, 1:370.

As the war dragged on through the summer of 1862, with little or no Northern military success, Sumner and Stevens became even more convinced that a firm stand from the administration on emancipation was necessary to rally the North behind the war. Stevens wrote to a colleague on September 5, "It is plain that nothing approaching the present policy will subdue the rebels." He looked for a policy that would "treat this [conflict] as a radical revolution, and remodel our institutions." Sumner was apparently surprised when Lincoln released the preliminary Emancipation Proclamation on September 22, for he had written Francis Lieber on September 16, "I despair of any thing definite until the Genl. Govt. boldly strikes Slavery." But at last the Lincoln administration had acted. About the proclamation Sumner wrote John Bright on October 28, "from this time forward our whole policy will be more vigorous." As the date for the official signing drew near, Sumner described how he had personally urged Lincoln the previous evening "to dwell on the importance & grandeur of the act & how impatient we all are that it should be done in the way to enlist the most sympathy & to stifle opposition." Sumner remarked in a subsequent speech in February that the whole climate of opinion had changed from the time when the "very mention of Slavery in Congress was forbidden. . . . Now Emancipation is an accepted watchword." The sardonic Stevens was less enthusiastic about Lincoln's edict, stating in a speech to the Union League of Lancaster in April 1863 that the "'Proclamation of Freedom,' as it is charitably called, although indicative of a sound heart does not reach the evil. It exempts from its operations every place where it could be enforced," that is, areas actually occupied by federal armies. Stevens wondered, "What will the slaves of unconquered places think when they see those in the territory occupied by our troops held in bondage?"[19]

Stevens held doubts about Lincoln's resolve and worried about the appeasement policies of his cabinet members. In the one letter during the Civil War from Stevens to Sumner that has been recovered, Stevens asked Sumner to bring a recent speech from the Unionist Postmaster General Montgomery Blair to the attention of Lincoln. Clearly, Stevens viewed Sumner as the liaison to Lincoln. Blair's speech of October 3, 1863, criticized the

---

[19]TS to Simon Stevens, Sept. 5, 1862, TS, *Papers*, 1:323; CS, *Letters*, 2:125, 128; CS to John Murray Forbes, Dec. 28, 1862, CS, *Letters*, 2:135. CS, Senate Speech on Missouri Emancipation, CS, *Works*, 7:270. TS, Speech on War Legislation, TS, *Papers*, 1:391.

"ultra-Abolitionists" as being "equally despotic" and as much a threat to the Union as the rebels. He specifically attacked a recent Sumner pronouncement asserting that the Confederate states had committed "state suicide," as Sumner had phrased it, by leaving the Union. Blair's speech, maintained Stevens, was so "vulgar" and "infamous" that the president should dismiss Blair from the Cabinet. "If the President persists in retaining such men . . . we must take care that his reign shall not be prolonged." Despite Blair's personal attack, Sumner was more conciliatory. In a letter to the postmaster general specifically addressing Blair's hostile speech, he asked Blair to "Put forth yr system. Let it work, if it will constitutionally." Sumner admitted to John Bright on December 15, 1863, "Any plan which fastens Emancipation beyond recall will suit me."[20]

As a key ingredient of emancipation, these two Radicals sought equal treatment for the blacks now enlisted in the Northern armies, enlisted by virtue of the Confiscation Act of 1862. In the winter of 1863 both men turned their attention to legislation authorizing equal pay for African Americans with their white fellow soldiers. In January 1863, Stevens introduced a bill by which blacks would be armed and equipped to "suppress the present rebellion" and would receive "the same rations, clothing, and equipments as other volunteers." This provision would update the provision in the Confiscation Act of 1862 that blacks receive seven dollars a month, as opposed to the thirteen-dollar monthly pay of white soldiers. Cleverly appealing to the racist attitudes of some of his fellow congressmen, Stevens asked, "Why should our race be exposed to suffering and disease, when the African might endure his equal share of it?" But Congress did not enact any legislation for equal pay for black troops until 1864. As the House debated the equal pay issue, Stevens once again demanded of his fellow congressmen in April of that year, "Why should [the black troops] not be all paid alike? why should they not all charge the rebels alike, and die in defense of the Union?" In February, Sumner had introduced an amendment that blacks should receive the same pay as white soldiers, and that the pay should be retroactive to the date of their enlistment. Although this amendment failed, and retroactive pay was established only as far back as January 1, 1864, Sumner

---

[20]TS to CS, Oct. 9, 1863, *Thaddeus Stevens Papers*, reel 2, fr. 890; "Judge Blair's Speech," *New York Times*, Oct. 17, 1863; CS to Montgomery Blair, Oct. 28, 1863, CS, *Letters*, 2:204–5; CS to John Bright, Dec. 1863, CS, *Letters*, 2:214.

could still exult, as he did in an April letter to Governor Andrew, that some "justice to colored troops" had been established. "God be praised!"[21]

Finally, amid increasing discussion of the fate of the slaves at war's end, the time became ripe for moving from exhortation and incremental legislative steps to major legislative action. Emancipation must be official federal policy, optimally part of the U.S. Constitution. Sumner presented to the Senate in February 1864 a petition containing a hundred thousand signatures from the Women's National League for "an act of Universal Emancipation." Writing Susan B. Anthony on March 2, Sumner expressed his disappointment that the petition had received little publicity: "It would have been an advertisement of the movement, which would have acted powerfully on the country." Despite their leadership advocating universal emancipation, neither man was the first to introduce in Congress what would become the Thirteenth Amendment. Ohio Congressman James Ashley did so in December 1863, followed on January 11, 1864, by Senator John Henderson of Missouri. Soon after, Sumner introduced his version on February 8. In a long Senate speech on April 8, Sumner argued for both congressional legislation abolishing slavery and a Constitutional amendment. Sumner believed (erroneously as it turned out) that outright legislation was more expedient, because "such an Amendment cannot be consummated at once.... Even under most favorable circumstances, it is impossible to say when it can become part of the Constitution." The Senate, however, moved relatively promptly to enact the amendment in May.[22]

The straightforward language of the resolution that Stevens offered on March 28, 1864, closely resembles the amendment that ultimately became part of the Constitution: "Slavery and involuntary servitude, except for the punishment of crimes whereof the party shall have been duly convicted, is forever prohibited in the United States and all its Territories." The Thirteenth Amendment reads: "Neither slavery nor involuntary servitude, except as punishment for crime whereof the party shall have been duly convicted, shall exist within the United States, or any place subject to their jurisdiction." Once again, Stevens did not speak as the House debated the amendment that the Senate had passed. Here his silence is noteworthy, given

---

[21]TS, "Bill to Authorize Black Soldiers," Jan. 27, 1863; Negro Soldiers," Feb. 2, 1863; Remarks on Black Soldiers, Apr. 30, 1864, TS, *Papers*, 1:354–55, 356, 457; CS to Francis W. Bird, Feb. 22, 1864; to John Andrew, Apr. 30, 1864, *Letters*, 2:227–28, 237.
[22]CS, *Works*, 8:80–83, 386; CS, *Letters*, 2:229.

his commitment to the cause. The House failed to obtain the necessary two-thirds vote on the Senate version before Congress adjourned. Stevens addressed this failure in a campaign speech in Lancaster on September 7, 1864. As he rallied his fellow Republicans, he warned against the possible victory of the peace Democrats, including presidential candidate George McClellan, in the forthcoming election: "Every Republican voted in favor of the measure; every vote against it came from the peace McClellan Copperheads. They are responsible for the continued, misery and bloodshed which this nation shall endure."[23]

The Union's "continued misery and bloodshed" made Lincoln's reelection prospects problematic. Sumner regretted that the June Republican convention nominating Lincoln had met so early in the 1864 campaign. "Into the darkness of the Presidential contest I am not prepared to enter," he wrote Lydia Maria Child on August 7. "The whole subject might have been postponed till Sept. when we should have seen more clearly who ought to be the candidate." Later that month, he wrote Governor Andrew that he hoped Lincoln would withdraw *"patriotically & kindly so as to leave no breach in the party."* Sumner emphatically opposed any action against the president unless he withdrew. Although Stevens received letters from constituents concerned about Lincoln's weakness and reelection prospects, no letters from him on the subject have been recovered. An outburst came in July 1864, however, when Lincoln declined to sign the Wade-Davis bill. This bill established conditions for returning states, including the abolition of slavery and the banning of any Confederate supporter from holding office. Instead of approving the bill, Lincoln instead issued a statement that he was not "inflexibly committed to any single plan of restoration." Of Lincoln's pocket veto, Stevens exclaimed, "What an infamous proclamation! . . . How little of the rights of war and the law of nations our Presdt. knows! But what are we to do? Condemn privately and applaud publicly!"[24]

When the Democrats nominated McClellan and endorsed a platform to end the war as soon as possible with the preservation of all states' rights "unimpaired," Sumner wrote John Bright that the Democrats' platform "& our victories have settled the Presidential election beyond question." And

---

[23] TS, *Papers*, 1:448, 503.
[24] CS, *Letters*, 2:249; CS to John Andrew, Aug. 24, 1864, CS, *Letters*, 2: 251; CS to Francis Lieber, Sept. 3, 1864, CS, *Letters*, 2:252, n. 3; TS to Edward McPherson, July 10, 1864, TS, *Papers*, 1:500.

Stevens—willing now to "applaud publicly"—stated in his Lancaster speech, "Elect McClellan, and the Republic has ceased to exist. On its ruins will spring up numerous petty empires, whose future condition will be one of perpetual wars and of grinding Slavery. Re-elect the calm statesman who now presides over the nation, and he will lead you to an honorable peace and to permanent liberty."[25]

In his annual message of December 1864, the newly reelected Lincoln recommended that the House follow the Senate and pass the Thirteenth Amendment, moving the nation, in Stevens's words, to "permanent liberty." In a December letter to Francis Lieber, Sumner confidently predicted that that body would approve it. Stevens, speaking on January 5, 1865, the day before the House would officially address this legislation, praised the president's message: "Sir, I give the President all honor for his course on this question. Never had a man to decide so important a question under such difficulties." In remarks on January 13, the pragmatic Stevens resorted to legal, as opposed to political, argument to convince skeptical colleagues that the amendment was constitutional. Asking the clerk to read Article V from the Constitution on Congress's power to amend that document, he stated, "[W]e are not now inquiring whether we have jurisdiction over slavery. We are inquiring whether the States have granted to us the power of amendment." On January 31, the House, by a vote of 119 to 56, 8 abstaining, sent the constitutional amendment to the states for ratification.[26]

Once all the slaves in rebel and Border States alike were emancipated, what did these two men believe should be done for them? Both, not surprisingly, argued for suffrage. Eric Foner rightly contends that along the spectrum of attitudes toward black rights, Sumner with his "egalitarian vision" is the more extreme. During the Thirty-Seventh and Thirty-Eighth Congresses, Sumner regularly offered a series of resolutions which would gradually chip away at legal discrimination against African Americans—for example, abolishing black codes in the District of Columbia; preventing the disqualification of mail carriers because of color; permitting blacks to testify in court cases; integrating streetcars. A few of these were enacted. Later, in 1871, Sumner sponsored his Supplemental Civil Rights bill which

---

[25]CS to John Bright, Sept. 27, 1864, CS, *Letters*, 2:252; TS, *Papers*, 1:503.
[26]CS to Francis Lieber, Dec. 18, 1864, CS, *Letters*, 2:259; TS, "Remarks on the President's Message and Emancipation"; "Abolition of Slavery," TS, *Papers*, 1:513, 523.

would end all racial discrimination in juries, schools, inns, restaurants, and all modes of transportation. Not, however, until the Civil Rights Act of 1965 did African Americans gain the rights that Sumner sought. For his part, Stevens emphasized equal economic rights for the freed slaves. In his Reconstruction speech in Lancaster on September 6, 1865, he introduced his elaborate plan to confiscate the assets of former rebels, and stated, "Give, if you please, forty acres to each male freedman." Yet Stevens publicly stated that he would draw the line at the kinds of social equality that Sumner sought. For example, when asked by Ohio congressman Samuel Cox in January 1865 whether he would give up his "doctrine of negro equality," he answered, "not equality in all things—simply before the laws, nothing else." Nevertheless, Stevens's statement on his legacy perhaps more accurately reflects his view of all suppressed people. In another Reconstruction speech on December 18, 1865, he declared, "This is not a 'white man's Government.' . . . This is man's Government; the Government of all men alike. . . . [E]qual rights to all the privileges of the Government is innate in every immortal being, no matter what the shape or color of the tabernacle which it inhabits."[27]

In his biography of Stevens, Hans Trefousse relates a story which may be apocryphal but is nevertheless appropriate to Stevens's and Sumner's quest for universal emancipation. Apparently in the summer of 1862, Lincoln complained how Sumner, Stevens, and Senator Henry Wilson of Massachusetts were continually pressing him about some kind of an emancipation proclamation. As Lincoln spoke with Missouri Senator John Henderson, he looked out the window to see the three approaching the White House. In typical fashion, Lincoln resorted to a story, a story ending in the punch line: "There comes them same damned fellows again."[28]

---

[27]Foner, *Fiery Trial*, p. 293; See CS, *Works*, 6:122, 385, 442, 8:103–17. TS, "Reconstruction," Sept. 6, 1865, TS, *Papers*, 2:19; "Remarks on the President's Message and Emancipation," Jan. 5, 1865, TS, *Papers*, 1:516; "Reconstruction," TS, *Papers*, 2:54.
[28]Hans L. Trefousse, *Thaddeus Stevens: Egalitarian* (Chapel Hill, 1997), p. 120.

L. Diane Barnes

Frederick Douglass and the Complications of Emancipation

His CONTEMPORARIES AND modern scholars alike expected much of Frederick Douglass as the most famous and influential African American of the nineteenth century in the years surrounding the Civil War and emancipation. As a recognized leader of his race, his words and actions spoke to black and white Americans through his prolific stream of newspaper editorials and speeches. During the war he agitated for reform, recruited soldiers, and met many times with government officials, including Abraham Lincoln. But for some contemporaries and modern scholars, these actions were not enough. In his lifetime and in modern scholarship, Douglass's words and actions have been subjected to close scrutiny. He emerged from the war as a stalwart Republican, and despite the party's failure to push for full equality, he remained a loyalist for the remainder of his career. That adherence to party and other actions left Douglass open to criticism from contemporaries in the black community and from modern scholars, both of whom have faulted him for various reasons. For Douglass, the Civil War was an era fraught with complications as he walked a fine line between Republican politicians and black activists who each expected something different from this spokesman for African Americans.

Much was anticipated of Douglass because he was such an exceptional figure in the antebellum and Civil War eras. Escaping slavery at the age of twenty in 1838, he quickly emerged as an antislavery lecturer, author, and

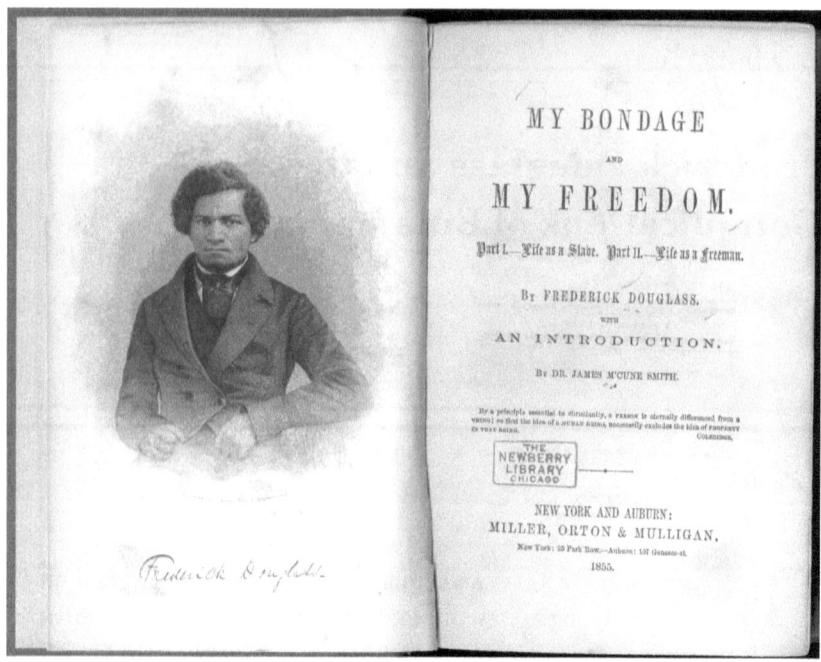

Fig. 1. Frontispiece and title page of *My Bondage and My Freedom. (Newberry Digital Collections for the Classroom; http://dcc.newberry.org/collections/representing-american-revolution)*

newspaper editor. His eloquence as an orator led some to doubt that he had ever been enslaved. Partly to satisfy his critics, he penned a narrative of his life in slavery. Although his was one of numerous slave autobiographies in print, *Narrative of the Life of Frederick Douglass* (1845) became the most widely read in both the United States and Britain, selling thousands of copies. The brief book elevated Douglass to celebrity status in the reform community, and opened doors to other possibilities. After a successful tour of Ireland and Britain, in late 1847 he began publishing his own weekly newspaper, the *North Star*, in Rochester, New York. For the next fifteen years, Douglass wielded the editorial pen through a succession of publications. In 1855 he published a second autobiography, *My Bondage and My Freedom* (fig. 1), in which he detailed his reform activism and offered expanded details of his experience of enslavement. Although this second volume sold fewer copies than the shorter *Narrative*, it established him as a man of letters as well as an orator and editor. Giving constant voice to his own brand of reform and advocating on behalf of African American civil rights as well as the abolition of slavery, Douglass was a leader among blacks as well as among abolitionists. In the late 1840s and 1850s he was a well-known organizer in a series of state and national conventions that gathered the nation's leading African Americans to debate issues of importance to their race, including voting rights, education, and business opportunities. He also became associated with political abolitionists in upstate New York and struggled to locate his political identity in the changing climate of the 1850s, which saw most, but not all, political abolitionists gravitate to the Republican Party.

Even before the Civil War, Douglass's prominence in so many arenas sometimes resulted in clashes with contemporaries, especially within the black convention and abolition movements. On several occasions prominent black abolitionists disputed Douglass's positions on a number of issues. Through the editorial pages of his own newspaper and another in 1849, Douglass and Henry Highland Garnet came to verbal blows over the usefulness of spending their limited resources on a campaign to send Bibles to southern slaves. Douglass declared Garnet and fellow Bible advocate Henry Bibb to be out of touch with reality, rightly noting that Bibles would be generally useless to illiterate slaves. He suggested instead sending spelling books, "since the former would be useless without a knowledge of the latter."[1] In 1851 he shocked William Lloyd Garrison (fig. 2) and his followers with his declaration that after considerable study, he had come to believe that the Constitution was not, as Garrison believed, a "covenant with death and assessment with hell," but in fact was useful in the toolbox of abolitionists. The personal animosity between Douglass and Garrison grew until the two old friends ceased speaking to each other for an extended period of time.[2] Although Douglass initially partnered with Pittsburgh physician and editor Martin R. Delany when establishing the *North Star*, in the 1850s the pair sparred verbally and in print over the ability of African Americans to advance economically in U.S. society. Delany supported the notion that in order to achieve their full potential blacks should consider emigrating to Central or South America, or perhaps the Caribbean. In contrast, Douglass firmly argued that the United States offered the best possibilities for

---

[1] Henry Highland Garnet to Frederick Douglass, June 16, 1849, John R. McKivigan et al., eds., *The Frederick Douglass Papers*, ser. 3: *Correspondence*, vol. 1: *1842–1852* (New Haven, Conn., 2009), pp. 382–83; "Frederick Douglass vs. Henry Bibb," *North Star*, June 22, 1849.

[2] Henry Mayer, *All on Fire: William Lloyd Garrison and the Abolition of Slavery* (New York, 1998), p. 371.

FIG. 2. William Lloyd Garrison. *(Prints and Photographs Division, Library of Congress)*

black advancement.³ Although he claimed to speak for his race, Douglass's most prominent mentors before the Civil War were the white reformers William Lloyd Garrison and Gerrit Smith. While he debated many in the black community on a host of issues, Douglass spent most of his time in the company of white reformers. On numerous occasions other black leaders condemned Douglass for his espousal of biracial cooperation and desire for racial integration.⁴

Modern scholarly analysis of Douglass's actions in the antebellum and Civil War eras echoes many of his nineteenth-century critics. Examining his words and actions, historians have found Douglass to be a complex man who fought selflessly for the abolition of slavery and black civil rights, but also an ambitious individual who saw in the war effort and the Republican Party avenues for personal gain. Historian Waldo Martin has called him too optimistic and argues that Douglass failed his race because he did not cry out for larger structural changes. Martin argues that Douglass "advocated and came to symbolize the integrationist-assimilationist and protest traditions in black uplift ideology." He believes that Douglass could and should have pushed harder for civil rights and the breakdown of racial barriers.⁵ Literary scholar Peter F. Walker goes even further, arguing that Douglass betrayed black America by embracing and espousing the norms of white civilization as universal and appropriate models for African Americans. Walker even suggests that Douglass wanted to be white.⁶

Although there is some validity in all of these criticisms, they do not offer a full picture of Douglass's thoughts and actions during the Civil War era. Modern scholars look at Douglass and all he accomplished in life, his writings, his persuasive oratory, the place he held among his white and black coadjutors, and expect something miraculous. It is easy to project Douglass as something he was not. Should he have pushed for more structural change? Maybe. But what would that have gotten him during the Civil War and after? Would he have been invited to meet with Lincoln? Probably not. Would more agitation on race issues have gotten him the

---

³Robert S. Levine, *Martin Delany, Frederick Douglass, and the Politics of Representative Identity* (Chapel Hill, 1997), pp. 59–61.
⁴Peter C. Myers, *Frederick Douglass: Race and the Rebirth of American Liberalism* (Lawrence, Kans., 2008), pp. 12–13.
⁵Waldo E. Martin, *The Mind of Frederick Douglass* (Chapel Hill, 1984), pp. x–xi.
⁶Peter F. Walker, *Moral Choices: Memory, Desire, and Imagination in Nineteenth-Century American Abolition* (Baton Rouge, 1978), pp. 224–28, 244–61.

officer's commission he so desperately wanted? Not likely. And what of the racial issue? Did he have many relations across the color line, including with white women? Indeed he did. Did Douglass support integration and aspire to emulate the dominant white society? Yes he did. But in a world where African Americans held little economic or political sway, he came to believe that only by working within the existing system could he persuade those with political power and influence to consider the needs of African Americans. During the Civil War the Republican Party dominated the political system and, in his mind, provided the most likely means for achieving his brand of emancipation, which meant full citizenship for blacks as well as an end to slavery.

Perhaps Douglass understood what W. E. B. Du Bois so clearly articulated a generation later: achieving the goals of civil rights and racial equality required that he adopt a double self. To be a proper advocate for his race, he had to navigate a careful path both as a spokesman for African Americans and as an adherent to the Republican Party. He had to be both a black man and an American.[7] Although sometimes critical in his intellectual biography, Waldo Martin also describes this duality as one of Douglass's main strengths. He roots Douglass's intellectual significance in his ability to glean insight from "both the intrinsic interrelationship between the Afro-American and Euro-American minds and the pervasive impact of race on American life."[8] Throughout the war era, he fought to put the abolition of slavery and the advancement of black rights at the forefront of the national consciousness. At the same time, however, he understood that increasingly, achieving those aims required interracial cooperation. During the Civil War, he came to the realization that the best hope for his race (and for his own personal advancement) required him to cast his lot with the Republican Party. If we could ask Douglass to explain his actions in the years surrounding emancipation, he might say simply, "it's complicated." Since we cannot ask him directly, it is helpful to explore his words and actions to determine what that means.

Douglass's actions in the Civil War era provide a key to understanding the dual path he took to effect the changes so crucial to himself and his race. At the outset of the war, what Douglass wanted more than anything was an

---

[7]W. E. B. DuBois, *The Souls of Black Folk: Essays and Sketches* (Chicago, 1903), pp. 3 4.
[8]Martin, *Mind of Frederick Douglass*, p. ix.

end to slavery, and he was willing to make significant compromises in order to reach that goal. He did agitate for structural change, and he did eventually place his optimistic hope in the powers of the Republican Party to bring about emancipation and other rights for African Americans, but his support was not a given in 1860. The southern political coalition known as the Slave Power held tremendous sway in antebellum politics, and attempts at maintaining a fragile connection to the upper South made slavery a delicate issue during the early part of the war. It became apparent that it would take much agitation to convince Lincoln and other Republicans that slavery should be a war aim, but Douglass was willing to press the issue. Although the era did not result in the kinds of real racial equality Douglass wanted, the Civil War did end slavery, and in 1865 that *was* a very radical change.[9] Douglass worked tirelessly before and during the war to make emancipation possible, and during and afterward to secure citizenship and voting rights for the freedpeople. Douglass's loyalty to the Republican Party evolved gradually during the war and was linked to his growing belief that the party offered the most enduring partnership for African Americans. Although in hindsight one might argue that it was irrational for Douglass to remain loyal to the Republicans and that his adherence to the party muted his ability to push for structural changes and decry racism, especially following Reconstruction, nevertheless his practical nature saw him adhere when some black leaders began deserting the party. He believed that the advancement of black rights and suffrage could only be attained through the existing political system, and he believed his dual existence as a black man and a Republican Party loyalist made it more likely that those goals would be achieved.

Tracing Douglass's path into the Republican Party sheds additional light on the difficult dual path he followed. His struggle to make emancipation a war aim was complicated and fraught with personal and political challenges. Douglass and other abolitionists urged politicians, and the Republican Party especially, to take up the cause of the slave. At first he was indifferent to Lincoln and the Republican Party, then outright hostile in late 1861 and 1862. Gradually, as the war escalated, however, Douglass moved toward support for the Republicans, especially after the issuance of the Emancipation Proclamation. Events during the war cemented his support

---

[9] See Eric Foner, *Reconstruction: America's Unfinished Revolution, 1863–1877* (New York, 1988).

for the party and for President Lincoln, but even then his relationship with both was complicated by his desire to see more of a commitment to racial equality than the party was willing to provide. Through speeches and dozens of editorials he agitated for larger structural changes, including suffrage and full equality before the law, but those goals were only incompletely realized.

In some senses it is surprising that Douglass became such a stalwart Republican. He was never very good at attaching to a particularly dogmatic position in his reform thought. Unlike William Lloyd Garrison, who was willing to stick to his mantra, "no union with slaveholders," and to reject the Constitution as a proslavery document, Douglass explored a variety of positions. When he first entered the abolitionist lecturing field in 1841, Douglass adopted the Garrisonian view that condemned both organized religion and political action as corrupted by the influences of the slave system. Although he maintained his skepticism of established Protestant denominations' commitment to reform, he did change his mind about political means to affect abolition. After moving to Rochester, New York, and beginning his own newspaper venture in 1847, connections with the region's political abolitionists, and especially Gerrit Smith, led Douglass to think differently about politics. He eventually broke with Garrison to promote a brand of political abolitionism that proclaimed slavery had never and could never be legal under the Constitution. But he also found it hard to remain steadfastly committed to the idea of immediate abolition espoused by the Liberty Party, as did his friend Gerrit Smith. While he followed Smith from the Liberty Party into the Radical Abolition Party at its formation in 1855, he flirted with the doctrines of the more practically based Free Soil Party, attending their conventions in the early 1850s. In 1852, Douglass even acted as secretary at a convention of Free Democrats, although he did not endorse their candidate that fall. Then, as at most election times, he was still wavering when ballots were to be cast, and often took the more moderate position in the end.[10]

Douglass followed a similar pattern of vacillation in the months leading up to the 1860 election. The Republican Party's lukewarm commitment to

---

[10] John R. McKivigan, "The Frederick Douglass-Gerrit Smith Friendship and Political Abolitionism in the 1850s," in *Frederick Douglass: New Literary and Historical Essays*, ed. Eric J. Sundquist (New York, 1990), pp. 217–19.

antislavery concerned him. He was worried that electing Abraham Lincoln would not help the abolitionist cause, but was cautiously optimistic that it could. Upon learning of Lincoln's nomination he editorialized in *Douglass' Monthly*: "For ourselves, we are sorry that the hosts of freedom could not have been led forth upon a higher platform, and have had inscribed upon their banners, 'Death to Slavery,' instead of 'No more Slave States.' But the people will not have it so, and we are compelled to work and wait for a brighter day, when the masses shall be educated up to a higher standard of human rights and political morality."[11] His concern that the Republican Party was only "negatively antislavery" was based in the party's expression of opposition to the politics of the Slave Power and its failure to declare outright opposition to the institution as morally wrong.[12] Despite offering a soft endorsement of Lincoln's nomination, in August Douglass attended the Radical Abolitionist Party's nominating convention, where his friend Gerrit Smith was named as the party's presidential candidate. He endorsed Smith's candidacy, and was chosen by the New York convention as an elector for the ticket, but privately both he and Smith believed Lincoln would be victorious.[13] Douglass campaigned little for either candidate, and it is not clear how he cast his ballot that fall.

Although he was frustrated with the Republicans, in the summer and fall of 1860 his agitation on an issue important to African Americans in New York monopolized most of Douglass's time and attention. Instead of the presidential election, his main concern was campaigning for the passage of a New York referendum to remove the $250 property qualification the state placed on black voters. While keeping a foot in the national debate through his monthly editorials, his time and energy was devoted to the black suffrage agenda. The measure failed to pass, even though the Republican Party gained widespread support throughout New York. He complained that the suffrage referendum's failure in the wake of Republican triumph was "inconsistent with every profession and principle of the triumphant party, and must surprise the enemies of equal rights as much as it certainly disappoints the expectations of colored citizens."[14] It was clear that on the eve of

---

[11]"The Chicago Nominations," *Douglass' Monthly*, June 1860.
[12]Ibid.
[13]McKivigan, "Frederick Douglass-Gerrit Smith Friendship," p. 223.
[14]"Equal Suffrage Defeated," *Douglass' Monthly*, December 1860.

secession, Douglass did not yet see the Republicans as the best hope for emancipation.

As historian David Blight has described in *Frederick Douglass' Civil War*, one of Douglass's enduring qualities was a hopeful outlook, but his hopeful nature was also tinged with a duality. He describes Douglass as wavering between a "duty of principle" and a "duty of hope," vacillating between two kinds of thinking, one moral and one political. This outlook, evident over and over again, eventually spurred Douglass's adherence to the Republican Party and guided his actions during the Civil War. But Douglass was not always hopeful; scholar Peter C. Myers explains Douglass's condition in the wake of Lincoln's 1860 election as "momentary pessimism," which was clearly evident in the winter of 1860–61.[15] Appalled that the new president chose to coddle the seceding South rather than stand strong against slavery, in February his moralism led him to uncharacteristically suggest accepting the southern states' decision to leave the Union. He editorialized, "If there is not wisdom and virtue enough in the land to rid the country of slavery, then the next best thing is to let the South go to her own place, and be made to drink the wine cup of wrath and fire, which her long career of cruelty, barbarism and blood shall call down upon her guilty head."[16] Although he had railed against those abolitionists who had espoused disunion for more than a decade, his frustration found him momentarily in line with the likes of Wendell Phillips, the strongest abolition voice for dissolution of the Union.[17]

Douglass's cynicism also led him to reconsider the place of African Americans in northern society. For the first time, as the secession winter crept on, he seriously considered emigrating outside the United States. He had spent almost two decades arguing vehemently against the likes of his former business partner Martin R. Delany that black Americans did not have to leave their homeland to prosper, but that they should stay and fight for their rightful place as American citizens. Yet in 1861 he was finalizing plans to embark on April 25 with his daughter, Rosetta, for an extended exploratory trip to Haiti. The firing on Fort Sumter interrupted his plans.

---

[15]David W. Blight, *Frederick Douglass' Civil War: Keeping Faith in Jubilee* (Baton Rouge, 1989), p. 51; Myers, *Frederick Douglass: Race and Rebirth*, p. 9.

[16]"The Union and How to Save It," *Douglass' Monthly*, February 1861.

[17]James Brewer Stewart, *Wendell Phillips: Liberty's Hero* (Baton Rouge, 1986), pp. 218–19.

Once the war was under way, Douglass canceled his travel plans and threw himself into doing what he did best: he agitated, trying to get Lincoln and anyone who would listen to believe that emancipation was necessary and should be made the war's most important goal. For him, moral and political thought were again poised to merge. Following the fighting at Fort Sumter, his despair evaporated and he rejoiced: "Thank God! The slaveholders have saved our cause from ruin! They have exposed the throat of slavery to the keen knife of liberty, and have given a chance to all the righteous forces of the nation to deal a deathblow to the monster evil of the nineteenth century. *Friends of freedom! be up and doing; now is your time.*"[18] He reversed his earlier flippant endorsement of disunion and pushed instead for an abolition war. Already seeing the world-shattering possibilities in the conflict, in early May he compared the Civil War to other important conflicts across history, telling a large crowd gathered at Rochester's A.M.E. Zion Church, "revolutions never go backwards."[19] His hope was revived, at least temporarily, and he looked toward the new president and the Republican Party as potential partners in the moral work of abolition.

Two months before the First Battle of Bull Run, Douglass was already goading Lincoln's government to go after slavery: "*The simple way to put an end to the savage and desolating war now waged by the slaveholders, is to strike down slavery itself,*" which he called "the primal cause of that war."[20] As Blight has argued, Douglass quickly assumed a new role as a war propagandist. His editorials attacked the character of slaveholders and Southern society, and coaxed the Northern public to see Southerners as violent enemies to be defeated in the name of justice. Not yet in line with the Republican Party, which took a more moderate line early in the war, Douglass even proclaimed poor whites to be ignorant, servile tools of the slaveholders.[21]

Just after the war was under way, Douglass also began to agitate for a military role for African Americans. He urged blacks to organize themselves into informal militia companies, to buy arms and learn how to use them. In a May 1861 editorial he urged, "LET THE SLAVES AND FREE COLORED PEOPLE BE CALLED INTO SERVICE, AND FORMED

---

[18]"The Fall of Sumter," *Douglass' Monthly*, May 1861.
[19]John Blassingame et al., eds., *The Frederick Douglass Papers*, ser. 1: *Speeches, Debates, and Interviews*, 5 vols. (New Haven, Conn., 1979–92), 3:428–35.
[20]"How to End the War," *Douglass' Monthly*, May 1861.
[21]Blight, *Frederick Douglass' Civil War*, pp. 83–84.

INTO A LIBERATING ARMY," to march into the South where the banner of emancipation could be quickly raised.[22] But his early calls for black participation fell on deaf ears in Washington and among most Union military commanders. Later in the conflict, black participation and the treatment of U.S. Colored Troops caused Douglass to waver in his support for the president and to temper his connection with the Republican Party. His commitment to racial equality reflected his dual concern to navigate between the best path to freedom for his race and the role of political activism in achieving both emancipation and civil rights.

Even in the first two years of the war, however, Douglass was not yet ready to commit to a single plan or party, and his hopeful outlook began to wane. He became increasingly angry at the Republicans' inability to see the necessity of addressing the concerns of black Americans. He praised John C. Frémont's proclamation freeing the slaves of Confederates in Missouri and condemned Lincoln's veto of the provision. He railed against a government that "is still in bondage to fear, not that which the battle field inspires, but of the political power of slavery."[23] He urged abolitionists to keep agitating to "make the Government and people an abolition Government and an abolition people, for until both shall become such, it is quite plain that this land is doomed to see no peace."[24] Throughout the fall of 1861 and well into the spring of 1862, Douglass hit the lecture circuit, traveling thousands of miles across Northern states speaking before large and small crowds, trying to educate the public and galvanize the government into action against slavery. He supported the formation of the Emancipation League, which pushed for both an end to slavery and the advancement of black civil rights through the war effort. He worried over various proposals about what to do with the freedmen when freedom finally came. He continued to push for employing black troops.

Two weeks before Lincoln issued the preliminary Emancipation Proclamation, however, Douglass's pessimism about both the president and the war reached an all-time low in a private note sent to Gerrit Smith. He feared that the war effort was coming to naught and agreed that the nation was deeply under the sway of the Slave Power. He told his old friend, "I shudder

---

[22]"How to End the War," *Douglass' Monthly*, May 1861.
[23]"The Real Peril of the Republic," *Douglass' Monthly*, October 1861.
[24]"The Duty of Abolitionists," *Douglass' Monthly*, October 1861.

at what the future may still have in store for us. . . . This government is now in the hands of the Army, and the Army is in the hands of the very worst type of American Democracy, the chief representative of which is now doing his utmost to destroy the country."[25] Douglass was particularly angry with the president's recent address to a gathering of black leaders, in which he outlined a plan for removing freed African Americans from American shores. In the September issue of his monthly, Douglass's editorials condemned Lincoln and his plans to colonize blacks freed by the war effort, and those freed by Congress when it abolished slavery in the District of Columbia in April. By simultaneously appropriating six hundred thousand dollars for the colonization of freed blacks to Liberia or elsewhere, these actions tempered any ability to celebrate the end of slavery in the nation's capital, which had long been a goal of the immediate abolition movement. He likewise refused to be flattered by an invitation to lead the effort to resettle thousands of former slaves in Central America. "Mr. Lincoln is quite a genuine representative of American prejudice and Negro hatred," he told his readers; the president's actions demonstrated that he was "far more concerned for the preservation of slavery, and the favor of the Border Slave States, than for any sentiment of magnanimity or principle of justice and humanity."[26]

Once the Emancipation Proclamation had been issued, however, Douglass's hope was cautiously revived, and he was ready for action. He editorialized: "Now for the work," and called on Northerners to rally behind Lincoln's policy. He rejoiced to his British readers, many of whom relied on his monthly for an honest abolitionist assessment of the war effort: "The Proclamation of President Lincoln is the first chapter of a new history. The object of the Government is no longer to preserve, but to destroy slavery, no longer to recapture fugitive slaves, but to set them at Liberty, no longer to prevent slaves from rising against their cruel masters, but to see that nothing is done for such prevention."[27]

Although he first approached the party with the same questioning concern, following the issuance of the Emancipation Proclamation in 1862 and

---

[25]Douglass to Gerrit Smith, Sept. 8, 1862, in Philip Foner, ed., *The Life and Writings of Frederick Douglass*, 5 vols. (New York, 1950–55), 3:260.
[26]"The President and His Speeches," *Douglass' Monthly*, September 1862.
[27]"Address to Our Readers and Friends in Great Britain and Ireland," *Douglass' Monthly*, October 1862.

its implementation in 1863, Douglass's pragmatism led him closer to the Republican Party, and although he was still sometimes critical of Lincoln's administration, he remained attached to the Republicans for the remainder of his public career, even when the party failed to meet his expectations.

Despite his early hopefulness, as emancipation approached, Douglass was dismayed to see the abolition movement change and begin to drift apart. With the onset of war, abolition groups found that they were no longer in the rogue minority. The American Anti-Slavery Society (AASS) gained membership from mainstream America and attracted some who had wandered away back into its fold. Douglass, Gerrit Smith, Lewis Tappan, and others returned from the realm of political antislavery. But the movement also began to fragment as some members, notably Maria Weston Chapman and her sisters, left to pursue or prepare for missionary work among former slaves.

At the issuance of the Emancipation Proclamation, William Lloyd Garrison and Wendell Phillips argued over dissolving the AASS, because Garrison believed the group's work was nearly done. At the society's 1863 annual meeting, Douglass argued (as did Phillips) that the work of the society would not be finished until African Americans achieved full political and social equality. When Garrison declared their work to be done and the society no longer necessary, Douglass countered that the society was needed until "the black man of the South, and the black man of the North, shall have been admitted fully and completely into the body politic of America."[28] It seemed this beginning of the end to slavery formed a polarizing division within the abolition community. With his old colleagues arguing in this fashion, it is perhaps not surprising that Douglass looked to the Republican Party as an imperfect but nevertheless more likely entity for achieving his desired goals.

Douglass quickly moved from an advocate of black troops to an active recruiter once African American enlistments were approved. In early January 1863, Massachusetts Governor John A. Andrew put out a call for recruits to the newly forming Fifty-Fourth Massachusetts Infantry. He watched proudly as his sons Charles and Lewis joined that unit, and he began to lecture and recruit in earnest. In March 1863 he issued the famous broadside, "Men of Color, to Arms!"—an emotional call for African Americans far and wide to join the Fifty-Fourth. With only a small African

---

[28]Quoted in Stewart, *Wendell Phillips*, p. 244.

American population, Douglass and other black leaders tapped as recruiters spread out among northeastern states, quickly filling the initial regiment and then another, the Fifty-Fifth. Douglass concentrated his efforts in New York, while others traveled to Pennsylvania, Ohio, and other points west.

Although some Union personnel raised a few black regiments in 1862 in areas of the Deep South, such as Louisiana, in compliance with the Militia Act, it was in the wake of the Emancipation Proclamation that Douglass's push for black troops began to be realized. Northern states such as Massachusetts and Rhode Island answered the call, raising regiments early in the year. A formal designation for all black troops came with the issuance of General Order No. 143 on May 22, 1863, which established the U.S. Colored Troops, and reassigned regiments such as the Massachusetts Fifty-Fourth within the new designation. By war's end, 133 infantry regiments of U.S. Colored Troops were raised, in addition to cavalry units and heavy and light artillery regiments, accounting for approximately one-tenth of the Union army.[29] Secretary of War Edwin Stanton called on a number of abolitionists, including Douglass's acquaintance George L. Stearns (fig. 3), to recruit troops. It was Stearns who would directly involve Douglass in recruiting outside New England.

But even as he worked tirelessly to recruit Northern blacks into the Union army, Douglass was concerned about the growing tide of anti-black sentiment across the Northern states, reflecting another dimension in his dual struggle between responsibility to his race and his desire to fulfill a role within the Republican Party's war strategy. He knew that black soldiers were not going to be treated equally or given important assignments. He warned, "we shall be fighting a double battle, against slavery at the South and against prejudice and proscription at the North." Yet he could not help but be hopeful: "Whoever sees fifty thousand well drilled colored soldiers in the United States, will see slavery abolished and the union of these States secured from rebel violence."[30]

In the late spring and summer of 1863, Douglass acted along with his former recruiting partner, Massachusetts abolitionist George L. Stearns, now a major in the Union volunteer forces, in recruiting across the North.

---

[29]John David Smith, "Let Us All Be Grateful That We Have Colored Troops That Will Fight," in *Black Soldiers in Blue: African American Troops in the Civil War Era*, ed. John David Smith (Chapel Hill, 2002), pp. 8–9.
[30]"Condition of the Country," *Douglass' Monthly*, February 1863.

Fig. 3. George L. Stearns. *(Boyd B. Stutler Collection, West Virginia State Archives)*

Early in the recruiting process, however, Douglass became angry over unfair pay policies and the unequal treatment afforded colored troops. He wrote to Stearns in early August 1863, saying he could no longer continue to recruit under present circumstances. Despite their training and ability equal to whites, African American troops were often put to manual labor, and were paid only ten dollars a month, with three dollars withheld for clothing, while white soldiers were paid thirteen dollars. At the urging of Stearns, Douglass determined to go to Washington to intervene with on behalf of black troops.

Using various connections to important men, Douglass managed to get an audience with Secretary of War Stanton on August 10, 1863. The two met for about thirty minutes, and Douglass came away with the understanding that he would be given a commission to aid General Lorenzo Thomas with recruiting in the Mississippi Valley. He then met with President Lincoln and discussed the issues of concern with black troops, coming away from the meeting feeling fairly satisfied that the president intended to offer African American soldiers a fair deal. Hopeful once again, Douglass returned to Rochester and closed his newspaper, expecting his officer's commission to arrive any day. When he finally received word to report to Thomas in Vicksburg, Mississippi, however, there was no mention of a commission. He wrote to Stanton, but no commission came, and a deeply disappointed Douglass chose not to go south. The Republican Party, and Stanton in particular, had proved to be a great disappointment once again, but Douglass came away from his meeting with Lincoln impressed and with a new understanding of the president's position.

After 1863, with the Conscription Act in place and the anti-black violence that erupted in antidraft riots in cities such as New York, recruiting in the North largely dried up. From that point forward, most black troops were drawn from the South. Removing himself from the recruiting field altogether, Douglass spent the remainder of the war as an outspoken advocate for the rights of the freedpeople and colored troops. He continued to press for an "abolition war" that would completely eradicate slavery, but was soon becoming perturbed with Lincoln and the Republican Party once again.

Frustration found Douglass wavering with dual allegiance, torn between the needs of African Americans and the future promise of the Republican Party. As the 1864 election approached, Douglass seriously considered supporting the nomination of John C. Frémont to replace Lincoln on the Republican ticket, even signing a call for an alternative Republican convention. The war effort appeared to be at a standstill, and African Americans were making few gains. In the end, however, Douglass campaigned for Lincoln's reelection, once again taking a more practical political position. Although he continued to worry that the president was putting aside emancipation, Douglass's support for Lincoln and his allegiance to the Republican Party were probably greatly influenced by his second meeting with the president.

Douglass was summoned to meet with Lincoln for a second time in August 1864. Considering that the president's war was not going so well and that he was facing an uphill struggle toward reelection in the fall, Douglass was certainly flattered that Lincoln sought his advice. Eagerly traveling to the nation's capital for the meeting, Douglass found the president in a dismal state and close to bowing to the will of the growing tide of antiwar sentiment in the North. Lincoln showed Douglass a letter he had written declaring he would not stand in the way of peace or demand an end to slavery if the people of his country did not wish it to be abolished. Aghast that his hopes for abolition were about to be dashed, Douglass urged the president to remain steadfast against slavery and to set aside the letter. During the meeting Lincoln also outlined a plan similar to John Brown's original scheme to lure slaves out of the South via a type of government-sponsored Underground Railroad, and requested Douglass's advice on the plan's implementation. Although Douglass devised such an outline, the turning fortunes of battle in the fall of 1864 made it unnecessary.[31] Even though the plan never materialized, the fact that the president was considering such a radical measure demonstrates that Lincoln's policies regarding the freedpeople had changed dramatically from his earlier advocacy of colonization. Still, in the fall of 1864, Douglass was dismally concerned that the Republicans would leave slavery intact if that would bring an end to the awful war.

During the last part of the war, Douglass acted as an important black leader and patriot. Although he flirted with supporting Frémont as an opposition candidate for the Republican nomination in 1864, he eventually did campaign on Lincoln's behalf. By the time he met Lincoln for a third and final time during the second inauguration, at a reception at the executive mansion, his allegiance to the Republican Party was firmly secured. Here, famously, he recalled in his third autobiography that he was initially refused entry by guards because of his race. Telling the guards, "I shall not go out of this building till I see President Lincoln," Douglass determined to overcome racial convention. Standing in the doorway to the executive

---

[31]Douglass to Lincoln, Aug. 29, 1864, in Foner, *Life and Writings of Frederick Douglass*, 3:405–6.

mansion's East Room, where he had been detained, he was soon spotted by the president himself. Calling out, "here comes my friend Douglass," and taking him by the hand, Lincoln cemented the black man's party affiliation.[32] For the remainder of his career, Douglass never again wavered between support for his race and the Republican Party, believing their fates to be intimately linked.

When Lincoln was assassinated a month later, Douglass was devastated and offered an impromptu speech on the steps of the Rochester Court House. A few months after Lincoln's death, Mary Todd Lincoln sent Douglass one of her husband's favorite walking sticks, conveying in her letter that Lincoln had said before he died that he would like to do something to show his regard. Douglass assured her that he would cherish the gift, "not merely of the kind consideration in which I have reason to know that the president was pleased to hold me personally, but as an indication of his humane interest in the welfare of my whole race."[33]

By the time of Lincoln's assassination, Douglass's complicated struggle with his personal political allegiance was largely cemented; he subdued his dual nature and made a permanent home in the Republican Party. Regardless of the party's wavering on issues of slavery and abolition during the war, in January 1865 it was the Republican-led Congress that passed the Thirteenth Amendment banning slavery throughout the nation. In December it was the party's secretary of state, William H. Seward, who declared it to be the law of the nation. The Republican Party had been an imperfect partner for African American freedom and civil rights, and only reluctantly brought about an end to slavery. But in Douglass's mind, emancipation and the Union victory made the Republican Party the only logical home for him and for all African Americans. Douglass remained loyal to the party, even though it continued to disappoint him, especially by failing to push for a more painful and equitable Reconstruction.

Douglass's actions during the war and afterward left him open to criticism from some abolitionists (and later historians) and to self-doubt about his own actions and beliefs. In the end, the events of the war years and his interactions with political leaders fostered in him an eventual unwavering

---

[32]Frederick Douglass, *Life and Times of Frederick Douglass* (1892; reprint ed., New York, 1962), p. 366.
[33]Douglass to Mary Todd Lincoln, Aug. 17, 1865, in Foner, *Life and Writings of Frederick Douglass*, 4:174.

support for the Republican Party, even when it disappointed him. Although some have taken Douglass's loyalty to the Republican Party in the decades following the Civil War as evidence that he had become a political "yes man," more interested in his own prosperity than the advancement of his race, his adherence to the party of Lincoln was actually seated in a realism that had characterized his political alliances from the 1840s. Above all, Douglass was a pragmatist.

Michael Burlingame

Abraham Lincoln

Reluctant Emancipator?

IT IS FASHIONABLE in some circles to describe Lincoln as a reluctant emancipator who delayed issuing the Emancipation Proclamation because his heart was not in the antislavery cause.[1] Professor Julius Lester of the University of Massachusetts–Amherst insisted that "Blacks have no reason to feel grateful to Abraham Lincoln. Rather, they should be angry with him. After all, he came into office in 1861. How come it took him two whole years to free the slaves? His pen was sitting on his desk the whole time. All he had to do was get up one morning and say, 'Doggonnit! I think I'm gon' free the slaves today. It just ain't right for folks to own other folks.' It was that simple."[2] Professor Robert W. Johannsen of the University of Illinois cast doubt on the sincerity of Lincoln's antislavery professions, noting that his first speech attacking the peculiar institution was delivered in 1854, when the political climate seemed favorable. "Nearly all of his public statements on the slavery question prior to his election as president were delivered with political intent and for political effect," Professor Johannsen insisted.[3]

---

[1] See, for example, Lerone Bennett Jr., *Forced into Glory: Abraham Lincoln's White Dream* (Chicago, 2000).
[2] Julius Lester, *Look Out, Whitey! Black Power's Gon' Get Your Mama!* (New York, 1968), quoted in Allen C. Guelzo, *Lincoln's Emancipation Proclamation: The End of Slavery in America* (New York, 2004), p. 247.
[3] Robert W. Johannsen, *Lincoln, the South, and Slavery: The Political Dimension*, Walter Lynwood Fleming Lectures in Southern History (Baton Rouge, 1991).

In September 1862, a year and a half after Lincoln's inauguration, when he finally announced his intention to free the bondsmen of rebel slaveholders, he allegedly was responding only to political and diplomatic pressure. But in fact, Lincoln rejoiced in the liberation of slaves as enthusiastically as any abolitionist. In discussing the Emancipation Proclamation with his closest friend, Joshua Speed, he said: "I believe that in this measure my fondest hopes will be realized."[4] Constitutional and political constraints had compelled him to delay issuing the document; if he had acted solely on his own convictions and inclinations, it would have been issued much sooner. (In fact, as Professor James Oakes points out in his trailblazing study of emancipation, the Lincoln administration began liberating slaves without compensation in August 1861. By the time the Emancipation Proclamation was promulgated, tens of thousands of slaves had been freed by the administration's action.[5] Political or diplomatic considerations did not force Lincoln to issue the proclamation; on the contrary, such considerations led him to postpone doing so. In fact, as Professor Allen C. Guelzo has persuasively argued, in September 1862 it was politically and diplomatically hazardous for Lincoln to announce his intention to issue an emancipation proclamation.[6]

Rather than rehashing the familiar history of Lincoln's treatment of the slavery issue between 1854 and 1865, I propose to examine Lincoln's pre-1850 record of hostility to the peculiar institution. In 1864, Lincoln insisted that he was "naturally antislavery. If slavery is not wrong, nothing is wrong. I can not remember when I did not so think, and feel."[7] Six years earlier, as he began his campaign for Stephen A. Douglas's Senate seat, he declared: "I have always hated slavery, I think as much as any Abolitionist. . . . I have always hated it, but I have always been quiet about it until this new era of the introduction of the [Kansas-]Nebraska Bill began. I always believed that everybody was against it, and that it was in the course of ultimate extinction."[8]

---

[4]Joshua Speed to William H. Herndon, Louisville, Feb. 7, 1866, Douglas L. Wilson and Rodney O. Davis, eds., *Herndon's Informants: Letters, Interviews, and Statements about Abraham Lincoln* (Urbana, Ill., 1998), p. 197.
[5]James Oakes, *Freedom National: The Destruction of Slavery in the United States* (New York, 2012).
[6]Guelzo, *Lincoln's Emancipation Proclamation*.
[7]Lincoln to A. G. Hodges, Washington, Apr. 4, 1864, in *The Collected Works of Abraham Lincoln*, ed. Roy P. Basler, 9 vols. (New Brunswick, N.J., 1953–55), 7:281 (hereafter *CW*).
[8]Speech at Chicago, July 10, 1858, *CW*, 2:492.

Lincoln seldom used the word *hate*, but he did so repeatedly in 1854, when he delivered his first extended analysis of slavery. Alluding to Senator Douglas's neutrality on the slavery expansion issue, he said: "This *declared* indifference, but as I must think, covert *real* zeal for the spread of slavery, I can not but hate." "I hate it because of the monstrous injustice of slavery itself. I hate it because it deprives our republican example of its just influence in the world—enables the enemies of free institutions, with plausibility, to taunt us as hypocrites—causes the real friends of freedom to doubt our sincerity, and especially because it forces so many really good men amongst ourselves into an open war with the very fundamental principles of civil liberty—criticizing the Declaration of Independence, and insisting that there is no right principle of action but *self-interest*."[9]

When in 1855 Lincoln's friend Joshua Speed, a Kentucky slaveholder, criticized his attack on slavery, arguing that only Southerners were entitled to deal with that issue because they alone were directly affected by it, Lincoln protested: "You know I dislike slavery; and you fully admit the abstract wrong of it. . . . But you say that sooner than yield your legal right to the slave—especially at the bidding of those who are not themselves interested, you would see the Union dissolved. I am not aware that any one is bidding you to yield that right; very certainly I am not. I leave that matter entirely to yourself. I also acknowledge your rights and my obligations, under the constitution, in regard to your slaves. I confess I hate to see the poor creatures hunted down, and caught, and carried back to their stripes, and unrewarded toils; but I bite my lip and keep quiet. In 1841 you and I had together a tedious low-water trip, on a Steam Boat from Louisville to St. Louis. You may remember, as I well do, that from Louisville to the mouth of the Ohio there were, on board, ten or a dozen slaves, shackled together with irons. That sight was a continual torment to me; and I see something like it every time I touch the Ohio, or any other slave-border. It is hardly fair for you to assume, that I have no interest in a thing which has, and continually exercises, the power of making me miserable. You ought rather to appreciate how much the great body of the Northern people do crucify their feelings, in order to maintain their loyalty to the constitution and the Union."[10]

---

[9]Speech at Peoria, Oct. 16, 1854, *CW*, 2:260.
[10]Lincoln to Speed, Springfield, Aug. 14, 1855, *CW*, 2:321.

There is good reason to believe that Lincoln was not exaggerating when he claimed that he had always hated slavery. In 1858, he said: "the slavery question often bothered me as far back as 1836–1840. I was troubled and grieved over it."[11] Four years later, he remarked: "I have hated slavery from my childhood."[12] That same year he told Wendell Phillips that he had instructed Border State congressmen and senators "not to talk to him about slavery. They loved it & meant it should last—he hated it & meant *it should die*."[13] Similarly, Lincoln declared to Frederick Douglass: "I hate slavery as much as you do, and I want to see it abolished altogether."[14]

But we need not rely solely on Lincoln's later assertions that he hated slavery well before it became politically expedient to denounce it. Contemporary evidence supports his claim. In 1837, as a twenty-eight-year-old member of the Illinois state legislature, Lincoln and a colleague, Dan Stone, filed a protest against antiabolitionist resolutions that the General Assembly had adopted six weeks earlier by the lopsided vote of 77–6 in the House and 18–0 in the Senate. Lincoln and Stone were part of the tiny minority who opposed the resolutions—less than 6 percent of the entire legislature. Those overwhelmingly popular resolutions were introduced at the behest of southern state legislators who were outraged by the American Anti-Slavery Society's pamphlets depicting slave owners as cruel brutes. Equally objectionable to those southerners was the society's petition drive calling for the abolition of slavery in the District of Columbia. The resolutions that enjoyed the near-unanimous support of the Illinois General Assembly stated that its members "highly disapprove of the formation of abolition societies, and of the doctrines promulgated by them," that "the right of property in slaves is sacred to the slave-holding States by the Federal Government, and that they cannot be deprived of that right without their consent," and that "the General Government cannot abolish

---

[11]Robert H. Browne, *Abraham Lincoln and the Men of His Time*, 2 vols. (Cincinnati, 1901), 1:285.

[12]Vincent Colyer, *Report of the Services Rendered by the Freed People to the United States Army in North Carolina, in the Spring of 1862, after the Battle of Newbern* (New York, 1864), p. 51.

[13]Wendell Phillips's speech in Boston, Apr. 18, *New York Tribune*, Apr. 19, 1862; Phillips to his wife Ann, en route from Milwaukee to Madison, Wis., Mar. 31, 1862, Phillips Papers, Harvard University, Cambridge, Mass.

[14]Don E. Fehrenbacher and Virginia Fehrenbacher, eds., *Recollected Words of Abraham Lincoln* (Stanford, Calif., 1996), p. 145.

slavery in the District of Columbia, against the will of the citizens of said District."[15]

Lincoln wrote a protest against these resolutions and circulated it among his colleagues. None would sign except Stone, a native of Vermont and a graduate of Middlebury College who was not seeking reelection. (He would soon become a judge.) Lincoln declared in the document, which he and Stone entered into the journal of the House of Representatives, "that the institution of slavery is founded on both injustice and bad policy."[16]

To assert that "slavery is founded on both injustice and bad policy" took nerve in 1837, when antislavery views were unpopular throughout most of the nation, including central Illinois. Not long after Lincoln and Stone introduced their protest, Illinois Governor Joseph Duncan condemned efforts "to agitate the question of abolishing slavery in this country, for it can never be broached without producing violence and discord," even in the North. Duncan stated that "if I read my Bible right, which enjoins peace and goodwill as the first Christian duties, it must be wicked and sinful to agitate this subject in the manner it has been done by some Abolitionists, especially after our Southern neighbors have repeatedly and earnestly appealed to us not to meddle with it, and assured us their having done so has not only jeopardised their own safety and domestic peace, but in many cases has caused bloodshed and rebellion, which has compelled them, as a measure of prudence and protection, to use more rigidity and severity with their slaves." Duncan also contended that it would "neither be consistent with sound policy or humanity by a single effort to free all the slaves in the Union, ignorant, vicious, and degraded as they are known to be, and then turn them loose upon the world without their possessing the least qualification for civil government, or knowledge of the value of property, or the use of liberty."[17]

Henry Clay, whom Lincoln called his "beau ideal of a statesman," denounced abolitionists as "extremely mischievous" boat-rockers who "would see the administration of the Government precipitate the nation into absolute ruin" and "nullify the Constitution." He feared that "if they are not checked in their progress," people in "the free States will have to decide on

---

[15]Illinois General Assembly, *House Journal*, 1836–37, pp. 241–44.
[16]*CW*, 1:75.
[17]Duncan to Gideon Blackburn, Jacksonville, Dec. 12, 1837, in Julia Duncan Kirby, *Biographical Sketch of Joseph Duncan, Fifth Governor of Illinois*, Fergus Historical Series No. 29 (Chicago, 1888), pp. 50–51.

the alternative of repudiating them or repudiating the Union."[18] In 1836, Edward Everett, the governor of Massachusetts, declared: "Everything that tends to disturb the relations created by this compact [i.e., the Constitution] is at war with its spirit, and whatever by direct and necessary operation is calculated to excite an insurrection among the slaves has been held by highly respectable legal authority an offence against the peace of this Commonwealth."[19] Similarly, the governor of New York, William L. Marcy, described abolitionists as "sinister, reckless agitators" and recommended that the Free States provide "for the trial and punishment by their own judicatories, of residents within their limits, guilty of acts therein, which are calculated to excite insurrection and rebellion in a sister State."[20]

Several months after Lincoln and Stone entered their protest, Springfielders condemned abolitionism. During a session of the Presbyterian synod, citizens there tried to disrupt an antislavery speaker. Though violence was averted, townspeople announced that "as citizens of a free State and a peaceable community, we deprecate any attempt to sow discord among us, or to create an excitement as to abolition which can be productive of no good result . . . the doctrine of immediate emancipation in this country, (although promulgated by those who profess to be christians,) is at variance with christianity, and its tendency is to breed contention, broils and mobs, and the leaders of those calling themselves abolitionists are designing, ambitious men, and dangerous members of society, and should be shunned by all good citizens."[21] Springfield's Whig newspaper, for which Lincoln wrote anonymous and pseudonymous contributions, predicted "that public opinion in the frontier states is likely to check at once the perfidy of these fanatical men [abolitionists]." Westerners "could not be induced to visit upon the South such an accumulation of horrors as is embraced in the meaning of those two words—'universal emancipation.'"[22]

---

[18]Clay to Calvin Colton, Lexington, Sept. 2, 1843, and to John Sloane, Lexington, Oct. 27, 1843, in James F. Hopkins et al., eds., *The Papers of Henry Clay*, 11 vols. (Lexington, Ky., 1959–92), 9:852, 874.
[19]Paul Revere Frothingham, *Edward Everett: Orator and Statesman* (Boston, 1925), p. 132.
[20]*Albany Argus*, Jan. 7, 1837, quoted in Lorman Ratner, *Powder Keg: Northern Opposition to the Antislavery Movement, 1831–1840* (New York, 1968), p. 72; Marcy, message of Jan. 5, 1836, quoted in Ivor Debenham Spencer, *The Victor and the Spoils: A Life of William L. Marcy* (Providence, R.I., 1959), p. 104.
[21]Springfield, Ill., *Sangamo Journal*, Oct. 28, 1837.
[22]Andy Van Meter, *Always My Friend: A History of the* State Journal-Register *and Springfield* (Springfield, Ill., 1981), p. 30.

The abolitionist movement came late to Illinois. To be sure, in the late 1810s and early 1820s, some of its citizens had effectively fought against the introduction of slavery into their state, but after their triumph in 1824, antislavery zeal cooled dramatically. In 1837, the year of the Lincoln–Stone protest, a campaign to circulate antislavery petitions was thwarted. Four years later, Springfield authorities denied an agent of the Illinois Anti-Slavery Society permission to speak. Three years thereafter, a howling Springfield mob disrupted an abolitionist's attempt to lecture, while police passively stood by and laughed. Lincoln's close friend Simeon Francis, who edited the *Illinois State Journal* (Springfield's Republican newspaper), wrote that the word *abolitionist* "is an odious epithet among us; and we do not believe that there are a dozen men to be found in Sangamon county to whom it can be properly applied."[23]

In 1845, an abolitionist writing from central Illinois noted that "quite a large portion of western people, who are anti-slavery in principle and who will subscribe to all the views of the abolitionists when presented to them in private conversation, still abhor the name *abolitionist*." It conjured up "amalgamation, circulating inflammatory papers among the negroes in order to instigate them to insurrection, and a desire to do away with slavery by physical force."[24]

In a region where such views were widespread, Lincoln knew that speaking out against slavery would not help him politically. Yet by 1837 he clearly loathed slavery. In 1860, he wrote that the protest which he and Stone had introduced twenty-three years earlier "briefly defined his position on the slavery question; and so far as it goes, it was then the same that it is now."[25]

Lincoln's friend and political ally Samuel C. Parks thought that "Lincoln told the truth when he said he had 'always hated slavery as much as any Abolitionist' but I do not know that he deserved a great deal of credit for that for his hatred of oppression & wrong in all its forms was constitutional—he could not help it."[26] Indeed, Lincoln had an unusually sensitive conscience, and as a youngster growing up in southwestern Indiana,

---

[23] Springfield *Illinois State Journal*, Oct. 19, 1854.
[24] E. M. to Messrs. Leavitt and Alden, Morgan County, Ill., June 22, Boston *Emancipator and Weekly Chronicle*, July 16, 1845.
[25] Autobiography written for John Locke Scripps [ca. June 1860], *CW*, 4:65.
[26] Samuel C. Parks to Herndon, Mar. 25, 1866, Wilson and Davis, *Herndon's Informants*, p. 239.

he had chastised his playmates for their cruelty to animals. On the Midwestern frontier, such cruelty was common. At log-rollings, men would "round up a chipmunk, a rabbit, or a snake, and make him take refuge in a burning log-heap and watch him squirm and fry."[27] In one of his early bouts of schooling, Lincoln wrote an essay on that subject. As an adolescent he upbraided his stepbrother John Johnston for smashing the shell of a land turtle against a tree, leaving the suffering animal quivering and defenseless. When his mother urged him to kill a snake, Abe replied: "No, it enjoys living just the same as we do."[28] His stepsister Matilda remembered Abe saying that "an ant[']s life was to it, as sweet as ours to us."[29] A youngster who was so offended by cruelty to animals would doubtless have been offended by cruelty to slaves.

But Lincoln's hatred of slavery was rooted in something more than his God-given conscience. He called slavery "monstrous" because, among other things, it represented the systematic theft of the fruits of hard labor, a kind of institutionalized robbery. It was outrageous that someone worked hard in the hot sun all day and someone else derived all the profits of that labor. Slaveholders blasphemously rewrote the word of God Almighty, who upon expelling Adam from the Garden of Eden, said: "In the sweat of thy face shalt thou eat bread." The slaveholders' version of that divine injunction read: "In the sweat of someone else's face shalt thou eat bread."

In 1860 Lincoln remarked: "I always thought that the man who made the corn should eat the corn."[30] Thirteen years earlier, upon first meeting the Virginia-born-and-bred Ward Hill Lamon, he had made disparaging remarks about white Southerners' work ethic. To Lamon's protest, Lincoln remarked: "Oh, yes; you Virginians shed barrels of perspiration while standing off at a distance and superintending the work your slaves do for you. It is different with us. Here it is every fellow for himself, or he doesn't

---

[27] William Riley McLaren, "Reminiscences of Pioneer Life in Illinois," quoted in John Mack Faragher, *Sugar Creek: Life on the Illinois Prairie* (New Haven, Conn., 1986), p. 153.

[28] *Charleston* (Illinois) *Plaindealer*, Feb. 1892, photocopy, Abraham Lincoln Association reference files, folder marked "Coles County," Lincoln Presidential Library (LPL), Springfield, Ill.

[29] Matilda Johnston Moore, interview with Herndon near Charleston, Ill., Sept. 8, 1865, in Wilson and Davis, *Herndon's Informants*, p. 109.

[30] Cassius M. Clay in Allen Thorndike Rice, ed., *Reminiscences of Abraham Lincoln by Distinguished Men of His Time* (New York, 1886), p. 458.

get there."[31] For the rest of his life, Lincoln would stress this theme often, most memorably in his second inaugural address: "It may seem strange that any men should dare to ask a just God's assistance in wringing their bread from the sweat of other men's faces; but let us judge not that we be not judged."[32] A few weeks earlier he told a Tennessee woman who was pleading for the release of her Confederate spouse from prison: "You say your husband is a religious man; tell him when you meet him, that I say I am not much of a judge of religion, but that, in my opinion, the religion that sets men to rebel and fight against their government, because, as they think, that government does not sufficiently help some men to eat their bread on the sweat of other men's faces, is not the sort of religion upon which people can get to heaven!"[33]

That theme resonated with Lincoln because he himself had been treated like a slave by his father Thomas, who rented young Abraham out to neighbors. Around 1825, Thomas Lincoln found himself in greater financial trouble than usual. To help pay off his debts, Thomas removed Abe from school and hired him out to neighbors. For several years, Lincoln toiled like a slave as a butcher, ferry operator, riverman, store clerk, farm hand, wood chopper, distiller, and sawyer, receiving from ten cents to thirty-one cents a day. This money he turned over to Thomas, in compliance with the law stipulating that children's earnings belonged to their father. Understandably, Abraham came to feel as if he were a chattel on a southern plantation. "I used to be a slave," he declared in 1856.[34] Eighteen years earlier, he had related to a friend how he had courted a woman and then regretted his decision to become engaged to her: "Through life I have been in no bondage, either real or immaginary from the thraldom of which I so much desired to be free."[35] The painful experience of quasi-slavery in his youth led Lincoln to identify with the slaves and to denounce human bondage even when it was politically risky to do so.

In addition to the 1837 Lincoln–Stone resolution attacking slavery, there is another piece of legislative evidence illustrating Lincoln's pre-1850

---

[31]Ward Hill Lamon, *Recollections of Abraham Lincoln, 1847–1865*, ed. Dorothy Lamon Teillard, 2d ed. (Washington, D.C., 1911), pp. 14–15.
[32]*CW*, 8:333.
[33]Ibid., 8:155.
[34]Reminiscences of John E. Roll, *Chicago Times-Herald*, Aug. 25, 1895.
[35]*CW*, 1:118.

FIG. 1. Daguerreotype of Congressman-Elect Abraham Lincoln, attributed to Nicholas H. Shepherd, taken in 1846 or 1847; it is the earliest known photograph of Lincoln. *(National Photo Company Collection, Prints and Photographs Division, Library of Congress)*

hostility to slavery. In January 1849, as a member of the U.S. House of Representatives (fig. 1), he framed a statute abolishing slavery in the District of Columbia (fig. 2). Congress was then debating a motion introduced by Daniel Gott of New York outlawing the slave trade in the District.

FIG. 2. *United States Slave Trade*, 1830; depicts a slave coffle in the shadow of the U.S. Capitol in Washington, D.C. As a member of Congress, Lincoln could see slave pens from the Capitol. *(Prints and Photographs Division, Library of Congress)*

Lincoln and three other Northern Whigs unsuccessfully voted to table it. Ohio Representative Joshua R. Giddings (fig. 3), the foremost opponent of slavery in Congress, called Lincoln's vote "direct support of the slave trade."[36] Lincoln evidently believed that the preamble to Gott's resolution (which asserted that slave trading in the District was "contrary to natural justice" and "notoriously a reproach to our country throughout Christendom and a serious hindrance to the progress of republican liberty among the nations of the earth") was too inflammatory.[37] Antislavery Congressman Caleb B. Smith of Indiana criticized its tendency to "inflame or excite the people of the South" and "hold them up to the odium of the country."[38]

Gott's resolution, the first congressional measure aimed at restricting the domestic slave trade, alarmed southern senators and representatives, who warned that their states might secede in response to such action. Scared by those threats, the House on January 10, 1849, voted to reconsider Gott's

---

[36] Joshua Giddings to Charles Sumner, Washington, D.C., Dec. 22, 1848, Sumner Papers, Harvard University, Cambridge, Mass.; Joshua R. Giddings, *History of the Rebellion: Its Authors and Causes* (New York, 1864), pp. 286–88.
[37] *House Journal*, 30th Cong., 2d sess., Dec. 21, 1848, p. 132.
[38] *Congressional Globe*, 30th Cong., 2d sess., Jan. 10, 1849, appendix, p. 214.

FIG. 3. Joshua R. Giddings, Lincoln's colleague in the House of Representatives and his collaborator on the bill to provide compensated emancipation in the District of Columbia. This photograph taken by Mathew Brady's studio, dates to between 1855 and 1865. *(Brady-Handy Photograph Collection, Prints and Photographs Division, Library of Congress)*

measure, thus killing it. Lincoln's stand on the Gott resolution prompted Horace Greeley to term him "one of the very mildest type of Wilmot Proviso Whigs from the free States," and Radical Congressman George W. Julian of Indiana to deem him "a moderate Wilmot Proviso man" whose "anti-slavery education had scarcely begun."[39]

Lincoln's antislavery education, in truth, was well advanced, as he showed on the same day that he joined the House majority to scuttle Gott's resolution; he announced his intention to offer a substitute that was more far-reaching than the New Yorker's measure, one calling for the abolition of slavery—not simply slave trading—in the District. He evidently shared the view of abolitionist firebrand William Lloyd Garrison, who wrote that eliminating "the slave traffic . . . is impractical while slavery exists. There is no reason why slave-trading should be prohibited if slave-holding is justified and allowed."[40] Lincoln's measure provided that, beginning in 1850, babies born to slave mothers would be free; that their masters would have to support and educate them; that the children "would owe reasonable service, as apprentices, to such owners . . . until they respectively arrive at the age of ____ years when they shall be entirely free"; that Congress would compensate the owners; and that runaway slaves reaching the District would be extradited. The measure would be implemented only after a majority of the District's voters approved it. Lincoln declared "that he was authorized to say, that among fifteen of the leading citizens of the District of Columbia to whom this proposition had been submitted, there was not one but who approved of the adoption of such a measure."[41]

Among those citizens were the mayor of Washington, Joseph Gales, and William Seaton, coeditor of the influential *National Intelligencer*. Eleven years later, Lincoln recalled: "I visited Mayor Seaton, and others whom I thought best acquainted with the sentiment of the people, to ascertain if a bill such as I proposed would be endorsed by them. . . . Being informed that it would meet with their hearty approbation I gave notice in Congress that I should introduce a bill. Subsequently I learned that many leading southern members of Congress, had been to see the Mayor and the others who favored my bill and had drawn them over to their way of thinking. Finding that I

---

[39] Horace Greeley, "Greeley's Estimate of Lincoln," *The Century Magazine*, July 1891, p. 374; George W. Julian, *The Life of Joshua R. Giddings* (Chicago, 1892), p. 261.
[40] *The Liberator* (Boston), Feb. 9, 1849.
[41] *CW*, 2:20–22.

was abandoned by my former backers and having little personal influence, I *dropped* the matter knowing it was useless to prosecute the business at that time."[42] (In 1862, Lincoln would propose to Congress a plan of gradual, compensated emancipation, also providing federal support for any freed slaves who desired to leave the country. No such clause was included in his 1849 measure.)

A Mississippi newspaper condemned Lincoln as an abolitionist, while the antislavery militant Wendell Phillips called Lincoln's measure "one of the poorest and most confused specimens of pro-slavery compromise."[43] Joshua Giddings, who opposed slavery as strongly as did Phillips, lauded Lincoln's bill, which he had helped write. On January 8, 1849, Giddings confided to his diary: "Mr. [John] Dickey of P[ennsylvani]a and Mr. Lincoln of Illinois were busy preparing resolutions to abolish slavery in the D C this morning. I had a conversation with them and advised them to draw up a bill for that purpose and push it through. They hesitated and finally accepted my proposition.... Mr. Lincoln called on me this evening and read his bill and asked my opinion which I freely gave." Soon thereafter, Giddings recorded in his diary that "our whole mess remained in the dining-room after tea, and conversed upon the subject of Mr. Lincoln's bill to abolish slavery. It was approved by all; I believe it as good a bill as we could get at this time, and am willing to pay for slaves in order to save them from the Southern market."[44]

Giddings's view was shared by the abolitionist Gamaliel Bailey, who wrote: "we should like to see a bill [emancipating slaves in the capital] prepared, submitting the question to the [legally] qualified [i.e., adult white male] voters of the District, with the distinct information that a liberal appropriation would be made to aid in the act of emancipation. Such a bill, we doubt not, would pass Congress, and we have just as little doubt as to the decision of the citizens of this District under it." A measure like that "would be giving to thousands of citizens, unrepresented in any legislative body, an opportunity to do a high act of justice, with some grace; and would

---

[42] James Quay Howard's notes of an interview with Lincoln [May 1860], Abraham Lincoln Papers, Manuscript Division, Library of Congress, Washington, D.C.

[43] "Another Abolition Appointment by Taylor," *Vicksburg Sentinel*, n.d., copied in the *Yazoo Democrat* (Yazoo City, Miss.), Oct. 10, 1849; *The Liberator*, July 13, 1860.

[44] Giddings diary, Jan. 8 and 11, 1849, Ohio Historical Society, Columbus.

also result in the *emancipation*, not *transfer*, of the victims of Slavery. Pass an act of abolition, without such provision as we have suggested, and before it could take effect, almost every slave in the District would be sold to the South."[45]

Some abolitionists opposed compensating slaveholders, but others disagreed. In the District of Columbia, William L. Chaplin and Jacob Bigelow, the foremost conductors on the local Underground Railroad, had at first rejected compensated emancipation but in time changed their minds. In 1848, Chaplin urged opponents of slavery to "reject the dogma, that money is lost which is paid for slaves. Every dollar thus paid is a most effective sermon to the conscience of the guilty." A few years thereafter, Bigelow stated that on "the subject of paying for slaves, to secure their freedom, I acknowledge that I once *theorised* against it; but was, long ago very summarily cured of my theory, when I came to practice upon it."[46] Prominent antislavery politicos, including William Henry Seward of New York and Salmon P. Chase of Ohio, favored compensating Washington slaveholders. (Seward supported compensated emancipation in the District provided that a majority of its citizens supported the measure.)

Horace Greeley criticized the provision in Lincoln's bill requiring the voters of the District to approve emancipation before it could be implemented: "it seemed to me much like submitting to a vote of the inmates of a penitentiary a proposition to double the length of their respective terms of imprisonment."[47] But some District residents opposed slavery and slave trading, including several hundred who in 1828 had urged Congress to abolish the peculiar institution. Because the District was controlled by Congress, which contained no representatives speaking for its citizens, many believed that it would be unfair to deny them a voice in the matter. The electorate of a state—or its representatives—controlled the fate of slavery within its limits. While Congress might legally have the authority to outlaw slavery in the District without the voters' approval, the *Baltimore Sun* opined that it would be unwise to do so: "it is well to have a giant's strength, but

---

[45] Washington, D.C., *National Era*, Dec. 28, 1848.
[46] *Albany Patriot*, Mar. 22 and 24, 1848, and *Anti-Slavery Reporter*, May 1, 1853, quoted in Stanley Harrold, *Subversives: Antislavery Community in Washington, D.C., 1828–1865* (Baton Rouge, 2003), pp. 102–3.
[47] "Greeley's Estimate of Lincoln," p. 374.

tyrannous to use it like a giant. We submit, however, that to abolish slavery in the District without the consent of a majority of the white population would be a wanton exercise of that absolutism with which Congress has been vested in its legislative relation to the people of the District. . . . For our part, we believe it would be greatly conducive to the peace of the nation on this subject, if slavery was abolished there by their own consent and free will."[48] In late 1847 an Illinois representative observed that "a very large party in the District" favored "the *gradual* abolition of slavery in the District, and a small party in favor of the *immediate* abolition. A majority of Congress is disposed to leave this matter to the voters of the District."[49] Three years later another Illinois congressman, alluding to abolition in the nation's capital, wrote from Washington that "it is well understood here that if the question was submitted to the people of the *District* a large majority would vote in favour of it."[50] In 1854, Lincoln declared that six years earlier he had "heard no one express a doubt that a system of gradual emancipation, with compensation to owners, would meet the approbation of a large majority of the white people of the District."[51]

Majority opinion favored compensating slaveholders if the peculiar institution were to be abolished. When Lincoln announced his intention to submit a proposal for compensated emancipation, a journalist reported that it was "believed that there is a large majority of the House in favor of some such proposition" and "that the sooner some step of the kind is taken, the better it will be for the peace and union of the country." It was widely understood that "whatever action may be had in the premises, *compensation* must follow. This may be the ground of compromise that will continue. We must take men and the laws as they are, not as one would have them, and regulate our legislation on those principles of justice and expediency, which so marked and honored the national councils of our fathers."[52] An antislavery journalist insisted that it would be "dishonorable in the extreme" to "free at once all slaves, without compensating their owners."[53] The Speaker of

---

[48] *Baltimore Sun*, n.d., copied in *The National Era* (Washington, D.C.), Jan. 4, 1849.
[49] [John Wentworth], Washington correspondence, Dec. 22, 1847, *Chicago Daily Democrat*, Jan. 4, 1848.
[50] William Bissell to Joseph Gillespie, Washington, Apr. 19, 1850, Joseph Gillespie Papers, LPL.
[51] Speech at Peoria, Oct. 16, 1854, *CW*, 2:255.
[52] Washington correspondence by "Athenian," Jan. 10, 1849; *Boston Atlas*, Jan. 15, 1849.
[53] Washington correspondence, Feb. 2, 1849; *New York Herald*, Feb. 6, 1849.

the House of Representatives, Robert C. Winthrop of Massachusetts, believed that "compensation must go hand in hand with emancipation. It is this view which takes away the idea of selfishness from Northern philanthropy. If we admit that we are to unite with the South in bearing the burdens & defraying the cost of Abolition, we make it a matter of joint interest in regard to which our voices may fairly be heard." Convincing slaveholders to accept abolition would require an offer of compensation, Winthrop believed. "Those who oppose such a course, however philanthropic they may be in theory, are practically riveting the bonds which they desire to break."[54] Abolition in the British West Indies, as well as in Pennsylvania, New Jersey, and New York, had been accompanied by compensation to slaveholders.

In 1860, Wendell Phillips denounced the fugitive slave clause in Lincoln's 1849 emancipation bill and called its author "the slave hound of Illinois."[55] In a public letter that has curiously escaped the attention of most historians, Joshua Giddings stoutly defended Lincoln: "his conversing with the people of the District, the preparation of his bill, the avowal of his intention to present it, were important." Such actions placed him among "those who were laboring in the cause of humanity. He avowed his intention to strike down slavery and the slave trade in the District; to strike from our statute book the act by which freemen were transformed into slaves; to speak, and act, and vote for the right," and "cast aside the shackles of party, and took his stand upon principle." Chiding Phillips, Giddings added: "You speak of that act with great severity of condemnation. I view it as one of high moral excellence, marking the heroism of the man. He was the only member among the Whigs proper [as opposed to the handful of antislavery Whigs] of that session, who broke the silence on the subject of those crimes."[56]

Sydney Howard Gay, managing editor of the *New York Tribune* and a militant opponent of slavery, also challenged his old friend Phillips. In August 1860, William Herndon, probably speaking for Lincoln, told Gay: "Your reply to Wendell Phillips's article in the Liberator was correct." Gay,

---

[54]Winthrop to John H. Clifford, Washington, D.C., Jan. 20, 1849, and to his son Robert, Washington, D.C., Feb. 18, 1849, Winthrop Papers, Massachusetts Historical Society, Boston, Mass.
[55]*The Liberator* (Boston), June 30, 1860.
[56]Giddings to Phillips, Jefferson, Ohio, July 30, 1860, *Ashtabula* (Ohio) *Sentinel*, n.d., copied in *The Liberator* (Boston), Aug. 24, 1860.

Herndon said, was "familiar—too familiar—with legislative business not to know that . . . no one man can possibly get his own ideas put into any statute—any law, or any Constitution." Passing bills involved "concession—compromise." When "Lincoln was in Congress this State of affairs Existed: he was then a strong Anti-Slavery man and is now the same. This I know, though he wishes and will act under the Constitution: he is radical in heart, but in action he must Conform to Law & Constitution as Construed in good old times." Herndon, a conspicuous admirer of Phillips, concluded: "Lincoln, in reference to the Bill about which Mr. Phillips wrote his articles, was actuated by Anti-Slavery sentiments alone. . . . In doing this he had to consult his friends' feelings and ideas or he could do nothing; and so his bill was drawn up with a reference to all the aforesaid Conditions—conflicting sentiments & ideas." Lincoln "wanted the slave trade in the District of Columbia cut up by the roots and slavery gradually abolished."[57]

In the fall of 1849 a *New York Tribune* correspondent called Lincoln "conspicuous in the last Congress—especially during the last session, when he attempted to frame and put through a bill for the gradual Abolition of Slavery in the District of Columbia. He is a strong but judicious enemy to Slavery, and his efforts are usually very practical, if not always successful."[58] Eleven years later, Joshua Giddings recalled that when he and Lincoln served in Congress together "they became intimately acquainted—boarding at the same house, and sitting opposite each other at meals; that he thought he knew the heart of Abraham Lincoln as well as any living man, and speaking from that knowledge, he believed that every beat of 'honest Abe's' heart was a throb of sincerity and truth—in a word, that he is that noblest work of God—an honest man. He believed Lincoln's loyalty to republican principles, and to the cause of freedom and humanity, was unquestionable and beyond suspicion."[59]

Instead of regarding Lincoln as a reluctant emancipator who lacked strong antislavery feeling, it would be more appropriate to consider him

---

[57]Herndon to Sydney Howard Gay, Springfield, Aug. 10, 1860, Gay Papers, Columbia University, New York.

[58]Washington correspondence by C.B.A., Sept. 20, 1849; *New York Tribune*, Sept. 22, 1849.

[59]Speech of May 22, 1860, at Oberlin, Ohio, *Springfield* (Massachusetts) *Republican*, May 28, 1860.

"emphatically the black man's President," which is what Frederick Douglass called him in a June 1865 speech that is too little known today. According to Douglass, Lincoln was the first president "to show any respect for their rights as men . . . the first American President who . . . rose above the prejudice of his times, and country."[60]

---

[60]Frederick Douglass, speech delivered at the Cooper Union in New York, June 1, 1865, manuscript in Douglass's hand, Douglass Papers, Library of Congress Manuscript Division.

Paul Finkelman

Lincoln's Long Road to Freedom

How a Railroad Lawyer Became the Great Emancipator

COMING TO TERMS with Lincoln and emancipation was once a relatively easy task. He crossed American history like a meteor, preserving the Union, freeing the slaves, and then becoming our first martyred president. The image of the Great Emancipator is everywhere, even in our purses and pockets. His face is on the front of every penny and every five dollar bill. For more than a half century the Lincoln Memorial—our secular temple dedicated to the Union and freedom—was on the back of every penny, and although the grand statue of Lincoln in the memorial is not visible on that small copper disk, most Americans instantly recognize any picture of it. But if we need a refresher of that magnificent marble tribute to Lincoln, we can see it clearly (although it is small) on the back of the five dollar bill.

For most Americans the image of Lincoln remains secure. But some scholars and commentators reject the image of Lincoln as the Great Emancipator. The critique can be easily summarized.

1. *Lincoln was a reluctant emancipator.* Lincoln was slow to move against slavery, waiting almost two years before issuing the Emancipation Proclamation on January 1, 1863. During this period he countermanded orders by his own generals in Missouri and South Carolina who tried to free slaves in their military districts. Even when he ordered the liberation of slaves, the Emancipation Proclamation only applied to slaves still under Confederate control, ignoring the million or so slaves in the loyal slave states, Tennessee,

and parts of Virginia and Louisiana excluded from the reach of the proclamation.[1] Some critics argue that because of these exemptions, Lincoln only freed the slaves he had no power to emancipate, while ignoring those slaves under the control of the United States, whom he could free.

2. *Lincoln never really supported black freedom.* This point dovetails with the previous argument about his slow move to emancipation. Support for this argument is found in Lincoln's first inaugural address, in which he said he had "no inclination" to end slavery where it already existed.[2] In addition, those who accept these arguments point to Lincoln's support for colonization and his assertions in the first inaugural and at the beginning of the war that his only goal was to preserve the Union.

3. *Emancipation was purely a military act disconnected from any commitment to freedom.* Proponents of this analysis argue that Lincoln issued the proclamation only when forced to do so by a dwindling supply of white soldiers and by reverses on the battlefield, especially the defeat at Second Bull Run in August and the disaster at Fredericksburg in December 1862. Supporters of this argument claim that only when the military situation became dire did Lincoln finally use emancipation to hurt the Southern war effort and to recruit blacks to fill the ranks of his army. Some critics also tie this to foreign policy, asserting that Lincoln issued the proclamation because he feared Britain would recognize the Confederacy. Supporters of this analysis claim that emancipation was simply a desperate act of a desperate military commander.

4. *Self-emancipation, and not Lincoln, ended slavery.* Some scholars object to the emphasis on Lincoln as the Great Emancipator in the American narrative. They argue that emancipation was a function of black agency, that slaves running away from their owners forced Lincoln to take a stand against slavery. This analysis is often paired with the previous ones on Lincoln's timing and his lack of enthusiasm for emancipation, leading to the conclusion that emancipation stemmed from the actions of slaves running to freedom, which forced Lincoln to issue the proclamation.

---

[1] In 1860 there were 439,000 slaves in the four slave states that did not secede and about 276,000 in Tennessee. Lincoln excluded those states, as well as parts of Virginia and Louisiana, from the proclamation.

[2] Abraham Lincoln, "First Inaugural Address—Final Text," Mar. 4, 1861, in *The Collected Works of Abraham Lincoln*, ed. Roy P. Basler, 9 vols. (New Brunswick, N.J., 1953–55), 4:262–63 (hereafter *CW*).

5. *The Emancipation Proclamation lacked any moral purpose or meaning.* Critics argue that in ending slavery Lincoln failed to use the "bully pulpit" of the presidency because the Emancipation Proclamation did not set a moral goal of the war. How can the emancipator be "Great," we might ask, if he failed to be great and inspiring when he issued the document? Lincoln was one of the greatest craftsmen of the English language in American political history. But in the proclamation, the most important moment of his life, Lincoln appears as a pettifogger, drafting a boring, almost incomprehensible legal document. Unlike almost everything else he wrote, the proclamation itself was dull and uninspiring. Even historians who admire Lincoln think it was "boring" and "pedestrian."[3] Historian Richard Hofstadter encapsulated this notion more than a half-century ago, arguing that with its turgid language the Emancipation Proclamation had "all the moral grandeur of a bill of lading."[4]

In sum, critics question Lincoln's commitment to black freedom and the nature and timing of the Emancipation Proclamation. It took Lincoln more than a year to propose emancipation, and when he finally did so, Lincoln seemed to vacillate, offering to withdraw the preliminary proclamation if the rebellious states would return to the Union.[5] When he issued the final Emancipation Proclamation, nearly two years into the war, it did not free all the slaves in the United States.

On the surface, these criticisms of Lincoln are somewhat plausible. In the end, however, a careful understanding of Lincoln's own ideology and philosophy, the constraints of the United States Constitution, and the nature of the Civil War suggest that the criticisms ultimately miss their mark. Lincoln's strategy and policy turns out to be subtle and at times brilliant. Ultimately his strategy worked, as slavery came to an end everywhere in the nation.

---

[3]Allen C. Guelzo, "'Sublime in Its Magnitude': The Emancipation Proclamation," in *Lincoln and Freedom: Slavery, Emancipation, and the Thirteenth Amendment*, ed. Harold Holzer and Sara Vaughn Gabbard (Carbondale, Ill., 2007), p. 66.

[4]Richard Hofstadter, *The American Political Tradition* (New York, 1948), pp. 110, 115, 131.

[5]Lincoln indicated that the proclamation would go into effect only if the Confederate states did not return to the Union. He had no expectation that any of the Confederate states would accept this offer, so his vacillation is more apparent than real. Had the Confederate states returned to the Union before the proclamation went into effect, he would have had no constitutional power to end slavery in them.

I

Lincoln came to the White House after a long career as a practicing attorney. He served in the Illinois legislature for a number of years and served one term in the U.S. House of Representatives. But his pre-presidential profession was as a lawyer.[6] He studied the law, learned the law, and had an almost religious faith in the Constitution. Thus, Lincoln began his presidency with a strong sense of the limitations that the Constitution placed on any emancipation scheme. In his first inaugural he implored the seven seceding states to reassume their proper political relationship within the nation. Lincoln reminded these Deep South states that under the Constitution the U.S. government—including the president of the United States—had no power or authority to end slavery. Quoting from a speech he made before his election, Lincoln declared: "I have no purpose, directly or indirectly, to interfere with the institution of slavery in the States where it exists. I believe I have no lawful right to do so, and I have no inclination to do so." He then reiterated the point by quoting from the Republican Party platform:

> *Resolved,* That the maintenance inviolate of the rights of the States, and especially the right of each State to order and control its own domestic institutions according to its own judgment exclusively, is essential to that balance of power on which the perfection and endurance of our political fabric depend; and we denounce the lawless invasion by armed force of the soil of any State or Territory, no matter what pretext, as among the gravest of crimes.

He promised "that all the protection which, consistently with the Constitution and the laws, can be given, will be cheerfully given to all the States when lawfully demanded, for whatever cause—as cheerfully to one section as to another."[7] Critics of Lincoln quite naturally point to these passages to prove, at least to their satisfaction, that Lincoln had no interest in ending slavery.

---

[6] Even after he won the presidency, Lincoln continued his law practice before he moved to Washington because it was his only source of income. See Paul Finkelman, "Abraham Lincoln: Prairie Lawyer," in *America's Lawyer Presidents: From Law Office to the Oval Office,* ed. Norman Gross (Evanston, Ill., 2004), pp. 128–37.

[7] Abraham Lincoln, "First Inaugural Address—Final Text," *CW,* 4:262–63.

Lincoln's position, as set out in the first inaugural address, reflected an orthodox and almost universally accepted understanding of the U.S. Constitution. In 1787 the understanding of the Constitution by all parties was quite clear: the national government had no power to interfere with the "domestic institutions" of the states. Thus the states, and not the national government, had sole power to regulate all laws concerning personal status, such marriage, divorce, child custody, inheritance, voting, and freedom—whether one was a slave or a free person. As General Charles Cotesworth Pinckney told the South Carolina House of Representatives after the Constitutional Convention: "We have a security that the general government can never emancipate them, for no such authority is granted and it is admitted, on all hands, that the general government has no powers but what are expressly granted by the Constitution, and that all rights not expressed were reserved by the several states."[8]

The development of American constitutional law before 1860 reaffirmed Pinckney's analysis of the Constitution: that it created a government of limited powers and that any powers not explicitly given to the national government were retained by the states. Constitutional jurisprudence under Chief Justice Roger B. Taney had strengthened this understanding, but also had expanded it to actually encroach on the powers of Congress. Thus, the Court interpreted the Constitution to limit federal power that might encroach on a state's power to regulate immigration in order to protect slavery, but also limited the power of the states to protect their free black citizens from kidnapping.[9] Except for a few constitutional outliers, such as Lysander Spooner, no antebellum politicians or legal scholars believed Congress had the power to end slavery in the states. Indeed, such a claim was simply unthinkable for someone like Lincoln, who took law and constitutionalism seriously.

---

[8]Pinckney, quoted in Jonathan Elliot, ed., *The Debates in the Several State Conventions on the Adoption of the Federal Constitution*, 5 vols. (1888; reprint ed., New York, 1987), 4:286. For a more elaborate discussion of this issue at the convention see Paul Finkelman, *Slavery and the Founders: Race and Liberty in the Age of Jefferson* (3rd ed., New York, 2014).

[9]*Mayor of New York v. Miln*, 36 U.S. (11 Pet.) 102 (1837), allowing New York to tax immigrants and explicitly allowing southern states to limit in right of free blacks to enter their jurisdictions, and *Prigg v. Pennsylvania*, 41 U.S. (16 Pet.) 539 (1842), striking down Pennsylvania's personal liberty law of 1826. For more discussion of this, see Paul Finkelman, "Teaching Slavery in American Constitutional Law," *Akron Law Review* 34 (2000):261–82, and Paul Finkelman, "Story Telling on the Supreme Court: *Prigg v. Pennsylvania* and Justice Joseph Story's Judicial Nationalism," *Supreme Court Review* 1994 (1995):247–94.

Any federal attempt to end slavery where it already existed would also have run counter to the Fifth Amendment to the Constitution, which provides that "No person . . . shall be deprived of life, liberty, or property, without due process of law; nor shall private property be taken for public use without just compensation." Freeing slaves would have constituted taking "private property . . . for public use" and thus required "just compensation." In *Dred Scott v. Sandford* (1857), Chief Justice Taney had used this amendment to strike down federal legislation banning slavery in the territories. Lincoln and most Republicans rejected the legitimacy of that portion of the decision,[10] arguing that Congress could ban slavery from the territories. But there was a huge difference between banning slavery in new territories and taking slave property from people in the states or even in federal jurisdictions, including Washington, D.C., where slavery was legal. Lincoln, like almost all lawyers at the time, understood that even *if* Congress had the power to take slaves from American citizens, it could only be done through compensation, as required by the Fifth Amendment. But in 1861 no one could have contemplated the cost—perhaps two to three billion dollars—of purchasing all the slaves in the United States. Where would such sums have come from? As Southerners constantly pointed out, slavery produced most of the nation's exports and created much of the nation's wealth. Southerners argued that freeing all those slaves would undermine the national economy, and buying all those slaves would bankrupt the nation.[11]

Thus, when Lincoln entered office he understood that he had "no lawful right" to "interfere with the institution of slavery in the States where it exists." His task as he took office was to preserve the Union and prevent a civil war, and he could hardly accomplish this by freeing the slaves in the South, which would have been an unconstitutional act. Not surprisingly, he told the nation he had "no inclination to" interfere with slavery.

Some scholars and critics interpret this passage in his inaugural address to mean that Lincoln had no personal interest or desire in ending slavery.

---

[10]Paul Finkelman, Dred Scott v. Sandford*: A Brief History* (2d ed., Boston, 2016); Joseph R. Fornieri, "Lincoln's Critique of *Dred Scott* as a Vindication of the Founding," in Holzer and Gabbard, *Lincoln and Freedom*, pp. 20–36.

[11]In retrospect, of course, it would have been far cheaper to purchase all the slaves and free them than pay for the Civil War and suffer all the costs in lives and wealth. But in 1861 no one imagined such costs or expenditures by the national government.

But these critics clearly misunderstand the position Lincoln took in 1861, and the one he had taken his whole life. In his inaugural address Lincoln chose his words carefully. His personal views on slavery were clear: he hated slavery and had always believed that "If slavery is not wrong, nothing is wrong."[12] But his personal desires could not overcome the constitutional realities of his age. Because he had no constitutional power to touch slavery where it existed, he could honestly say he had no inclination to attempt to do so. Consistent with his long-standing reverence for the American government and his understanding of the nature of limited government, Lincoln rejected the idea of acting outside the Constitution. Reflecting his sense of the politically possible, Lincoln willingly reassured the seceding states that he had no "inclination" to do what he could not constitutionally, legally, or politically accomplish. When circumstances changed, so would Lincoln's "inclination." But in March 1861 Lincoln had no reason to think that circumstances would change.

Lincoln's constitutional understandings in 1861, and his personal hatred for slavery, were hardly new. In 1837, as a twenty-eight-year-old freshman in the Illinois state assembly, Lincoln proposed a resolution declaring that slavery was "founded on both injustice and bad policy." Here Lincoln asserted the traditional understanding that the national government had "no power, under the constitution, to interfere with the institution of slavery in the different States." However, Lincoln also argued, again consistent with traditional constitutional understanding, that Congress did have "the power under the constitution, to abolish slavery in the District of Columbia."[13] This early foray into the constitutional issues of slavery suggests that Lincoln, even as a young man, understood the constitutional limitations as well as the constitutional possibilities of fighting slavery.

A decade later, in his single term in Congress, Lincoln proposed a bill for the gradual abolition of slavery in the District of Columbia. This proposal avoided the Fifth Amendment problem of taking property without due process or just compensation because gradual emancipation did not free any existing slaves, but only guaranteed that their as-yet-unborn children would be free. Lincoln read the proposed emancipation bill on the floor of Congress, but in the end did not introduce it. A powerless freshman

---

[12]Lincoln to Albert G. Hodges, Apr. 4, 1864, *CW*, 7:281.
[13]Protest in the Illinois Legislature on Slavery, Mar. 3, 1837, *CW*, 1:74–75.

congressman, he explained, "I was abandoned by my former backers."[14] Nevertheless, this bill, like his state legislative resolution, underscores that Lincoln always hated slavery and was always interested in ending slavery where it could be constitutionally accomplished.

The new president personally hated slavery—he was "naturally antislavery" and could "not remember when" he "did not so think, and feel."[15] But he also recognized that the Constitution severely limited his ability to directly confront the institution. Indeed, Lincoln was firm in his opposition to the admission of new slave states because this was one area of law where the Constitution allowed the national government to take a stand against slavery.

Lincoln also knew, as all Americans did, that slavery was the reason for secession. Documents and debates from the secession conventions made this clear. After Lincoln took office, Alexander Stephens, the vice president of the Confederacy, articulated that slavery and the belief that blacks were inferior to whites constituted the "cornerstone" of the Confederacy.[16] By mid-April secession had led to Civil War. When it became clear that the war would not be over quickly, many in the North called for an end to slavery. Lincoln was surely sympathetic to this goal. He had always articulated his hatred for slavery. Furthermore, many Northerners believed that attacking it was the best way to end the crisis: root out the problem, destroy the institution, and the Union could be restored. But such a simplistic response did not, however, comport with the reality of the crisis Lincoln faced. As much as he hated slavery and would have liked to destroy it, Lincoln understood that an assault on slavery required the complete or partial fulfillment of four essential preconditions.

---

[14]Benjamin Quarles, *Lincoln and the Negro* (New York, 1962), p. 30.
[15]Lincoln to Hodges, Apr. 4, 1864, *CW*, 7:281.
[16]"Our new government is founded . . . its foundations are laid, its corner-stone rests, upon the great truth that the negro is not equal to the white man; that slavery, subordination to the superior race is his natural and normal condition" (Alexander Stephens, "Cornerstone Speech," Mar. 21, 1861, in Henry Cleveland, *Alexander H. Stephens, in Public and Private: With Letters and Speeches, before, during, and since the War* [Philadelphia, 1886], pp. 717–29). For an analysis of the proslavery nature of secession, see Paul Finkelman, "States' Rights, Southern Hypocrisy, and the Coming of the Civil War," *Akron Law Review* 45 (2012):449–78.

II

From the moment the war began, Lincoln faced demands for emancipation. Abolitionists and antislavery Republicans wanted Lincoln to make the conflict a war against slavery. Northern free blacks were anxious to serve in a war of liberation. Even before the conflict started, slaves escaped to U.S. Army lines, where they assumed that they would find freedom.[17] But in 1861 there were relatively few seriously committed opponents of slavery in the North, and southern slaves had no political influence. Most Northerners wanted a quick end to the conflict and a restoration of the Union. Emancipation did not fit into that formula, just as it did not fit into any generally recognized interpretation of the Constitution.

Thus, immediately before the war began and during the first few weeks of the conflict, military commanders returned fugitive slaves to their Confederate masters. These acts led *Harper's Weekly* to complain that the "Fugitive Slave Act" was not "found in the Army Regulations."[18] However, this was not entirely correct. The federal Fugitive Slave Law of 1850 in fact authorized the military to help return fugitive slaves. Because Lincoln did not recognize the legality of secession, the administration initially believed it was constitutionally obligated to return escaped slaves. This analysis also meant it was legally improper for federal troops to harbor fugitives. In calling for seventy-five thousand volunteers to suppress the rebellion, Lincoln said the army would take "the utmost care . . . to avoid any devastation, any destruction of, or interference with, property."[19] Suppressing the rebellion, and bringing the seceding states back into the Union, was Lincoln's only goal at this point. Furthermore, he believed he had no constitutional power to interfere with slavery or any other form of property in the South.

This position dovetailed with Lincoln's goal of restoring the Union. The politics of secession also required Lincoln to carefully avoid a crisis over fugitive slaves. Even after the firing on Fort Sumter, Lincoln hoped the conflict would end quickly, without much bloodshed. Thus returning fugitive

---

[17]James Oakes, *Freedom National: The Destruction of Slavery in the United States, 1861–1865* (New York, 2013), pp. 89–90; Eric Foner, *The Fiery Trial: Abraham Lincoln and American Slavery* (New York, 2010), p. 166.

[18]Foner, *Fiery Trial*, p. 166.

[19]Abraham Lincoln, "Proclamation Calling Militia and Convening Congress," Apr. 15, 1861, in *CW*, 4:331–32.

slaves to the Confederacy was an act of good faith to help end the secession crisis. This early fugitive slave policy also helped Lincoln secure the loyalty of the four slave states—Delaware, Maryland, Missouri, and most of all Kentucky—that had not seceded.[20]

Early attempts at emancipation—such as General John C. Frémont's precipitous proclamation freeing slaves in Missouri—illustrate the complex and delicate nature of achieving black freedom. Many abolitionists (and some modern-day critics of Lincoln) bristled at the idea that achieving freedom could be delicate.[21] Their position was relatively straightforward: slavery was immoral and wrong and slavery was the cause of the war. Ending slavery would be a great humanitarian act, and secession, treason, and civil war gave the president the opportunity to immediately free the slaves. Lincoln could not accept such a facile and simplistic solution. Emancipation required the convergence of four preconditions in the context of the war effort, legal understanding, and popular ideology. Without these preconditions emancipation was both meaningless and impossible.

A. *Constitutional Interpretation.* First, Lincoln had to develop a constitutional or legal framework for taking slaves—a valuable form of private property—from their owners. Mere hostility to the United States by slave owners was not a sufficient reason for taking their property from them. Even making war on the United States could not justify seizing private property. The law of war, as understood at the time, did not allow an army to take property owned by the citizens of an enemy nation (assuming that the Confederacy was dignified as a "nation").[22] Ending slavery required reconceptualizing the Constitution and the role of slaves in American society, and then

---

[20]Stanley Harrold, *Border War: Fighting over Slavery before the Civil War* (Chapel Hill, 2010), pp. 206–7.

[21]For modern critical assessments of Lincoln and emancipation, in addition to Hofstadter, see Lerone Bennett Jr., *Forced into Glory: Abraham Lincoln's White Dream* (Chicago, 2000); LaWanda Cox, "Lincoln and Black Freedom," in *The Historian's Lincoln: Pseudohistory, Psychohistory, and History,* ed. Gabor S. Boritt and Norman O. Forness (Urbana, Ill., 1988); Ira Berlin, "Who Freed the Slaves? Emancipation and Its Meaning," in *Union and Emancipation: Essays on Politics and Race in the Civil War Era,* ed. David W. Blight and Brooks D. Simpson (Kent, Ohio, 1997); Julius Lester, *Look Out Whitey! Black Power's Gon' Get Your Mama!* (New York, 1968); Lerone Bennett Jr., "Was Lincoln a White Supremacist?" *Ebony* 23 (1968):35–42.

[22]For discussions of the law of war at the beginning of the Civil War, see Paul Finkelman, "Francis Lieber and the Modern Law of War," *University of Chicago Law Review* 80 (2013):2071–132; and John Fabian Witt, *Lincoln's Code: The Laws of War in American History* (New York, 2012).

developing a legal and constitutional framework that would allow the national government to emancipate slaves.

The different status of the slave states also complicated creating a legal framework for emancipation. Maryland, Delaware, Kentucky, and Missouri had not seceded and remained in the United States. Thus, their citizens still enjoyed all of the protections of the United States Constitution. Since neither Congress nor the president had any power to interfere with the local institutions of the states, Lincoln had no constitutional power to end slavery in those states. Furthermore, if slaves from those states ran away, the national government had an obligation to help return them under the Fugitive Slave Law of 1850 and the fugitive slave clause of the Constitution. Indeed, many slave owners in those states apparently made a conscious decision to remain in the Union because they believed their slave property was secure under the U.S. Constitution and they had a better chance of recovering fugitive slaves who ran north *if* they were still in the Union.[23]

Lincoln did believe Congress could end slavery in the District of Columbia, the Indian Territory, and other federal territories like Utah and Nebraska. However, emancipation in those places would presumably require paying masters for the value of their slaves, because the Fifth Amendment prohibited taking private property without just compensation. This provision of the Constitution would also hold true for ending slavery in the loyal slave states if Lincoln somehow found a constitutionally acceptable method of doing that.

The status of residents—and their slaves—in the new Confederacy was much less clear. Lincoln claimed that secession was illegal and that the Confederacy could not legally exist. If this were true, then presumably the residents of the Confederacy were still citizens of the United States and thus protected by the Constitution. Combatants, on the other hand, might not be as protected by the Constitution, but even here the legal issues were murky. Personal property used in combat—a weapon, a wagon, or a horse—could, of course, be confiscated on the battlefield. This would be true whether the combat was with Confederate soldiers in uniform or pro-Confederate guerrillas in civilian clothes. Presumably, slaves used in a combat situation—such as teamsters—might also be seized. Beyond that the government had no power to take property from combatants.

---

[23]This is one of the many important insights in Harrold, *Border War.*

Thus, at the beginning of the war there was no clear legal theory on which emancipation might proceed. Emancipation without such a theory would doubtless have been overturned by the Supreme Court, on which every one of the six justices was a proslavery Democrat.[24] Five of the justices, including Chief Justice Taney, had been part of the majority in *Dred Scott* and had held that the Fifth Amendment protected slave property in the territories. The sixth, Nathan Clifford, was a classic "doughface"—a Northern man with Southern principles—who could be expected to support slavery and oppose emancipation. Taney, a "seething secessionist," in fact drafted an opinion striking down emancipation just in case he had the opportunity to use it.[25] Lincoln could reasonably expect the Court to strike down any emancipation act that was not constitutionally impregnable.

B. *Political Support in the North.* Second, even if Lincoln could develop a coherent legal and constitutional theory to justify emancipation, he still needed to have political support to move against slavery. Most Northerners disliked slavery, but were not prepared for a long, bloody crusade to end it. Even Republicans who had been battling slavery all their adult lives, like Salmon P. Chase and William H. Seward, did not think there was sufficient public support to attack slavery at that time. Lincoln needed to create the circumstances necessary to make emancipation an acceptable wartime goal. The war began as one to save the Union, which commanded support among almost all Northerners. He could not afford to jeopardize that support by too quickly turning the war into an antislavery crusade, even though he deeply hated slavery. Lincoln understood, as his abolitionist critics (and modern critics) did not, that declaring the slaves to be free would be a meaningless gesture if he did not have the political support in the North to implement his new policy.

C. *Securing the Border Slave States.* Third, Lincoln needed to secure the four loyal slave states before he could move against slavery. The demographics were crucial. There were more than two and one-half million whites living in these states. If Missouri and Kentucky seceded they would become the second and third largest states in the Confederacy. More importantly, in

---

[24]There were three vacancies on the Court when Lincoln took office and he could not fill them right away. The seats could not be filled until Congress reconfigured the circuits for justices.

[25]Don E. Fehrenbacher, *The Dred Scott Case: Its Significance in American Law and Politics* (New York, 1978).

terms of the crucial white population that would provide troops for the Confederacy, they would be the largest and third largest states in the Confederacy. The border slave states could also provide three of the four largest cities in the Confederacy—Baltimore, St. Louis, and Louisville—dwarfing all other Confederate cities except New Orleans.[26] The added industrial capacity of those cities would have been a huge benefit to the South. While Delaware had no major city, it did have the militarily important E. I. du Pont de Nemours and Company, which was the nation's leading manufacturer of black powder.

Strategically the loyal slave states were even more important. If Maryland joined the Confederacy the nation's capital would be completely surrounded by the enemy. If Missouri joined the rebel nation there would be a Confederate army on the upper Mississippi, poised to threaten Lincoln's home state of Illinois and able to penetrate into Iowa and Minnesota.

Most crucial of all was Kentucky. A Confederate army on the southern bank of the Ohio River could interrupt east–west commerce and troop movements, threaten the vast agricultural heartland of Ohio, Indiana, and Illinois, and endanger key cities, including Cincinnati, Chicago, Indianapolis, and Pittsburgh. With more than two hundred thousand slaves in the state, Kentucky was vulnerable to Confederate entreaties. A precipitous movement toward emancipation would push the Bluegrass State into the hands of the enemy, and that would probably send Missouri into the Confederacy as well. Early in the war a group of ministers urged Lincoln to free the slaves, because God would be on his side. He allegedly responded, "I hope to have God on my side, but I must have Kentucky."[27] Early emancipation would almost certainly have cost him that crucial state and possibly the war.

D. *Military Victory as a Precondition to Emancipation.* This leads to the fourth precondition for emancipation: the likelihood of a military victory. Lincoln insisted that he could only move against slavery if he could win the war; if he attacked slavery and did not win the war, then he would have accomplished nothing. This analysis turns modern critiques of Lincoln on their

---

[26]Peggy Wagner, Gary W. Gallagher, and Paul Finkelman, *The Library of Congress Civil War Desk Reference* (New York, 2002), pp. 70–72.

[27]Lowell Hayes Harrison, *Lincoln of Kentucky* (Lexington, Ky., 2000), p. 135; see also David Lindsey, "Review of *The Civil War in Kentucky* by Lowell H. Harrison," *Journal of American History* 63 (1976):136.

head. Critics of Lincoln argue that he eventually moved toward emancipation for military and diplomatic reasons: because he needed black troops to repopulate his army and to prevent Britain and France from giving diplomatic recognition to the Confederacy.[28] Emancipation is explained as a desperate act to save the Union, reflecting the title of Lerone Bennett's book saying that Lincoln was "forced into glory" by circumstances.

Lincoln's constitutional evolution and his steps leading to emancipation do not support this analysis. Very early in the war the Lincoln administration allowed the military to free slaves who sought refuge with the army, and in the summer of 1861 Congress passed, and Lincoln signed, the First Confiscation Act,[29] which provided for the emancipation of slaves under some circumstances. Both Lincoln and Congress began to move more directly toward emancipation in the spring and summer of 1862 after a series of U.S. military victories. Lincoln then waited to announce emancipation until after a major victory that stopped Lee's army dead in its tracks—with huge casualties—at Antietam. Any move toward emancipation much before this would probably have thrown Kentucky and Missouri into the Confederacy and perhaps doomed the Union cause.

While emancipation may properly be seen as one of the elements of victory, it must also be seen as the legitimate fruit of victory over the Confederacy. Victory would probably have been possible without emancipation (and the use of black troops did not necessarily require it), although victory would have been more difficult and perhaps taken longer. But, while victory was possible without emancipation, emancipation was clearly impossible without victory. Conditions looked bright after Antietam, when Lincoln issued the Preliminary Emancipation Proclamation, and Lincoln assumed they would look just as bright in a hundred days,[30] when he planned to sign the

---

[28] See note 21 for modern critical assessments of Lincoln and emancipation.

[29] Obviously, when the law was passed no one knew there would be a "second" confiscation act, passed in 1862, and so it was simply called the "Confiscation Act." However, for clarity it will be referred to as it is known today, as the "First Confiscation Act."

[30] The military disaster at Fredericksburg in December 1862, of course, was not something Lincoln could anticipate. Because of it, some scholars misunderstand the proclamation as being issued in the wake of defeat. However, Lincoln issued the preliminary proclamation after a major Union victory, and that document committed Lincoln to issuing the final proclamation on January 1, 1863.

proclamation on January 1, 1863.[31] Thus, rather than being forced into glory when he announced emancipation, Lincoln understood that moral glory—emancipation—was now possible because his army was achieving military glory.

III

When the war began, none of the four preconditions for emancipation were in place. Nevertheless, the push for emancipation would not wait for the right circumstances. In the first half year of the war Lincoln faced three different models for attacking slavery. Two of these models satisfied the first three preconditions: there was a legal/constitutional basis for these two models; they would not undermine Northern support for the war; and they would not chase Kentucky and Missouri out of the Union. The third, General John C. Frémont's proclamation freeing slaves in Missouri, failed all of these tests, and Lincoln wisely overruled it.

The first model involved slaves who simply left their masters and fled to the safety and protection of the U.S. Army. This is part of the argument that the great emancipators were the slaves themselves. Even before the war began, slaves started to flee their owners for the sanctuary of U.S. military bases. Before the war began, and immediately after Fort Sumter, commanders returned these fugitives, properly understanding that the federal government had a constitutional obligation, reinforced by the Fugitive Slave Law of 1850, to return fugitives to their masters.[32]

In 1865, in his second inaugural, Lincoln would assert that four years earlier "All knew" that slavery "was somehow the cause of the war."[33] However, in 1861 when the war began, the administration could not focus its energies on destroying the cause of the war because of the lack of the preconditions necessary to attack slavery. The slaves, however, were under no such constraints. They knew, even more than their masters or the blue-clad enemies of their masters, that this war was about slavery—about them and their future. While Lincoln bided his time, waiting for the moment to strike

---

[31]See generally Louis P. Masur, *Lincoln's Hundred Days: The Emancipation Proclamation and the War for the Union* (Cambridge, Mass., 2012).
[32]Foner, *Fiery Trial*, pp. 166–69.
[33]Abraham Lincoln, "Second Inaugural Address," Mar. 4, 1865, *CW,* 8:332–33.

out against slavery, hundreds and then thousands of slaves struck out for freedom.

These fleeing slaves created the need for clever lawyering and a clear government policy, even when no one in the administration was ready to develop such a policy. To this extent those who argue that the slaves were a catalyst for emancipation are correct. But the development of a policy for dealing with runaways was only a first and temporary step in the process of emancipation. "By 1864, nearly 400,000 slaves had made their way to Union lines."[34] It is likely that most of these left their owners after Lincoln issued the Preliminary Emancipation Proclamation in September 1862. In any event, these slaves constituted only about 10 percent of all the slaves living in the United States in 1860. Most slaves lacked the opportunity, means, or ability to escape to U.S. Army lines. Self-emancipation was thus a catalyst for new policies, but not the key to ending slavery.

The war had hardly begun when slaves began to stream into the camps and forts of the U.S. Army (fig. 1). The army was not a social welfare agency and was institutionally unprepared to feed, clothe, or house masses of refugees. As I have noted, initially the army, acting under the Fugitive Slave Law of 1850 and the Constitution, returned slaves to their masters. However, this situation undermined the morale of the troops, who fully understood that they were returning valuable property to their enemies, and more importantly, those enemies would use that property to make war on them.[35] Slaves grew the food that fed the Confederate army, raised and cared for the horses the Confederates rode into battle, and labored in the workshops and factories that produced implements of war.[36] As Frederick Douglass noted, "The very stomach of this Rebellion is the negro in the form of a slave." Douglass correctly understood that "arrest that hoe in the hands of the Negro, and you smite the rebellion in the very seat of its life."[37] Returning slaves to Confederate masters was hardly different than returning guns or horses to them. Initially, however, some army officers did just that.

On May 23 three slaves—Frank Baker, Shepard Mallory, and James Townsend—owned by Confederate Colonel Charles K. Mallory escaped to

---

[34]Foner, *Fiery Trial*, p. 167.
[35]Ibid., pp. 168–69.
[36]Charles Dew, *Bond of Iron: Master and Slave at Buffalo Forge* (New York, 1994), pp. 264–311.
[37]Douglass, quoted in James M. McPherson, *Battle Cry of Freedom: The Civil War Era* (New York, 1988), p. 354.

FIG. 1. Fugitive slaves seeking sanctuary in Fortress Monroe were depicted in the June 8, 1861, issue of *Frank Leslie's Illustrated* newspaper. *(Prints and Photographs Division, Library of Congress)*

Fortress Monroe, under the command of General Benjamin F. Butler (fig. 2). A day later Butler faced the surrealistic spectacle of Confederate Major M. B. Carey, under a flag of truce, demanding the return of the slaves under the Fugitive Slave Law.[38] Major Carey, identifying himself as Mallory's agent, argued that Butler was obligated to return the slaves under the fugitive slave clause of the Constitution and the Fugitive Slave Law of 1850. A month earlier, both before and after Sumter, some commanders had returned fugitive slaves. But much had changed since then.

Butler was hardly an abolitionist. A Democrat before the war, he had supported the proslavery doughface James Buchanan in 1856 and had voted

---

[38]Adam Goodheart, *1861: Civil War Awakening* (New York, 2011), pp. 295–347; see also Masur, *Lincoln's Hundred Days*, pp. 16–18.

FIG. 2. Major General Benjamin F. Butler. *(Prints and Photographs Division, Library of Congress)*

for John C. Breckinridge, the proslavery southern Democrat, in 1860. But by May 1861 Butler no longer had any sympathy for slavery or the South. A successful Massachusetts lawyer before the war, Butler devoted some thought to Carey's demand. The next day he informed him that the slaves were contrabands of war, because they had been used to build fortifications for the Confederacy. Thus, he could not return them to Mallory.[39] Butler also told Carey "that the fugitive slave act did not affect a foreign country, which Virginia claimed to be and she must reckon it one of the infelicities of her position that in so far at least she was taken at her word." However, perhaps playing on the absurdity of Carey's demand, Butler offered to return the slaves to Colonel Mallory if he would come to Fortress Monroe and "take the oath of allegiance to the Constitution of the United States."[40] Butler knew, of course, that Mallory would not accept this offer.

This was the end of Colonel Mallory's attempt to recover his slaves, but it was the beginning of a new policy for the United States. Butler, in need of workers, immediately employed the three fugitives, who had previously been used by Mallory to build Confederate defenses. Because these slaves had been used for military purposes, he considered them contrabands of war, and taking them away from the Confederates served the dual purposes of depriving the enemy of labor while providing labor for the United States.

By the middle of the summer slaves were pouring into U.S. forts and camps, with some officers offering them sanctuary and others trying to chase them away or even return them to their masters. In this period more than 850 slaves escaped to Fortress Monroe,[41] where Butler happily gave them clothing—blue uniforms—and jobs. Other commanders returned slaves to all masters; others only returned them to loyal masters in Maryland, Kentucky, and Missouri. In Missouri, General William S. Harney declared that slavery was secure under the Constitution and the U.S. Army, while General George McClellan promised residents of western Virginia (which was still part of the Confederacy) that he would never interfere with slavery.[42] But other commanders offered sanctuary to all slaves who entered their lines.

---

[39] Benjamin F. Butler, *Butler's Book* (Boston, 1892), pp. 256–57.
[40] Maj. Gen. Benjamin F. Butler to Lt. Gen. Winfield Scott, May 24/25, 1861, in *The War of the Rebellion: The Official Records of the Union and Confederate Armies*, 127 vols., index, and atlas (Washington, D.C., 1880–1901), ser. 2, 1:752 (hereafter *OR*).
[41] Foner, *Fiery Trial*, p. 171.
[42] Oakes, *Freedom National*, p. 104.

Meanwhile, Lincoln quietly supported Butler's solution to self-emancipation, joking in his cabinet about "Butler's fugitive slave law."[43]

On August 8, Secretary of War Simon Cameron informed Butler of Lincoln's desire "that all existing rights in all the States be fully respected and maintained" and reaffirmed that the war was "for the Union and for the preservation of all constitutional rights of States and the citizens of the States in the Union." Because of this, "no question can arise as to fugitives from service within the States and Territories in which the authority of the Union is fully acknowledged."[44] This, of course, meant that military commanders could not free fugitive slaves in Missouri, Kentucky, Maryland, or Delaware. This position was thoroughly consistent with existing federal law and with Lincoln's primary short-term goal of completely securing the loyalty of the four slave states that had not joined the Confederacy.

The rest of Cameron's message, however, indicated an important shift in policy, because the president also understood that "in States wholly or partially under insurrectionary control" the laws could not be enforced, and it was "equally obvious that rights dependent on the laws of the States within which military operations are conducted must be necessarily subordinated to the military exigencies created by the insurrection if not wholly forfeited by the treasonable conduct of the parties claiming them." Most importantly, "rights to services" could "form no exception" to "this general rule."[45]

Under this policy the military would, or at least could, return fugitive slaves, but in the Confederate states the military would have no obligation to return them, and might—the orders are ambiguous on this point—be precluded from doing so. The slaves of loyal masters who lived in the Confederacy presented a "more difficult question." The solution was to have the army employ the fugitives, but to keep a record of such employment, so that at some point loyal masters might be compensated for the use of their slaves. Cameron, speaking for the president, admonished Butler not to encourage slaves to abscond nor to interfere with the "servants of peaceful citizens" even in the Confederacy, nor to interfere in the voluntary return of fugitives to their masters "except in cases where the public safety" would "seem to require" such interference.[46]

---

[43]Foner, *Fiery Trial*, p. 171.
[44]Simon Cameron to Maj. Gen. Benjamin F. Butler, Aug. 8, 1861, *OR*, ser. 2, 1:761–62.
[45]Ibid.
[46]Ibid.

These caveats were probably unnecessary. It was not the job of the army to rescue people from slavery, and it was a violation of the law of war to arbitrarily take property from enemy civilians. But the new policy was important as a first step to ending slavery and as a clear signal to those slaves near U.S. Army forts and camps that they were now free to make themselves free.

Thus, by late August, Butler's contraband policy had become the norm. The U.S. Army could employ any slaves who ran to its lines, provided they came from Confederate states. This was not a general emancipation policy, and the army had been admonished not to deliberately attempt to free slaves. But the army would not return fugitive slaves to masters in the Confederate states, even if the masters claimed to be loyal to the United States. Shrewdly, the Lincoln administration had become part of the process of ending slavery while professing not to be doing so. To abolitionists, the administration could point to the growing thousands of "contrabands" who were being paid a salary and often wearing the only clothing available, blue uniforms.[47] But in the loyal slave states, the administration could show it was not interfering with slavery.

An ad hoc policy by a lawyer turned general, responding to a demand for three slaves, had now morphed into a national policy, endorsed by the president and adopted by the Department of War. It was not a direct attack on slavery and it was not an emancipation policy *per se*. But it did protect the freedom of thousands of blacks who were developing their own strategy of self-emancipation by running to the U.S. Army.

These events undermine the claim that Lincoln was opposed to emancipation and black freedom. The evidence demonstrates that Lincoln jumped at Butler's contraband theory—Butler's new fugitive slave law—and thus the chain of command, from Lincoln to Secretary of War Cameron to General Henry Halleck and then to all army officers, now supported military emancipation. This brief history also illustrates the significance of blacks running from slavery in creating the circumstances for the beginning of emancipation. But this outcome was not preordained. The administration might have reprimanded Butler, or refused to implement his brilliant response to fugitive slaves. However, since the president had always believed that "If

---

[47]Special Orders No. 72, Oct. 14, 1861, and General Orders No. 34, Nov. 1, 1861, *OR*, ser. 2, 1:774–75 (setting out pay scale for black laborers).

slavery is not wrong, nothing is wrong,"[48] Lincoln happily seized the opportunity to free some slaves, even as the administration could not actually move against all slavery.

These events also illustrated the beginning of a new constitutional understanding. Butler's actions were based on military circumstances and on military necessity. Butler needed to take labor away from the Confederacy, and he needed laborers to fight the Confederate armies. Emancipating fugitives from the Confederacy accomplished both goals.

By the time Secretary of War Cameron spelled out the policy to General Butler, Congress had endorsed it and pushed it further along with the First Confiscation Act, which allowed for the seizure of any slaves used for military purposes by the Confederacy.[49] This was not a general emancipation act and was narrowly written to allow only the seizure of slaves in actual use by Confederate forces. No slave owners in the Border States, even those sympathetic to the Confederacy, were put in jeopardy unless they knowingly used their slaves to support Confederate military action. Freeing slaves under the Confiscation Act might have violated the Fifth Amendment, if it were seen as allowing a taking of private property without due process. But this law only applied to those in rebellion—who through secession (or specific acts of war in the Border States) had made war on the United States. While potentially applicable to Border State citizens who fought for or gave material aid to the Confederacy, it mostly applied to Confederate citizens who had renounced their American citizenship and rejected the protections of the U.S. Constitution. This law was also a military measure. Surely the army could seize a weapon in the hands of a captured Confederate soldier without a due process hearing, or take a horse from a captured Confederate. Similarly, slaves working on fortifications, or being used in other military capacities, might be taken.

The First Confiscation Act was ambiguous and cumbersome, and, like Butler's contraband theory, did not threaten slavery as an institution. It merely allowed for the seizure of those slaves—relatively few in number—being used specifically for military purposes. However, the Act did indicate a political shift toward emancipation. It was not decisive, because the

---

[48]Lincoln to Albert G. Hodges, Apr. 4, 1864, *CW*, 7:281.
[49]"An Act to confiscate Property Used for Insurrectionary Purposes," Act of Aug. 6, 1861, 12 *U.S. Statutes at Large* 319.

emancipatory aspects of the law were limited, but it did show that Congress was ready to support some kind of emancipation. Neither Congress nor the American people were ready to turn the military conflict into an all-out war against slavery; however, Congress had passed the first law in the history of the United States designed to emancipate slaves.[50] In that sense, it was truly a revolutionary act. Congress—which presumably reflected the ideology of its constituents—was ready to allow the government to free some slaves in the struggle against the Confederacy.

The contraband policy and the Confiscation Act of 1861 were major steps toward emancipation. Importantly, both signaled to the Northern public that national policy was evolving from simply a struggle to preserve the Union to a war against the true cause of the conflict: slavery. In the War Department's embrace of the contraband policy and in Congress's passage of the First Confiscation Act (which Lincoln signed), both Lincoln and Congress embraced the principle that the national government had the power to free slaves as a military necessity. The logical extension of this posture could be the total destruction of slavery in the Confederacy. If Congress could free some slaves through the Confiscation Act, or the executive branch could free some slaves through the contraband policy, then the two branches might be able to free all slaves if the military conditions warranted such a result. Such policies could not affect the slaves in the loyal Border States, but they could be used to abolish slavery throughout the Confederacy.

The action of Major General John C. Frémont (fig. 3), who declared martial law in Missouri on August 30, contrasted sharply with these evolving policies. In his declaration, General Frémont announced that all slaves owned by Confederate activists in that state were free.[51] This order went

---

[50]Laws banning the African slave trade provided that blacks illegally brought to the United States were to be taken back to Africa as free people. But this law presumed that the Africans were never legally slaves, and certainly never legally slaves in the United States. Similarly, the Northwest Ordinance banned slavery in the territories north of the Ohio, but at the time of its passage no one in Congress knew that there were actually any slaves in the territory. Furthermore, no slaves were actually emancipated by the Ordinance, and some slaves who had been in the region before the passage of the Ordinance remained in bondage until the 1840s. For a discussion of all these issues, see Finkelman, *Slavery and the Founders*.

[51]*OR*, ser. 1, 3:466–67. "The property, real and personal, of all persons in the State of Missouri, who shall take up arms against the United States, or who shall be directly proven to have taken active part with their enemies in the field, is declared to be confiscated to the public use, and their slaves, if any they have, are hereby declared free men."

FIG. 3. This ca. 1862–64 engraving by J. C. Buttre depicted Major General John C. Frémont surrounded by his exploits in Western exploration and the Civil War. *(Prints and Photographs Division, Library of Congress)*

well beyond the Confiscation Act and the contraband policy. It also violated the U.S. Constitution and undermined Lincoln's important policy goal of heading off secession in the Border States. It also was an outrageous act by a general trying to make public policy, which he had no authority to do.

Not surprisingly, Lincoln immediately and unambiguously urged Frémont to withdraw his proclamation, pointing out that it undermined efforts to keep Kentucky (and other Border States) in the Union. The president told the general: "I think there is great danger that the closing paragraph, in relation to the confiscation of property, and the liberating slaves of traitorous owners, will alarm our Southern Union friends, and turn them against us—perhaps ruin our rather fair prospect for Kentucky." Thus he asked Frémont to "modify" his proclamation "on his own motion," to conform with the Confiscation Act that Congress had just passed. This would allow for the confiscation of slaves actually used to further the Confederate war effort. Aware of the exaggerated egos of his generals, Lincoln noted, "This letter is written in a spirit of caution and not of censure."[52]

In the aftermath of Frémont's proclamation, letters poured in from Border State Unionists urging the president to directly countermand Frémont's order. One Kentucky Unionist told Lincoln, "There is not a day to lose in disavowing emancipation or Kentucky is gone over the mill dam."[53] Lincoln fully understood the issue. He told Senator Orville Browning of Illinois that "to lose Kentucky is nearly . . . to lose the whole game."[54] Lincoln hoped that Frémont—who had been the Republican candidate for president in 1856—would be politically savvy enough to withdraw the order.

But Frémont lacked any political sophistication on this issue. The vainglorious general hoped to score points with the abolitionist wing of the Republican Party, embarrass Lincoln, and set himself up to be the Republican candidate in 1864. Thus he refused to comply with the request of his commander in chief to withdraw the order. Refusing to withdraw his proclamation, Frémont asked—essentially dared—Lincoln to formally countermand the proclamation. This would allow Frémont to later blame the president for undermining emancipation. Lincoln "cheerfully" did so, ordering Frémont to modify the proclamation. Still playing politics, Frémont absurdly claimed he never received the order, but only read about it in the newspapers. Even after Lincoln publicly countermanded him, Frémont continued to distribute his original order.[55] Frémont's stubbornness, political

---

[52]Lincoln to John C. Frémont, Sept. 2, 1861, *CW*, 4:506.
[53]Both quotations in William E. Gienapp, *Abraham Lincoln and Civil War America: A Biography* (New York, 2002), p. 89.
[54]Lincoln to Orville H. Browning, Sept. 22, 1861, *CW*, 4:531–32.
[55]Lincoln to John C. Frémont, Sept. 11, 1861, *CW*, 4:517–18.

obtuseness, and military incompetence led to his dismissal by Lincoln on November 2, 1861.[56] He would get another command, and fail there, and by the end of the war, Frémont would be marginalized, irrelevant, and forgotten.

Critics of Lincoln point to his treatment of Frémont as "proof" of his insensitivity to black freedom. They argue that this was the perfect moment to strike a blow against slavery. Frémont was a national hero and a popular general. Proponents of this analysis argue that Lincoln could have turned the war into a crusade against slavery. Unlike the general, however, Lincoln saw four problems with Frémont's unauthorized attempt to end slavery in Missouri. First, it was flagrantly unconstitutional because Missouri was still part of the United States. Second, if sustained, the order would probably have pushed Kentucky into the Confederacy, and that would have made it virtually impossible for Lincoln to win the war. Third, the president understood that there was no possibility of ending slavery unless the United States actually defeated the Confederacy. Declaring an end to slavery and then losing the war would not end slavery; it would only destroy the Union and permanently secure slavery in the new Confederate nation. Finally, as a matter of authority and command structure, a general in the field should never set political policy. That was the job of the president. Generals could act in response to specific circumstances—as Butler had at Fort Monroe—but unlike Frémont, Butler did not try to create a national policy or even a local one. He simply dealt with the situation at hand.

Lincoln's comments to Frémont bear out his realistic assessment that if Kentucky, and perhaps Missouri, joined the Confederacy, the war might be lost. Frémont's proclamation jeopardized Kentucky, and Lincoln had to countermand it. The fall of 1861 was simply not the time to begin an attack on slavery, especially in the loyal Border States.

Lincoln did not respond to Frémont with a lecture on constitutional law, but he might have. Freeing slaves in the Confederacy who were being used for military purposes was probably constitutional. This was the contraband policy and the implication of the First Confiscation Act. Freeing slaves *within* the United States—which included Missouri—was unconstitutional unless those slaves were being used as part of active resistance against the

---

[56]General Order No. 28, Nov. 2, 1861, *OR, Additions and Corrections to Series 2*, 3:558–59.

government. Thus, the First Confiscation Act could have been used to free slaves being used by pro-Confederate forces in Missouri for military purposes; however, this is not what Frémont wanted to do. He wanted to emancipate slaves who were not being used directly for military purposes and were the property of people living in the United States. Because Missouri had not seceded, Confederate sympathizers who were not involved in direct combat were still protected by the Constitution. Thus Frémont's plan would have violated the Constitution by seizing property from U.S. citizens without due process or just compensation.

After countermanding the Missouri proclamation, Lincoln privately assured Senator Charles Sumner that the difference between the abolitionist wing of the Republican Party and Lincoln on emancipation was only a matter of time—a month or six weeks. This once more suggests that Lincoln was at heart an opponent of slavery and that he was simply trying to figure out how, and when, to move against slavery. Sumner understood this, and accepted Lincoln's pledge. The abolitionist senator from Massachusetts promised to "not say another word to you about it till the longest time you name has passed by."[57] The time would in fact be slightly more than a year, but there is little reason to doubt that Lincoln was moving toward some sort of abolition plan.

For Lincoln, emancipation was a process. If he moved too quickly against slavery he would lose the Border States and the war. If he moved against slavery before he had solid political support in Congress and the North he might lose the next election and be unable to complete the task. If he moved against slavery but lost the war he would have accomplished nothing. And if he had no constitutional and legal basis for ending slavery he would face a hostile Supreme Court, still led by the rabidly proslavery and deeply racist Chief Justice Taney.

Critics of Lincoln argue that he eventually moved toward emancipation because he needed black troops to win the war. But the evidence—starting with his correspondence with Frémont and Sumner and his response to Butler—demonstrates that he had his eye on how to end slavery and to do so when the time was right. Lincoln understood, as Frémont did not, that timing is everything. Lincoln could only move against slavery after he had

---

[57]Stephen Oates, *With Malice toward None: The Life of Abraham Lincoln* (New York, 1978), p. 292.

secured the Border States and made certain that victory was possible. Only then could be make emancipation actually work. Rather than a desperate act to save the war effort, emancipation became the logical fruit of victory. Frémont's proclamation surely did not fit that bill; consequently, Lincoln countermanded it.

IV

Lincoln clearly underestimated the time needed before he could move against slavery. The preconditions he needed for emancipation did not emerge in the month or six weeks he forecast to Sumner. A call for emancipation had to be tied to a realistic belief that the war could be won; there was no point in telling slaves they were free if the government could not enforce that freedom. The prospect of a military victory was not great in the fall of 1861. The embarrassing defeats at the First Battle of Bull Run and Ball's Bluff did not bode well for the future.[58]

Conditions for the Union and Lincoln began to change in the late fall. In November 1861, Admiral Samuel Du Pont successfully seized the South Carolina Sea Islands, with the important naval base at Port Royal. Once established, the United States would never be dislodged from this beachhead on the South Carolina coast. At least some of the war would now be fought in the heartland of the South.[59] Although Lincoln could not know it at the time, this was the beginning of the shrinking of the Confederacy.

The first half of the next year would be "one of the brightest periods of the war for the North."[60] In February, combined army and naval forces captured Roanoke Island, and by the end of April the navy and army had captured or sealed off every Confederate port on the Atlantic except Charleston, South Carolina, and Wilmington, North Carolina. Ports such as Savannah, Georgia, remained in Confederate hands, but the rebels no longer

---

[58]McPherson, *Battle Cry of Freedom*, pp. 358–68.
[59]One of the important results of this was the liberation of thousands of slaves on the Sea Islands, many of whom would later be enlisted when the United States began to organize black regiments in late 1862. See David Dudley Cornish, *The Sable Arm: Negro Troops in the Union Army, 1861–1865* (New York, 1966), and Willie Lee Rose, *Rehearsal for Reconstruction: The Port Royal Experiment* (New York, 1976).
[60]McPherson, *Battle Cry of Freedom*, p. 368.

had access to the ocean except by blockade runners, who had almost no effect on the Confederate war effort.

In the Mississippi Valley the United States won a series of crucial victories, securing Kentucky for the Union and putting the U.S. Army in the heart of the slave South.[61] Although the Kentucky legislature had voted in September to stay in the Union, support for the Confederacy remained strong in the Bluegrass State. In November General McClellan had told General Don Carolos Buell, "It is absolutely necessary that we shall hold all the State of Kentucky" and to make sure that "the majority of its inhabitants shall be warmly in favor of our cause." McClellan believed that the conduct of the "political affairs in Kentucky" was perhaps "more important than that of our military operations." He wanted to ensure that the U.S. Army respected the "domestic institution"—slavery—in the state.[62]

Underscoring McClellan's concern, later that month some two hundred Kentuckians organized a secession convention and declared their state to be in the Confederacy. In December the Confederate Congress admitted Kentucky into the Confederacy. This symbolic act had no impact on Kentucky politics or the war. On the other hand, during this period there were sometimes more than 25,000 Confederate troops in the state. This army could have undermined Unionist sentiment in the state and perhaps brought Kentucky into the Confederacy. As the New Year opened, Kentucky was hardly secure. That changed in a ten-day period in early February. On February 6, the obscure Brigadier General Ulysses S. Grant captured Fort Henry on the Tennessee River in northern Tennessee. On the 16th he captured Fort Donelson on the Cumberland River, along with more than 12,000 Confederate troops. These twin victories established what would be a permanent U.S. military presence in the Confederate state of Tennessee. More importantly, they emphatically secured Kentucky for the Union. By the end of the month the U.S. Army was sitting in Nashville, Tennessee, the first Southern state capital to fall. Instead of Kentucky possibly going into the Confederacy, it was more likely that Tennessee would be returned to the United States.

---

[61] Oakes, *Freedom National*, pp. 218–24, discusses the importance of U.S. military occupation of parts of Louisiana, with its huge and dense slave population.

[62] [General] George B. McClellan to Brig. Gen. D. C. Buell, Nov. 7, 1861, *OR*, ser. 2, 1:776–77.

Confederate forces suffered a devastating loss at Pea Ridge on the western side of the Mississippi in early March. The Confederates, led by Major General Earl Van Dorn, had planned to march into Missouri and eventually capture St. Louis. But Pea Ridge ended any chance of Missouri becoming a Confederate state. Instead, the outcome made it more likely that Arkansas would be brought back into the Union. A month later the United States won an important but bloody victory at Shiloh in southwestern Tennessee. On the same day combined naval and army forces seized Island No. 10 in the Mississippi River, capturing more than fifty big guns and some seven thousand Confederate soldiers. In April, Memphis fell, and on May 1, General Benjamin Butler, who had developed the contraband policy while commanding in Virginia, marched into New Orleans.

This truncated history of the first months of 1862 illustrates how circumstances allowed Lincoln to begin to contemplate emancipation. By June he knew that the border South was unlikely to join the Confederacy. There would be still be fighting in that region—especially horrible guerrilla warfare in Missouri[63]—but by June 1862 it was clear that Kentucky, Maryland, Delaware, and Missouri were secure. So too was a good piece of Tennessee as well as the cities of New Orleans, Baton Rouge, Natchez, and smaller river towns in Mississippi, Louisiana, and Arkansas. There could be no more realistic fears that emancipation would push Kentucky or Missouri into the Confederacy.

Lincoln now had a reasonable chance of implementing an emancipation policy for a substantial number of slaves. Even if the war ended with some part of the Confederacy intact, the president could break the back of slavery in much of the Mississippi Valley. Once free, these blacks could not easily be reenslaved.

By the spring of 1862 Lincoln had the third and fourth prerequisites in place for emancipation: security of the Upper South and a reasonable chance of military success that would make emancipation successful. He was also moving toward the first prerequisite: a legal theory that would justify emancipation. The theory had been developing since Butler discovered the legal concept of contrabands of war and brilliantly applied it to slaves. The First Confiscation Act had supplemented it. In March 1862 Congress

---

[63]Daniel E. Sutherland, *A Savage Conflict: The Decisive Role of Guerrillas in the American Civil War* (Chapel Hill, 2009).

prohibited the military from returning fugitive slaves, whether from enemy masters, loyal masters in the Confederacy, or masters in the Border States. Any officers returning fugitive slaves could be court martialed and if convicted, dismissed from military service.[64] None of these laws or polices had attacked slavery directly. Freeing contrabands required that the slaves take the initiative of running to the army *and* that the army be in close proximity to them. The Confiscation Act only applied to slaves being used for military purposes. Most slaves fit neither category.

But this congressional action signaled to Lincoln that he had political support for an attack on slavery. The new policies also weakened slavery in the Confederacy and the Border States. Most importantly, perhaps, these policies showed that Congress, like the president, saw emancipation as both a means to victory and a natural and legitimate consequence of victory.

The second of the four prerequisites—ensuring political support for emancipation—was still an open question at the beginning of 1862, but within a few months that had changed, starting with the law in March prohibiting the army from participating in the return of fugitive slaves. On April 10 Congress passed a joint resolution declaring the U.S. would "cooperate with," and provide "pecuniary aid" for, any state willing to adopt a gradual emancipation scheme.[65] In April Congress abolished slavery in the District of Columbia, providing compensation for the masters. This law was consistent with Lincoln's long-standing view that the Constitution granted Congress full power to govern the District, including the power to regulate or abolish slavery. The president happily signed this law. Fifteen years earlier Lincoln had hoped to end slavery in the District through a slow process of gradual emancipation. Now he did it with a single stroke of his pen.[66] By providing compensation to the masters, this law could survive a challenge on Fifth Amendment grounds.

In addition to providing payment to masters for their slaves, the D.C. Compensated Emancipation Act also provided money for colonization of former slaves in Africa or Haiti. Critics of Lincoln have often focused on this

---

[64]"An Act to Make an Additional Article of War," Mar. 13, 1862, 12 *Statutes at Large* 354. This law modified an important part of the Fugitive Slave Law of 1850, which had authorized the use of the military or the militia to return fugitive slaves.

[65]Joint Resolution No. 26, Apr. 10, 1862, 12 *Statutes at Large* 617.

[66]"An Act for the Release of Certain Persons Held to Service or Labor in the District of Columbia," Apr. 16, 1862, 12 *Statutes at Large* 376.

one provision as proof of Lincoln's racism and his insincerity with regard to both emancipation and black rights. However, a serious analysis of this provision undermines the strength of such claims.

The law provided up to $100,000 for the colonization of both free blacks already living in the District and the newly emancipated slaves. The operative language, however, was critical. The money was "to aid in the settlement and colonization of such free persons . . . as *may desire to emigrate* to the Republics of Hayti or Liberia, or such other country beyond the limits of the United States as the president may determine."[67] This language, which Lincoln had demanded, did not require or force anyone to leave the United States, and it allowed the president to prevent voluntary emigration if he was able to "determine" it was not suitable. The law also limited the amount to be appropriated for each emigrant to one hundred dollars.[68]

This provision was clearly a sop thrown to conservatives and racists, who feared a free black population. In 1860 there were 3,200 slaves in Washington and about 10,300 free blacks. The appropriation would have provided money for the colonization of only 1,000 blacks—less than a third of the newly freed slaves and less than 7 percent of the entire free black population of the city in 1860. Moreover, by 1862 the black population in the city was much larger than 14,000, which meant that an even smaller percentage of the population could leave under the appropriation. Furthermore, one hundred dollars was hardly an incentive for any free black or former slave to move to a new country. Not surprisingly, no record exists of *any* African American taking advantage of this offer. This law in fact may be unique in American history: the only time that Congress appropriated a substantial sum of money to be given out to individuals, and no one ever tried to obtain any of it.

The emancipation of slaves in the District of Columbia contained an important political message. In an election year the majority in Congress was prepared to begin to dismantle slavery. Members of the House, who were to stand for reelection in the fall, were willing to run on a record that included voting to abolish slavery in at least one corner of the United States.

---

[67] Ibid., p. 378 (emphasis added).
[68] Ibid. Misunderstanding of the colonization provision is common. John Hope Franklin, for example, asserts that the law "provided for the removal and colonization of the freedmen" (Franklin, *The Emancipation Proclamation* [Garden City, N.Y., 1963], p. 17), when in fact it did not provide for "removal" but merely allowed voluntary colonization.

In June Congress abolished slavery in the federal territories, this time without compensation.[69] It was in this context, with the war going relatively well, with the Border States secure, and with some emancipation taking place, that Lincoln began to work on the greatest issue of his life.

V

While Congress moved to end slavery in the territories and the District of Columbia, Lincoln contemplated a much larger issue: ending slavery in the Confederacy. However, before Lincoln could act, once again one of his generals began to move against slavery without authority. On May 9, 1862, Major General David Hunter (fig. 4), commander of U.S. forces in the Department of the South, issued General Order No. 11, declaring martial law in his military district, which comprised the states of South Carolina, Georgia, and Florida. Hunter's order declared all slaves in those states to be free because slavery was "incompatible" with a "free country" and with his imposition of martial law. This action went well beyond the authority of a general, and even if Lincoln had wanted to support Hunter's program, he could not possibly have approved of a general acting in this manner without authorization from the executive branch. Not only did Hunter lack authority for such an action, but he had not even consulted with his superiors, the War Department, or the president. No president could have allowed a military commander to assume such powers and, not surprisingly, ten days later Lincoln revoked the order.[70]

Hunter's actions were not like Frémont's action in Missouri in 1861. Lincoln did not have to placate Border State slaveholders. South Carolina, Georgia, and Florida were already out of the Union. The constitutional limitations that applied to Missouri were irrelevant to Hunter's military district. He was taking slaves from an enemy which had rejected the Constitution. Nor would such an order cause Lincoln any great political harm. Most Northerners were by this time ready to see the slavocracy of the Deep South destroyed, and Hunter's action was a step in that direction.

---

[69]"An Act to Secure Freedom to All Persons within the Territories of the United States," June 19, 1862, 12 *Statutes at Large* 432.

[70]"Proclamation Revoking General Hunter's Order of Military Emancipation of May 9, 1862," May 19, 1862, *CW*, 5:222.

FIG. 4. Major General David Hunter. *(Prints and Photographs Division, Library of Congress)*

Politically, it would not have cost Lincoln much to move against slavery, especially in South Carolina, where the rebellion began. But the need to preserve executive authority and maintain a proper chain of command, if nothing else, forced Lincoln to act. He simply could not let major generals set political policy.

Lincoln's response to Hunter differed dramatically from his response to Frémont, and contained an important hint of his evolving theory of law and emancipation. He rebuked Hunter for acting without authority, but he did not reject the theory behind Hunter's General Order: that slavery was incompatible with both a free country and the smooth operation of military forces suppressing the rebellion. Instead he told Hunter:

> I further make known that whether it be competent for me, as Commander-in-Chief of the Army and Navy, to declare the Slaves of any state or states, free, and whether at any time, in any case, it shall have become a necessity indispensable to the maintenance of the government to exercise such supposed power, are questions which, under my responsibility, I reserve to myself, and which I can not feel justified in leaving to the decision of commanders in the field.[71]

In the rest of his proclamation Lincoln urged the loyal slave states to take up Congress's offer of March 6 to give "pecuniary aid" to those states that would "adopt a gradual abolishment of slavery." He asserted that "the change" such a policy "contemplates" would "come as gentle as the dews of heaven, not rending or wrecking anything." He asked the leaders of the slave states—within the Union and presumably those who claimed to be outside the Union—if they would "not embrace" this offer of Congress to accomplish "so much good . . . by one effort."[72]

This document is a stunning example of Lincoln as a deft and subtle politician shaping public opinion in advance of announcing his goals. By this time he was fully aware that none of the Confederate states were ever going to end slavery on their own. But he was willing to continue to make conciliatory gestures, urging a peaceful and seemingly painless solution to the problem. He offered this to the Border States, even though he may have had little expectation that they would accept the offer. This made him look conservative on the issue of slavery while at the same time advocating abolition and preparing the public for an eventual end to slavery. Here Lincoln offered a solution to America's greatest problem with the least amount of social disruption. But he also hinted that there were alternative solutions. He did not exactly say he had the power to end slavery as commander in chief; he merely asserted that *if* such power existed, it rested with him, and

---

[71]Ibid., 5:222–23.
[72]Ibid., 5:223.

that if he felt emancipation had "become a necessity indispensable to the maintenance of the government" he was prepared to act against slavery.

Lincoln was preparing the public for what he would do. He was in no hurry. He was carefully laying the groundwork for public support, on the basis of military necessity. At the same time, he was laying the groundwork for a legal and constitutional rationale to justify emancipation. Like the superb courtroom lawyer he had been before becoming president, Lincoln was not ready to lay out his strategy all at once. He wanted to prepare his jury—the American public—for what he was going to do. He did not emphatically assert that he had the constitutional power to end slavery in the Confederacy; he merely raised it as a theoretical possibility, while at the same time making it clear that if such power existed, it rested with him.

A series of events in mid-July convinced Lincoln to move forward on emancipation at the executive level. On July 12 Lincoln met for the second time with representatives and senators from the Upper South, urging them to endorse compensated emancipation (with federal help) for their states. He implored them to return home to try to convince their state legislatures to accept the offer of Congress for compensated emancipation. Lincoln offered two strong arguments for cooperation on this matter. First, he asserted that by taking this stand the loyal slave states would help the war effort by showing the rebels "that, in no event, will the states you represent ever join their proposed Confederacy." Although Lincoln did not expect the Border States to join the rebellion, he believed that if those states voluntarily accepted compensated emancipation it would be a blow to Confederate hopes and morale. He then made a more practical argument, essentially telling these Border State politicians to make the best deal they could for their constituents. He famously told them that the "incidents of war" could "not be avoided" and that "mere friction and abrasion" would destroy slavery. He bluntly predicted—or more properly warned—that slavery "will be gone and you will have nothing valuable in lieu of it."[73]

He also hinted that beyond the "friction and abrasion" of war, emancipation might be more thorough. He told the Border State representatives that General Hunter's proclamation ending slavery in South Carolina had been

---

[73]"Appeal to Border State Representatives to Favor Compensated Emancipation," July 12, 1862, *CW*, 5:317–18; Gienapp, *Abraham Lincoln and Civil War America*, p. 110; McPherson, *Battle Cry of Freedom*, p. 503.

very popular and that he considered Hunter an "honest man" and "my friend."[74] This was in marked contrast to his view of Frémont. The Border State representatives and senators did not take the hint, indicating to Lincoln that they believed any move against slavery was unconstitutional. Two days later more than two-thirds of them signed a public letter denouncing any type of emancipation as "unconstitutional." Eight Border State representatives then published letters of their own supporting the president.[75]

On July 14, the same day that the Border State representatives denounced emancipation, Lincoln took a final stab at gradualism, although he doubtless knew the attempt would fail. He sent the draft of a bill to Congress that would provide compensation to every state that ended slavery. The draft bill left blank the amount of compensation for each slave, but provided that the money would come in the form of federal bonds given to the states. This bill was part of Lincoln's strategy to end slavery through state action where possible as a way of setting up the possibility of ending it on the national level. If he could get Kentucky or Maryland to end slavery, it would be easier to end it in the South. This was also consistent with prewar notions of federalism and constitutional interpretation that the states had sole authority over issues of property and personal status. Congress reported this bill, and it went through two readings, but lawmakers adjourned before acting on it.

Surely Lincoln knew that this bill, like his meeting with the Border State representatives, would not lead to an end to slavery in the Upper South. Nevertheless, this very public attempt to encourage the states—especially the Border States—to end slavery was valuable. Like his response to General Hunter, Lincoln demonstrated to the nation that he was not acting precipitously or incautiously. On the contrary, he was doing everything he could, at least publicly, to end slavery with the least amount of turmoil and social dislocation.

This proposed bill must also be seen in the context of Lincoln's actions on July 13, the day before he proposed the bill and the day after his meeting with the Border State representatives. On the 13th, Lincoln privately told Secretary of State William H. Seward and Secretary of the Navy Gideon

---

[74]"Appeal to Border State Representatives," *CW*, 5:317–18.
[75]Gienapp, *Abraham Lincoln and Civil War America*, p. 110; McPherson, *Battle Cry of Freedom*, p. 503.

Welles that he was going to issue an emancipation proclamation. This was not a sudden response to the Border State representatives rejecting compensated emancipation. Had they accepted Lincoln's proposal it would not have affected slavery in the Confederacy, where most slaves lived. Indeed, Lincoln told Welles that for weeks the issue had "occupied his mind and thoughts day and night."[76] Indeed, that was probably an understatement. Lincoln had probably been troubled by the issue since he had been forced to countermand Frémont's proclamation, or perhaps from the moment he first heard of Butler's contraband solution to runaways. Lincoln's conflicting views over emancipation—his desire to achieve it and his sense that the time was not right—was surely evident in his response to Hunter's proclamation, which Lincoln announced on May 19—nearly two months before he spoke with Welles.

Lincoln told Welles the issue was one of military necessity. "We must free the slaves," he said, "or be ourselves subdued." Slaves, Lincoln argued, "were undeniably an element of strength to those who had their service, and we must decide whether that element should be with or against us." Lincoln also rejected the idea that the Constitution still protected slavery in the Confederacy. "The rebels," he said, "could not at the same time throw off the Constitution and invoke its aid. Having made war on the Government, they were subject to the incidents and calamities of war."[77] Here Lincoln sounded much like Benjamin Butler in his response to Major Carey. Since Butler's response to Carey, the administration had accepted the idea that the fugitive slave clause of the Constitution could not be invoked by rebel masters. But why, Lincoln might have asked, was the fugitive slave clause different from any other part of the Constitution? If rebel masters were not entitled to the protection of that clause, then they were not entitled to the protection of any other part of the Constitution. Thus Lincoln had found a constitutional theory that would be acceptable to most Northerners. It might not pass muster with the U.S. Supreme Court, but that issue might not arise until after most slaves had been freed.

The military necessity argument is a more curious one. Lincoln did not begin to move toward an expansive emancipation policy until after the

---

[76]Lincoln, quoted in McPherson, *Battle Cry of Freedom*, p. 504. This chronology was emphatically confirmed by Eric Foner in *Fiery Trial*, pp. 217–18.

[77]Lincoln, quoted in McPherson, *Battle Cry of Freedom*, p. 504.

United States had achieved substantial military success in the first five months of 1862. He often said that he could not emancipate slaves until he knew he could win the war. Thus, Lincoln never saw emancipation as a military necessity; rather, it was an act that could only be accomplished by military success.

However, in framing its constitutionality, Lincoln argued simultaneously that emancipation grew out of military power—that is, his power as commander in chief—and that as commander in chief he could do whatever was necessary to win the war and preserve the Union. This was because he understood that constitutionally—and consistent with the laws of war—he could only attack slavery in the South as a military act. It would violate existing rules of war to take private property from enemy civilians *unless* it was for military necessity. So U.S. soldiers could take food from Southern farms, but not other property,[78] unless that other property was directly tied to Confederate war making. Thus, legally and constitutionally, emancipation had to be characterized as a war measure. There was nothing hypocritical about this, because in fact slavery was the cause of secession and the war, and the slaves themselves were, as Frederick Douglass noted, "[t]he very stomach of this Rebellion."[79]

Lincoln signed the Second Confiscation Act into law four days after his conversation with Welles and Seward.[80] This law was more expansive than the First Confiscation Act. The law provided the death penalty as well as lesser penalties—including confiscation of slaves—for treason; it also allowed for the prosecution of "any person" participating in the rebellion or who gave "aid and comfort" to it. The law also provided for the seizure and condemnation of the property of "any person within any State or Territory of the United States . . . being engaged in armed rebellion against the government of the United States, or aiding or abetting such rebellion." This would include Confederate sympathizers in the Border States as well as in the Confederacy. Two separate provisions dealt, in a comprehensive way, with the issue of runaway slaves and contrabands.

---

[78] General Sherman punished soldiers for looting. Joan E. Cashin, "Trophies of War: Material Culture in the Civil War Era," *Journal of the Civil War Era* 1 (2011):353. See also Finkelman, "Francis Lieber and the Modern Law of War," pp. 2101–8.

[79] Douglass, quoted in McPherson, *Battle Cry of Freedom*, p. 354.

[80] "An Act to Suppress Insurrection, to Punish Treason and Rebellion, to Seize and Confiscate the Property of Rebels, and for Other Purposes," July 17, 1862, 12 *Statutes at Large* 589.

Section 9 provided that slaves owned by anyone "engaged in rebellion against the government" who escaped to Union lines or were captured by U.S. troops would be "forever free of their servitude, and not again held as slaves." Section 10 prohibited the military from returning fugitive slaves to any masters, even those in the Border States, unless the owner claiming the slave would "first make oath that the person to whom the labor or service of such fugitive is alleged to be due is his lawful owner, and has not borne arms against the United States in the present rebellion, nor in any way given aid and comfort thereto." Like the Washington, D.C., emancipation act, this law allowed for the colonization of such blacks "as may be willing to emigrate" to other lands. This was a sop to conservatives who feared black freedom, but it did not require anyone to leave the United States.[81] Significantly, unlike the D.C. Compensated Emancipation Act, the Second Confiscation Act allowed colonization but did not appropriate any money for it.

The Second Confiscation Act was one more step toward creating a constitutional framework for emancipation while also preparing the public for an end to slavery. The law clearly confirmed that the national government had the legal and constitutional power to destroy slavery in the Confederacy, and that as a war measure both Congress and the president might emancipate slaves.

The act did not, however, actually free any slaves. The law provided numerous punishments for rebels, but their slaves would only become free after some judicial process. Had there been no Emancipation Proclamation or Thirteenth Amendment, the Second Confiscation Act might eventually have been used to litigate freedom, but it would have been a long and tedious process. The only certain freedom created by the Act came in Sections 9 and 10, which secured liberty to fugitive slaves escaping rebel masters. But this was not really much of a change from existing policy.

The same day he signed the Second Confiscation Act, Lincoln also signed a new militia act that, for the first time since the American Revolution, authorized the enlistment of black troops.[82] Unlike the Confiscation Act, this new law provided immediate freedom for any male slave who joined the U.S.

---

[81]Ibid.
[82]"An Act to Amend the Act Calling Forth the Militia to Execute the Laws of the Union, Suppress Insurrections, and Repel Invasions, Approved February Twenty-Eight, Seventeen Hundred and Ninety-Five, and the Acts Amendatory Thereof, and for Other

Army. Under this law, freedom would vest without any judicial process. Equally important, the law provided that the enlistee's "mother and his wife and children, shall forever thereafter be free" if they were owned by "some person who, during the present rebellion, has borne arms against the United States or adhered to their enemies by giving them aid and comfort."[83] A week later, Secretary of War Edwin M. Stanton authorized General Rufus Saxton, who was based at Hilton Head, South Carolina, to begin to enlist black troops.[84]

The Militia Act and the enlistment of black troops significantly altered the war and made emancipation inevitable. The slave South would never accept the legitimacy of black soldiers, and throughout the rest of the war Confederate armies violated existing rules of war in their treatment of black combatants and black prisoners.[85] Confederate Secretary of War James Seddon ranted that the "enlistment of negro slaves as part of the Army" was a barbarous act, "contrary to the usages of civilized nations."[86] This argument was nonsensical, since blacks and emancipated slaves had fought in the Revolution, the War of 1812, and even in South Carolina's colonial militia in the Yamasee War.[87] But Confederate anger over the enlistment of blacks changed the nature of the war. Later in the war, Confederate troops under Major General Nathan Bedford Forrest massacred surrendering black soldiers at Fort Pillow, shooting many while they attempted to surrender, mutilating some of the dead soldiers, and, according to many witnesses, burying alive or burning alive some captured black troops.[88] Confederate hostility to black enlistment ultimately led to a complete breakdown of prisoner exchanges during the war because General Grant and his subordinates, with the backing of Lincoln and Secretary of War Stanton, terminated all

---

Purposes," Act of July 17, 1862, chap. 201, 12 *Statutes at Large* 599. Blacks had been allowed to serve in the U.S. Navy.

[83]Ibid., secs. 12 and 13.

[84]Letter from Edwin M. Stanton to Brigadier General Saxton (Aug. 25, 1862), *OR*, 14:377, 377–78.

[85]Finkelman, "Francis Lieber and the Modern Law of War," pp. 2121–24.

[86]Letter from James A. Seddon to Robert Ould (June 24, 1863), *OR*, 6:41, 44.

[87]Finkelman, "Francis Lieber and the Modern Law of War," pp. 2121–24.

[88]John Cimprich, *Fort Pillow, a Civil War Massacre, and Public Memory* (Baton Rouge, 2011), pp. 81–84, 89, 95; Cornish, *The Sable Arm*, p. 175. For an example of burying captured prisoners alive, or allowing wounded prisoners to die untreated after the battle, see George S. Burkhardt, *Confederate Rage, Yankee Wrath: No Quarter in the Civil War* (Carbondale, Ill., 2007), p. 114 ; John Hope Franklin, *From Slavery to Freedom: A History of Negro Americans*, 3d ed. (New York, 1967), p. 292.

FIG. 5. Alexander H. Ritchie engraving of *The First Reading of the Emancipation Proclamation before the Cabinet*, by Francis B. Carpenter. *(Prints and Photographs Division, Library of Congress)*

such exchanges when the Confederates refused to exchange black prisoners.[89] Thus, the new Militia Act set the stage for a war to the end, with slavery and black freedom at the center of the conflict. No one, of course, knew this when the act was passed, but clearly Lincoln and Congress understood that enlisting former slaves, and freeing their mothers, wives, and children, would ultimately destroy slavery.

On July 22, five days after signing the Second Confiscation Act and the Militia Act, Lincoln presented his cabinet with his first draft of the Emancipation Proclamation (fig. 5). The draft began with a reference to the Second Confiscation Act, and contained a declaration warning "all persons" aiding or joining the rebellion that if they did not "return to their proper allegiance to the United States" they would suffer "pain of the forfeitures and seizures" of their slaves.[90] This language would not appear in the final proclamation. However, a few days after he showed this language to the cabinet, Lincoln recast it as a separate public proclamation.[91]

---

[89]McPherson, *Battle Cry of Freedom*, pp. 792–83.
[90]Emancipation Proclamation—First Draft [July 22, 1862], *CW*, 5:336.
[91]Proclamation of the Act to Suppress Insurrection, July 25, 1862, *CW*, 5:341.

The rest of the first draft of the proclamation focused on Lincoln's intent to urge Congress to give "pecuniary aid" to those states voluntarily ending slavery and "practically sustaining the authority of the United States." This was one more attempt to get the loyal slave states to end slavery. The last sentence of this draft proclamation finally went to the main issue. Lincoln declared that "as a fit and necessary military measure" he did "order and declare" as "Commander-in-Chief of the Army and Navy of the United States," that "all persons held as slaves within any state or states, wherein the constitutional authority of the United States shall not then be practically recognized, submitted to, and maintained, shall then, thenceforward, and forever be free."

This was the great change for Lincoln. He was now on record as asserting that he had the constitutional power to end slavery in the Confederacy. Lincoln had solved the third precondition of emancipation. Kentucky, Missouri, Maryland, and Delaware were securely in the United States, and while their leaders were not ready to end slavery, they clearly would not be joining the Confederacy. The first condition—a solid constitutional theory for ending slavery—had now been met as well. The fourth condition had been at least partially met. With United States troops controlling most of the Mississippi Valley, a good deal of Tennessee, and the islands off the coast of South Carolina and Georgia, and most Southern ports closed by the navy, Lincoln knew that an emancipation program would be successful in freeing a substantial number of slaves, even if somehow a shrunken Confederacy survived.

The only precondition that was left was the development of political support for emancipation. Here Lincoln was also close to achieving that precondition. Congress had been moving toward emancipation, as evidenced by the laws ending slavery in the District of Columbia and the territories, prohibiting the army from returning fugitive slaves, and the emancipation provisions of the Second Confiscation Act and the Militia Act. Meanwhile, generals such as Hunter were pushing for emancipation. Once he showed the proposed proclamation to the cabinet, only Postmaster General Montgomery Blair, who was from the slave state of Maryland, expressed any reservations. Blair did not oppose emancipation per se, but thought it would cost the Republican Party votes in the fall elections, and thus he urged Lincoln to postpone his announcement until after the election. Lincoln wisely did not follow his advice, understanding perhaps that the party in the White

House often lost seats in Congress in a midterm election, and that it would be even more problematic to announce emancipation after the November elections.

VI

During the summer and into the fall, Lincoln quietly set in motion the necessary conditions for emancipation. Illustrative of this was his famous letter to the *New York Tribune* on August 22. In an editorial titled "The Prayer of Twenty Millions," Horace Greeley had urged Lincoln to end slavery. Lincoln responded with a letter to the editor—probably the only time in the history of the nation that a sitting president has written a letter to an editor to be published in a paper—declaring his goal was to "save the Union," and that he would accomplish this any way he could. He told Greeley, and the nation, "If I could save the Union without freeing any slave I would do it, and if I could save it by freeing all slaves I would do it; and if I could save it by freeing some and leaving others alone I would also do that. What I do about slavery, and the colored race, I do because I believe it helps to save the Union; and what I forbear, I forbear because I don't believe it would help to save the Union." While he declared he would free some slaves, all slaves, or no slaves in order to save the Union, Lincoln made clear that this was a description of his "*official* duty." He then reiterated his "oft-expressed *personal* wish that all men every where could be free."[92]

Critics of Lincoln make much of this letter to show that Lincoln had no interest in ending slavery. But they misunderstand the letter in three ways. First, the end of the letter is a clear and unambiguous statement of Lincoln's lifelong hostility to slavery. Emancipation was clearly Lincoln's moral goal. Second, these critics forget (or fail to acknowledge) that by the time he wrote the letter to Greeley he had already drafted the Emancipation Proclamation and had the unanimous support of his cabinet to issue it. Thus, Lincoln clearly knew where he was headed. He could not constitutionally free the slaves in the United States, but he was planning to free all of them in the Confederacy. Third, as already noted, Lincoln had quietly begun to enlist black troops. He was encouraging his army in South Carolina to turn

---

[92]Lincoln to Horace Greeley, Aug. 22, 1862, *CW*, 5:388–89.

slaves into soldiers. He knew that this would almost certainly destroy slavery wherever the army could reach and enlist these slaves.

What then is the meaning of this letter? The letter was masterful, complicated, and politically shrewd. By this time at least 100,000 slaves had been liberated and more were being freed by a combination of the still-existing contraband policy and the new Militia Act. Thus, saying he would "save the Union without freeing *any* slave"[93] was simply a rhetorical sop to Northern conservatives and Border State slave owners. The letter to Greeley was just one more step in creating the political conditions for emancipation. Lincoln had now warned the nation that he would end slavery if it were necessary to preserve the Union. In fact, he had been quietly and secretly moving toward this result all summer. His letter was a prelude to what he had already determined to do. No Northerner could be surprised when he did it. Abolitionists could be heartened by having a president who believed, as they did, that "all men every where" should "be free." Conservatives would understand that they had to accept the necessity of emancipation.

A few weeks later, on September 13, Lincoln replied coyly to an "Emancipation Memorial" from a group of Chicago ministers.[94] He asserted that emancipation was useless without a military victory. If he freed the slaves without being able to implement his order by military force, he would simply look incompetent and foolish. He told these Protestant ministers his order would be "like the Pope's bull against the comet."[95] He asked how he "could free the slaves" when he could not "enforce the Constitution in the rebel States."[96] He also reiterated his need to secure the Border States, noting that precipitous emancipation would take "fifty thousand bayonets" from Kentucky out of the Union army and give them to the Confederates.[97] He also argued that he needed full public support to succeed. Thus, he urged

---

[93]Ibid., 5:388.

[94]Reply to Emancipation Memorial Presented by Chicago Christians of All Denominations, Sept. 13, 1862, *CW*, 5:419–25 [quotations, p. 420].

[95]Ibid., p. 420. According to various stories, in 1456 Pope Calixtus III issued a papal bull against Halley's Comet. This event was recounted in a biography of Calixtus III by Pierre-Simon Laplace published in 1475. Modern scholars believe this is not a true story, but it was believed at the time of Lincoln. For one discussion of this, see Andrew Dickson White, *A History of the Warfare of Science with Theology in Christendom* (New York, 1896), p. 177.

[96]Reply to Emancipation Memorial, *CW*, 5:420.

[97]Ibid., p. 423.

the ministers to be patient. Emancipation could only come with military success and the ability to "unite the people in the fact that constitutional government" should be preserved.[98]

Lincoln's reply to the ministers was very much like his letter to Greeley. He set out the conditions he needed to attack slavery—securing Kentucky and being likely to win the war—as though all this was off in the distant future. He responded to the ministers by evading any commitment and refusing to reveal his plans. In fact, Lincoln knew he had almost all his prerequisites on the table. To end slavery he needed the prospect of military success; the ability to secure the Border States; public support for black freedom; and a constitutional theory to justify his actions. In early September he had all of this except the first. The war had being going well since the previous December, but the disaster at Second Bull Run in August derailed that string of military successes. Had the Union won that battle he might have issued the preliminary proclamation then. Instead, he was biding his time until he had a significant battlefield victory. When he had that victory, emancipation would not in fact be a "necessity" to preserve the Union, as he has said in the Greeley letter; rather, it would be the fruit of victory. The victory at Antietam, just four days after he met with the ministers, was the last piece of the puzzle. He could now issue the proclamation as the logical fruit of the military successes that had taken place since the previous December.[99]

On September 22 he issued the preliminary proclamation, declaring that it would go into effect in one hundred days. He chose the date carefully, because it was exactly one hundred days until January 1, 1863, thus tying emancipation with the New Year. He now also had his constitutional/legal theory for issuing the proclamation.

He issued the proclamation in his dual capacity as "President of the United States of America, and Commander-in-Chief of the Army and Navy." The purpose of the proclamation was "restoring the constitutional relations" between the nation and all the states. The preliminary

---

[98]Ibid., p. 424.
[99]In hindsight it is, of course, clear that Antietam was not the knockout blow Lincoln was hoping for, and the end of 1862 and the first half of 1863 would be a period of enormous frustration for Lincoln as the war went badly. But Lincoln could not know or foresee this when he issued the preliminary proclamation.

proclamation put the nation on notice that in one hundred days he would move against slavery in any place that was still in rebellion against the nation.[100] Again, critics of Lincoln focus on the "hundred days," arguing that Lincoln was still vacillating. But in reality he was not.

By starting to enlist black troops he had guaranteed that no Southern state would return to the Union. But even without black troops there was not a shred of evidence to suggest that anyone in the Confederacy would take Lincoln up on his offer to end the war. The hundred days gave Lincoln the chance to once more offer a sop to conservatives, showing that he was reasonable and conciliatory. In addition, Lincoln was setting a special date—January 1—for Emancipation Day. The final proclamation would be dull and boring—"all the moral grandeur of a bill of lading"[101]—but the date of issue would be iconic and significant. He would begin the New Year with what he would later call "a new birth of freedom."

On January 1, 1863, the final proclamation was put into effect (fig. 6). Here Lincoln made the constitutional argument even more precise. He issued it "by virtue of the power in me vested as Commander-in-Chief, of the Army and Navy of the United States in time of actual armed rebellion." This was, constitutionally, a war measure designed to cripple the ability of those in rebellion to resist the lawful authority of the United States. It applied only to those states and parts of states that were still in rebellion. This was constitutionally essential. Lincoln only had power to touch slavery where, as he had told the ministers from Chicago, he could not "enforce the Constitution." Where the Constitution was in force, federalism and the Fifth Amendment prevented presidential emancipation. The document was narrowly written, carefully designed to withstand the scrutiny of the Supreme Court, still presided over by Chief Justice Taney. It applied narrowly only to the states in rebellion. It would not threaten Kentucky or Missouri, and it would not threaten the constitutional relationship of the states and the federal government.

A careful reading of the proclamation suggests that Professor Hofstadter was right. It did have "all the moral grandeur of a bill of lading." But Hofstadter failed to understand the significance of a bill of lading to a skilled railroad lawyer, which is what Lincoln had been before the war. A bill of

---

[100]Preliminary Emancipation Proclamation, Sept. 22, 1862, *CW*, 5:433.
[101]Hofstadter, *American Political Tradition*, pp. 110, 115, 131.

FIG. 6. "The Emancipation of the Negroes, January, 1863—The Past and The Future," drawn by Thomas Nast; *Harper's Weekly*, Jan. 24, 1863. *(Prints and Photographs Division, Library of Congress)*

lading was the key legal instrument used to guarantee the delivery of goods between parties who were far apart and may never have known each other. A bill of lading allowed a seller in New York to safely ship goods to a buyer in Illinois, with both knowing the transaction would work.

One contemporary living in Britain, Karl Marx, fully understood the highly legalistic nature of the proclamation. Shortly after Lincoln issued the preliminary proclamation, Marx wrote in an Austrian paper: "The most redoubtable decrees—which will always remain remarkable historical documents—flung by him at the enemy all look like, and intended to look like, routine summonses sent by a lawyer to the lawyer of the opposing party. . . . His latest proclamation which is drafted in the same style, the manifesto abolishing slavery, is the most important document in American history since the establishment of the Union, tantamount to tearing up the old American Constitution." Marx conceded that the proclamation was "aesthetically repulsive, logically inadequate, farcical in form, and politically contradictory," but he nevertheless asserted that "Lincoln's place in the history of the United States and of mankind, will, nevertheless be next to that of Washington!" He noted that in the Emancipation Proclamation "the significant is clothed in everyday dress in the new world."[102]

So, in the end, when all the preconditions were met—the Border States secured, military victory likely, political support in place, and the constitutional/legal framework developed—Lincoln went back to his roots as a railroad lawyer and wrote a carefully crafted, narrow document: a bill of lading for the delivery of freedom to some three million southern slaves. The vehicle for delivery would be the army and navy—of which he was commander in chief. As the armies of the United States moved deeper into the Confederacy, they would bring the power of the proclamation with them, freeing slaves every day as more and more of the Confederacy was redeemed by military success. This was the moral grandeur of the proclamation and of Lincoln's careful and complicated strategy to achieve his personal goal that "all men every where could be free."[103]

---

[102] Karl Marx in *Die Presse,* Oct. 12, 1862, in Karl Marx and Frederick Engels, *Collected Works,* 50 vols. (New York, 1975–2004), 19:250.

[103] Lincoln to Horace Greeley, Aug. 22, 1862, *CW,* 5:388–89.

Jenny Bourne

Double Take

Abolition and the Size of Transferred Property Rights

ABOLITION TRANSFERRED PROPERTY rights from former masters to former slaves. This regime change generates two mirror-image questions: How much did former slave owners lose after the government terminated their property rights? And how much did newly freed individuals lose before the government restored their right to self-ownership? Scholars have written about the former—often in the context of whether the Civil War was cost-justified—with lost property value estimated at about $3 billion in 1860 dollars.[1] Yet, if one considers freedom rather than slavery as the baseline, the latter amount is far more relevant.[2] The research presented here suggests that this number exceeds $8 billion in 1860 dollars.[3]

---

[1] See, for instance, Roger Ransom and Richard Sutch, "Capitalists without Capital: The Burden of Slavery and the Impact of Emancipation," *Agricultural History* 62 (1988):133–60.

[2] Kaimipono David Wenger, "Slavery as a Takings Clause Violation," *American University Law Review* 53 (2004):191–259, argues that slavery could be interpreted as a violation of the takings clause of the U.S. Constitution, building upon John Locke's argument that every person is entitled to the fruits of his labor. John Locke, *Two Treatises on Government*, ed. Mark Goldie (London, 1993).

[3] To transform this into dollars of today, multiply by 26. Price-level information from 1860 to 2003 appears in Peter Lindert and Richard Sutch, "Consumer Price Indexes, for All Items: 1774–2003," in *Historical Statistics of the United States, Earliest Times to the Present: Millennial Edition*, ed. Susan B. Carter, Scott Sigmund Gartner, Michael R. Haines, Alan L. Olmstead, Richard Sutch, and Gavin Wright (New York, 2006), table Cc1–2 (hereafter *HSUS*). For data from 2003 to the present, see http://data.bls.gov/.

Current calls for reparations to the descendants of slaves base arguments on uncompensated slave labor, at least in part.[4] These cases may have merit and certainly appeal to a sense of justice, but they encounter problems when it comes to plaintiffs' legal standing—no one living today suffered direct losses from slavery.[5] Yet former slaves alive in the mid-1860s would have faced no such difficulty with standing. Much as plaintiffs in a wrongful-death lawsuit might sue for lost future wages, former slaves who endured a sort of "social death"[6] might have claimed lost past wages.

The following sections estimate losses sustained by persons alive in 1860. Abolition stripped slave owners of something valuable that the law had previously allowed them to own. Prices of slaves, like the prices of other capital assets, reflected expected future earnings associated with the asset. Slave prices around the time of secession could therefore capture the size of pecuniary losses to former slave owners from abolition.[7] The

---

[4]The leading case is *In re: African-American Slave Descendants Litigation. Appeals of Deadria Farmer-Paellmann, et al. and Timothy Hurdle, et al.*, 471 F.3d 754 (U.S. Court of Appeals, 7th Cir., 2006). Most reparations advocates request compensation for discrimination against blacks after slavery ended, as well as unpaid wages for slaves. Identification of plaintiffs and defendants for these claims is challenging, as is the amount of damages. Alfred Brophy, *Reparations: Pro and Con* (New York, 2006), offers a sensitive and thorough review of the arguments on both sides of the reparations debate. See also Raymond Winbush, ed., *Should America Pay? Slavery and the Raging Debate on Reparations* (New York, 2003); Randall Robinson, *The Debt: What America Owes to Blacks* (New York, 1999); Boris Bittker, *The Case for Black Reparations* (New York, 1973); Symposium: "A Dream Deferred: Comparative and Practical Considerations for the Black Reparations Movement," *N.Y.U. Annual Survey of American Law* 58 (2003):447–698. Other writings focus on the magnitude of the loss suffered by African Americans. See, for example, James Marketti, "Black Equity in the Slave Industry," *Review of Black Political Economy* 2 (1972):43–68, and Marketti, "Estimated Present Value of Income Diverted during Slavery," in *The Wealth of Races: The Present Value of Benefits from Past Injustices*, ed. Richard F. America (New York, 1990), pp. 107–12.

[5]Nor are any potential defendants still living. Andrew Kull, "Restitution in Favor of Former Slaves," *Boston University Law Review* 84 (2004):1277–90, makes these points as well. Alfred L. Brophy, "The Cultural War over Reparations for Slavery," *DePaul Law Review* 53 (2004):1201–11, explores several arguments against reparations.

[6]This term is most closely associated with Orlando Patterson, *Slavery and Social Death: A Comparative Study* (Cambridge, Mass., 1982). Plaintiffs in wrongful-death cases are heirs and beneficiaries of the decedent who arguably would have enjoyed at least some of the fruits of the decedent's labor. If damages were constructed to generate optimal deterrence, however, they would instead focus on losses to the decedent. For discussion, see Steven Shavell, *Economic Analysis of Accident Law* (Cambridge, Mass., 1987), and Erin O'Hara, "Hedonic Damages for Wrongful Death: Are Tortfeasors Getting Away with Murder?" *Georgetown Law Journal* 78 (1990):1687–1721.

[7]Slaves were bought and sold throughout the Civil War—and even afterward—but prices during the war reflected expectations about victory, defeat, and the likelihood of

first section gives statistics on slave population and prices by age in 1860 as well as information on wealth by region in 1860 and 1870. Like previous studies, this one estimates lost property value to slave owners at just over $3 billion (in 1860 dollars). The second section focuses on forgone earnings to former slaves, offering information about slave hiring practices, hire rates by age over time, relationship of hire rates to prices, and manumission rates. At a real interest rate of 1 percent, the value of lost earnings (in 1860 dollars) to slaves enumerated in the 1860 census was $9.3 billion. The final section discusses less-quantifiable losses and offers conclusions.

Losses to Former Slave Owners

Number and Location of Slaves

Nearly four million slaves lived in the United States at the time of the Civil War, nine-tenths of them in the Confederacy. Table 1 reports the number of slaves by state enumerated in the 1860 federal census and the 1861 Confederate census; chart 1 shows the geographic concentration of slaves in the lower South and along the Mississippi River. Although Virginia boasted the largest number of slaves for any state, over half of the slave population resided in the five states of the Cotton South.[8]

Slave Prices and Productivity

Measuring the dollar loss to slave owners from abolition requires information about slave values. The largest and most complete data set on slave prices is available through the Inter-University Consortium for Political and Social Research; it was compiled under the direction of Robert Fogel and Stanley Engerman. These data pertain to slave sales and appraisals that took

---

abolition. Like others who have examined this issue, I therefore use prices reported from 1858 to 1860 as indicators of lost property value, even though the losses to slave owners arguably did not occur until at least the time of the Emancipation Proclamation or, more finally, upon passage of the Thirteenth Amendment.

[8]These states are South Carolina, Georgia, Alabama, Mississippi, and Louisiana. Parts of Texas and Florida are sometimes included in this region.

Table 1 Total slave population, 1860–61.

	1860 U.S. Census	1861 Confederate Census
Alabama	435,080	435,473
Arkansas	111,115	109,065
Florida	61,545	63,809
Georgia	462,198	467,461
Louisiana	326,726	312,186
Mississippi	417,390	479,607
North Carolina	331,059	328,377
South Carolina	402,406	407,185
Tennessee	275,719	287,112
Texas	181,618	184,956
Virginia	490,865	495,826
Total (Confederacy)	3,495,721	3,571,057
Delaware	1,798	
Kansas	2	
Kentucky	225,483	
Maryland	87,189	
Missouri	114,931	
Nebraska	15	
New Jersey	18	
Grand Total	3,925,157	

Sources: University of Virginia, Geospatial and Statistical Data Center, http://fisher.lib.virginia.edu/collections/stats/histcensus/index.html; Richard Todd, *Confederate Finance* (Athens, Ga., 1954), app. D, p. 199.

place from 1775 to 1865 in Virginia, Maryland, North Carolina, South Carolina, Louisiana, Tennessee, Georgia, and Mississippi.[9]

---

[9]Robert W. Fogel and Stanley L. Engerman, "1976: Slave Sales and Appraisals, 1775–1865" [computer file], ICPSR07421-v3 (Rochester, N.Y.: University of Rochester [producer], Ann Arbor, Mich.: Inter-University Consortium for Political and Social Research [producer and distributor], Oct. 11, 2006), http://doi:10.3886/ICPSR07421.v3 (hereafter Fogel and Engerman, ICPSR 7421). The data were obtained from probate records on deposit in the Church of Jesus Christ of Latter-Day Saints Genealogical Society Library, Salt Lake City, Utah. Variables document the sale locations and the appraised and sale values of the slaves, as

Not surprisingly, slave prices varied with slave productivity, which in turn varied with age, gender, and region of residence. Like free persons, slaves exhibited an inverse U shape in productivity as they aged—first becoming more productive as they grew from infants to young adults, then experiencing declining productivity as they aged further.[10] Female slaves of child-bearing ages were more valuable than comparably productive male slaves because owners of female slaves also owned any offspring.[11] Once slaves reached adulthood, male slaves tended to be more productive than females and thus were valued more highly; slaves in the Cotton South fetched higher prices than those in the older slave states.[12] Chart 2 depicts estimated 1860 prices for male and female slaves of various ages who resided in the Cotton South.[13] Chart 3 shows the age distribution of slaves by gender listed in the 1860 census; more than half of all slaves were under age twenty.

---

well as slave age, sex, occupational skills, and health. Additional data and statistics on slave prices appear in Ulrich Phillips, *Life and Labor in the Old South* (Boston, 1929); Alfred Conrad and John Meyer, "The Economics of Slavery in the Ante-Bellum South," *Journal of Political Economy* 66 (1958):95–122; Robert Evans, "The Economics of American Negro Slavery," in *Aspects of Labor Economics*, ed. H. Gregg Lewis (Princeton, N.J., 1962), pp. 185–243; Robert Fogel and Stanley Engerman, *Time on the Cross* (Boston, 1974); and Laurence Kotlikoff, "The Structure of Slave Prices in New Orleans, 1804 to 1862," *Economic Inquiry* 17 (1979):496–518.

[10] Fogel and Engerman argued that the age–sex and geographical patterns remained stable over the period from 1787 to 1860. See Fogel and Engerman, ICPSR 7421, 2:79. A comprehensive general survey on age and productivity is Vegard Skirbekk, "Age and Individual Productivity: A Literature Survey," Max Planck Institute for Demographic Research Working Paper WP 2003-028 (August 2003), http://www.demogr.mpg.de/papers/working/wp-2003-028.pdf.

[11] Infants were sold for a positive price, so the value of a female slave in child-bearing years was augmented by her expected fertility. Fogel and Engerman, ICPSR 7421, 2:83; refer to the "birthright" value of slaves, particularly after 1810.

[12] Males between the ages of twenty and fifty tended to cost 25 to 35 percent more than females of equivalent ages. Slaves in the Cotton South sold for about one-third more than those in Virginia and other slave states in the upper South. Not surprisingly, the slave population steadily moved—either with masters or via sales to new masters—into states farther south throughout the nineteenth century. For a comprehensive discussion, see particularly Michael Tadman, *Speculators and Slaves* (Madison, Wisc., 1989), and Jonathan Pritchett, "Quantitative Estimates of the United States Interregional Slave Trade, 1820–1860," *Journal of Economic History* 61 (2001):467–75.

[13] I obtained these estimates by regressing slave value on age, age squared, and dummy variables for gender, residence in the Cotton South, and decade in which the sale or appraisal occurred. I found similar results in regressions that used a second, smaller data set provided by Fogel and Engerman (Robert Fogel and Stanley Engerman, "New Orleans Slave Sale Sample, 1804–1862" [computer file], compiled by Robert W. Fogel and Stanley L. Engerman, University of Rochester, ICPSR07423-v2 (Ann Arbor, Mich.: Inter-University Consortium for Political and Social Research [producer and distributor], Aug. 4, 2008), http://doi:10.3886/ICPSR07423.v2). Regression results appear in the appendix to this chapter.

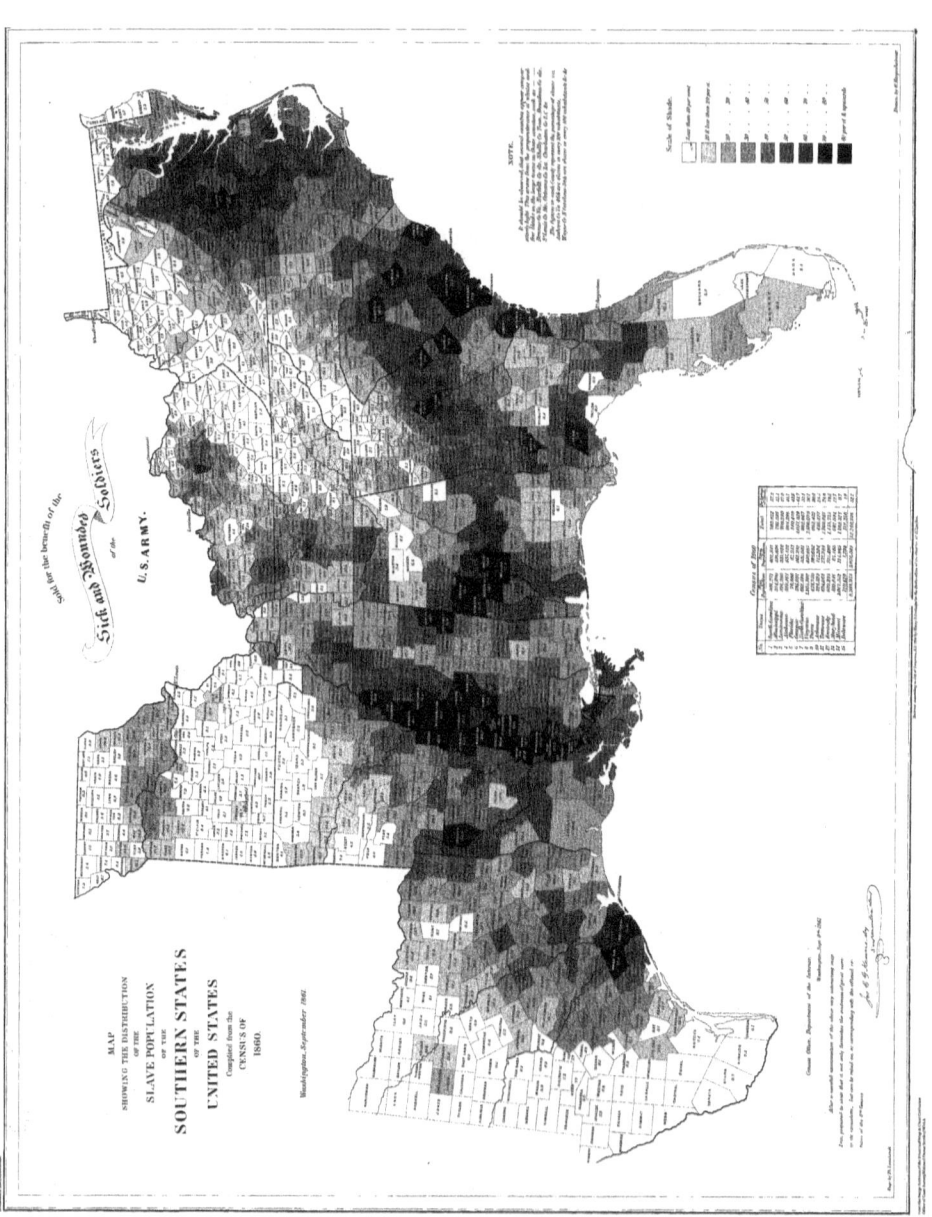

CHART 1. Slave population density by county, 1860.

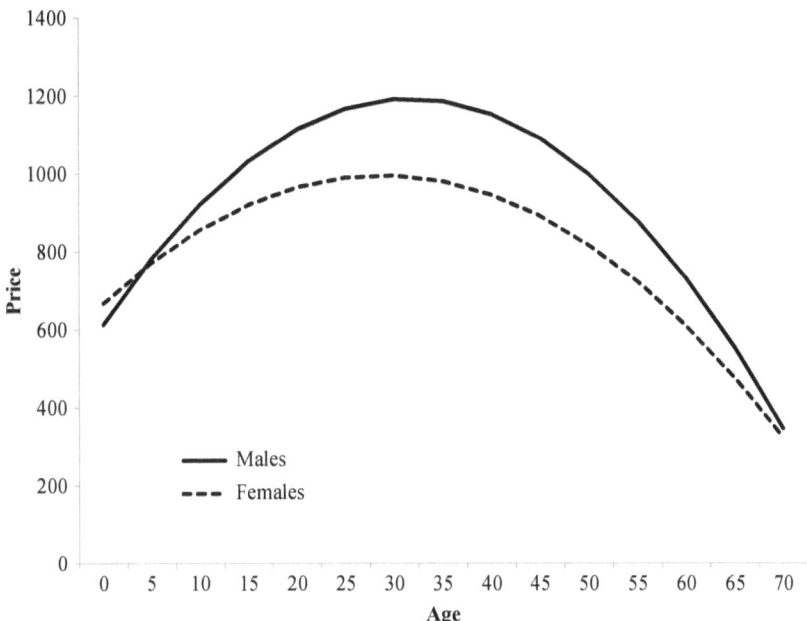

CHART 2. Estimated slave prices, cotton South, by age and gender, 1860.
Source: Fogel and Engerman, ICPSR 7421 data.

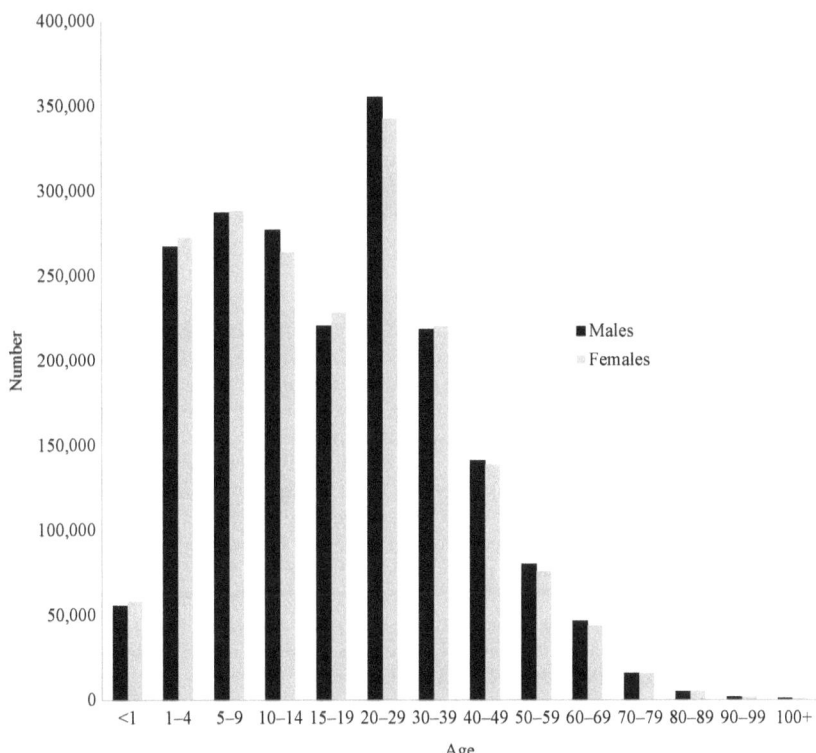

CHART 3. Age distribution of slaves, by gender, 1860.
Source: http://mapserver.lib.virginia.edu/php/state.php.

Losses to Slave Owners: My Estimates Compared to Others

Estimated total pecuniary losses to slave owners from abolition equals the sum of the age-specific, region-specific values of slaves multiplied by the number of slaves of a specific age in a given region.[14] My calculations yield a figure of about $3.27 billion in overall losses to slaveholders, with about $2.89 billion attributable to slaves held in the Confederate states.

These figures are comparable to estimates made by other scholars.[15] The Confederate census of 1861 reports total assessed slave value at only $2.37 billion, but it assigns a flat value of $600 per slave, whereas the Fogel and Engerman sample yields an average slave value of $833 in 1860.[16]

Other Methods of Estimating Slave Owner Losses

Reported wealth in the federal censuses is also consistent with my estimates of lost value to slave owners. Chart 4 shows total wealth by region (Confederacy, non-Confederate slave states, and nonslave states) in 1850, 1860, and 1870; Chart 5 shows assessed personal estate by region for 1860 and 1870.

The annual growth in wealth was essentially the same across regions from 1850 to 1860. Suppose this would have been true for 1860 to 1870 for both overall wealth and separate wealth components if the Civil War had not occurred. Slaves were typically considered personal property. Apply the growth rate in personal property in the nonslave states for 1860 to 1870 to the Confederate states, then subtract the reported 1870 personal property in the Confederate states: the result is about $3.39

---

[14]I use 1860 census figures to ascertain numbers of slaves in each age group and region. The loss to slave owners from abolition occurred slightly later on. I initially attempted to estimate the number of slaves in each age group and region as of 1863 and 1865 by interpolation between 1860 and 1870 census reports. Because I decided to use the more stable price values from around 1860, however, I simply used the 1860 population figures as well, rather than trying to fine-tune the overall estimate. Whether this method slightly over- or underestimates the loss to slave owners is unclear, given the inverted U shape of age-specific prices. I assigned the value of the average slave to slaves of unknown ages.

[15]Richard Sutch reports a figure of about $3.06 billion. Richard Sutch, "Appendix: The Value of the Slave Population, 1805–1860," in Ransom and Sutch, "Capitalists without Capital," pp. 141–60.

[16]Richard Todd, *Confederate Finance* (Athens, Ga., 1954), app. D., p. 199, reports assessed slave values; this information is replicated in Roger Ransom, "Taxable Property in the Confederacy, by State: 1861," in *HSUS*, Table Eh50–58.

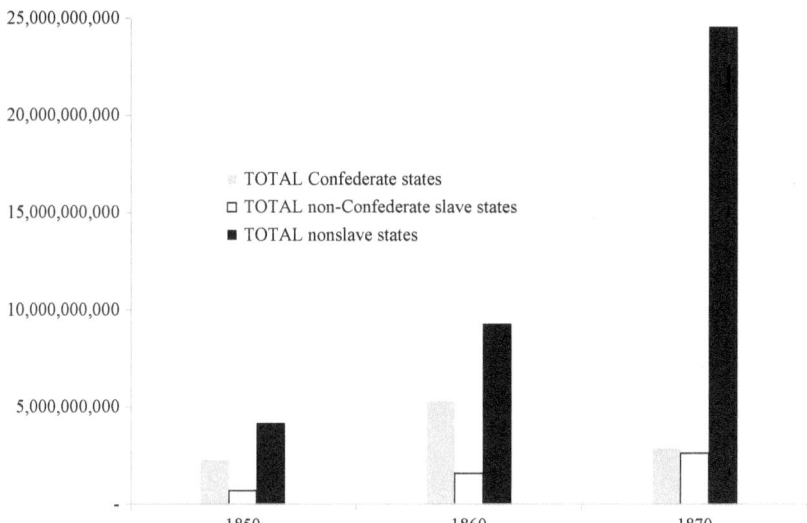

CHART 4. Wealth by region, 1850–1870.
Source: http://www2.census.gov/prod2/decennial/documents/1870c-01.pdf.

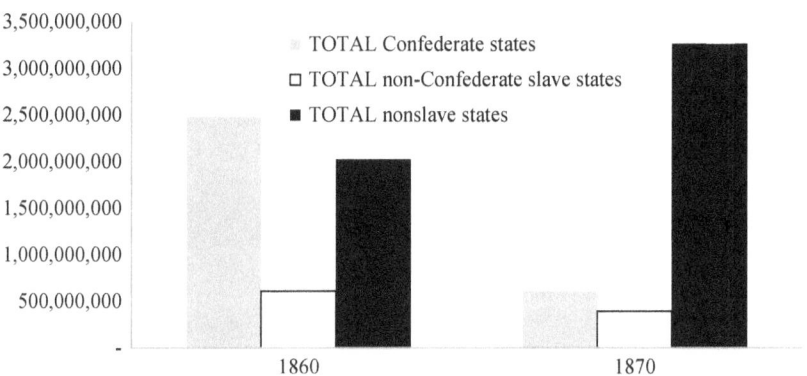

CHART 5. Assessed value of personal estate by region, 1860–70.
Source: http://www2.census.gov/prod2/decennial/documents/1870c-01.pdf.

billion. Including the non-Confederate slave states pushes the figure up to $3.6 billion. In other words, had slave property still been included in wealth in 1870, overall wealth would have been between $3 and $4 billion higher. This figure is probably an overestimate, because Confederates lost other sorts of personal property aside from slaves during the Civil War, which drives down the reported 1870 personal property figure relative to what it would have been without the war. It is therefore roughly consistent with my estimate for the loss in slave property value to former slave owners.

Losses to Emancipated Former Slaves
Why Hire Rates Are Useful Data

Abolition of slavery created a set of centaurs—persons entitled to the fruits of their future labors but who were previously considered property to be owned. Slaves who died before abolition and blacks born after were all of a piece. But slaves living at the time of abolition were both fish and fowl. The change in legal regime during their lifetime offers an intriguing possibility: if entitled to the future benefits of freedom, including wages, logically they might have a claim to past benefits as well. Just as claimants in wrongful-death lawsuits argue that the decedent had too few years to enjoy life at its end, former slaves might have said they had too few years to enjoy life at its beginning.[17]

Estimating the full loss from enslavement would entail speculation about the value of freedom—not impossible, but a daunting task. Evaluating lost wages is somewhat simpler: a robust hiring market for slaves existed from earliest days.[18] What is more, hirers generally paid for slave lodging, food,

---

[17]The plaintiffs in wrongful-death lawsuits are typically heirs of the decedent. Damages therefore pertain to their losses, including forgone inheritance due to the decedent's untimely death, which in turn arises because of forgone wages that the decedent would have earned had he or she lived. Former slaves could conceivably have sued on the basis of their own losses.

[18]Slave hiring took root by the Revolutionary period, according to Jonathan Martin, *Divided Mastery: Slave Hiring in the American South* (Cambridge, Mass., 2004). Also see Sarah Hughes, "Slaves for Hire: The Allocation of Black Labor in Elizabeth City County, Virginia, 1782 to 1810," *William and Mary Quarterly* 3d ser., 35 (1978):260–86. Information about slave hiring from 1830–60 appears in Evans, "The Economics of American Negro Slavery," pp. 185–243. Hiring was important in both industry and agriculture; it was frequently used to keep slaves occupied after an owner died but before the estate was settled. See Randolph Campbell, "Slave Hiring in Texas," *American Historical Review* 93 (1988):107–14; Charles Dew, ed., *Slavery in the Ante-Bellum Southern Industries* (Bethesda, Md., 1991); Robert Starobin, *Industrial Slavery in the Old South* (New York, 1970); Claudia Goldin, *Urban Slavery in the American South, 1820–1860* (Chicago, 1976). The slave hire system in Charleston, S.C., required slaves to wear badges—these items have now

and clothing, so slave hire rates actually reflect a measure of earnings net of basic consumption.[19] Court cases in which plaintiffs had been unlawfully held in slavery—most notably, *Hickham v. Hickham*—used hire rates as a basis for damages.[20]

Relationship of Sale and Hiring Markets

As for any other capital asset, hire and sale prices for slaves were intimately related. Hire rates for a particular period reflected slave productivity over that period and, like prices, varied with the age, gender, and region of residence of the slave. A slave's price at a given point in time mirrored expected productivity in future periods. Naturally, prices would have to account for expected mortality, as well as for expected child-bearing by women. Over time, both prices and hire rates could vary, in part due to changes in overall price levels and in part due to technological and demographic change that affected the productivity of slave labor.[21]

---

become collectibles. Harlan Greene, Harry S. Hutchins Jr., and Brian E. Hutchins, *Slave Badges and the Slave-Hire System in Charleston, South Carolina, 1783–1865* (Jefferson, N.C., 2004).

[19]See Evans, "The Economics of American Negro Slavery," pp. 194–96, and Martin, *Divided Mastery*, pp. 96–97. This is also apparent from court cases, for example, *Singleton v. Carroll*, 29 Ky. 527 (1831), *Harvey v. Skipwith*, 57 Va. 393 (1853), and *Hawkins v. Humble*, 45 Tenn. 531 (1868). That slave hirers bore these expenses may help explain why slave hire rates were lower than wages for free workers. Robert Margo, *Wages and Labor Markets in the U.S. 1820–1860* (Chicago, 2000), p. 42.

[20]46 Mo. App. 496 (Ct. App. 1891). In this case, the plaintiff was held as a slave because she allegedly did not know she had been freed. She submitted a claim for lost wages in the amount of $5 per month for twenty-four years and five days.

[21]Price-level information from 1860 to 2003 appears in Peter Lindert and Richard Sutch, "Consumer Price Indexes, for All Items: 1774–2003," in *HSUS*, table Cc1–2. The general price level spiked during the War of 1812 but then hovered around the level obtaining in 1860. In contrast, wage rates and slave hire rates trended up, both in nominal and in real terms. Slaves were increasingly native-born (particularly after the international slave trade closed in 1807–8), and native-born slaves were more valuable than imported slaves, all else equal, in part because they spoke English and had been born into slavery. David Galenson, "The Rise and Fall of Indentured Servitude in the Americas: An Economic Analysis," *Journal of Economic History* 44 (1984):1–26, argues that this partly explained why slaves took the place of indentured servants in the United States. Technology also enhanced the value of slaves—the cotton gin freed slaves to do other work, for example.

The task set forth here thus requires a look at more than slave prices in 1860—those numbers reflect expectations about future hire rates, whereas we want to know about past hire rates.[22] A historical time series of age-specific slave prices offers more information, but it has its own issue: prices reflected expected mortality and fertility, and I am focusing on individuals known to have lived. Nevertheless, slave prices over time might serve as a check on calculations of forgone hire. Estimates of the rate of return on slaves range from 12 percent to over 25 percent.[23] If slaves, like consol bonds, lived forever, then we would expect hire rates likewise to range from 12 to over 25 percent of prices.[24] But, due to finite lifespans, actual hire rates would exceed rates of return.[25]

Slave Hire Rates across Age Groups and over Time

Robert Fogel and Stanley Engerman have generously made available a large data set on slave hire rates, collected from eight southern states from 1775 to 1865.[26] Chart 6 depicts a scatter plot of average age-specific hire rates (all in 1860 dollars) for male slaves, along with a line that fits a second-order polynomial to the data. Like prices, hire rates appear first to increase and then to decrease with age. Chart 7 refines this analysis, comparing estimated hire rates to 12 percent of estimated prices for male slaves, by age, in the 1850s.[27] Not surprisingly, the peak for hire rates occurs at an older age—recall that

---

[22]Earlier studies, such as Marketti, "Estimated Present Value of Income Diverted during Slavery," had to rely on prices.

[23]See, for example, Evans, "The Economics of American Negro Slavery," table 19, p. 216, and table 21, p. 217, and Martin, *Divided Mastery*, pp. 80–81 n. 18.

[24]Consol bonds are bonds that do not have an expiration date. A consol bond with face value of $100 that pays a $10 coupon each year would therefore carry an implicit return of 10 percent.

[25]Court cases suggest that hire rates ranged from 10 to 17 percent of current price. See, for example, *Pryor et al. v. Ryburn*, 16 Ark. 671 (1856), *Baltzell v. Hall's Heirs*, 11 Ky. 97 (1822), and *Oustott v. Oustott*, 27 Tex. 643 (1864).

[26]Robert Fogel and Stanley Engerman, "Slave Hires, 1775–1865," ICPSR07422-v3 (Rochester, N.Y.: University of Rochester [producer], 1976, Ann Arbor, Mich.: Inter-University Consortium for Political and Social Research [producer and distributor], Oct. 11, 2006), http://doi.org/10.3886/ICPSR07422 (herafter Fogel and Engerman ICPSR 7422).

[27]I obtained the hire estimates from a regression of real hire rates (1860 dollars) on age, age squared, and dummy variables for gender, region of residence, decade of hire, and whether the hire contract was for a year. Price estimates are from the price regression discussed in note 13. Regression results are reported in the appendix.

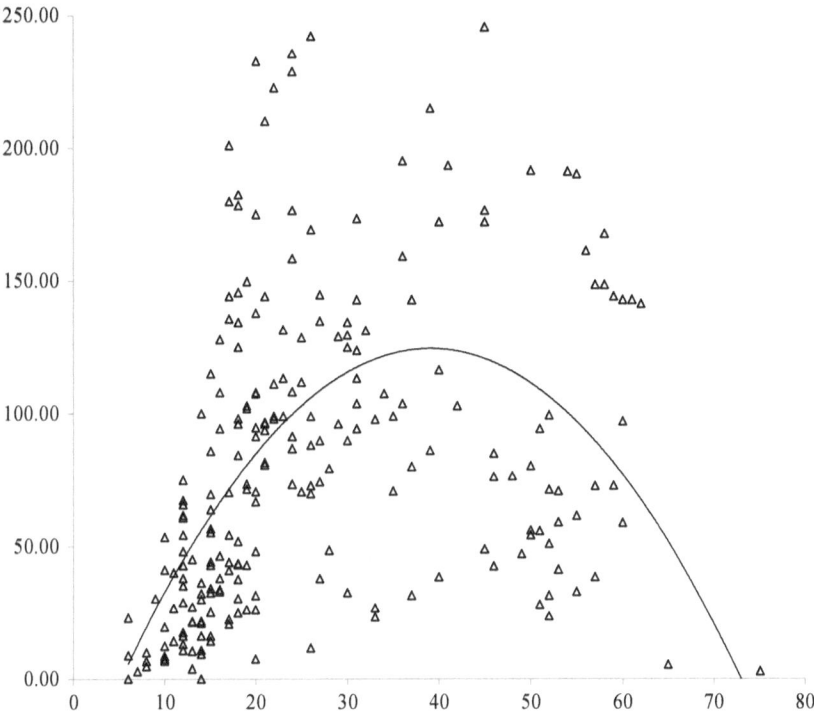

CHART 6. Annual hire rates, male slaves (1860 dollars).
Source: Fogel and Engerman, ICPSR 7422 data.

prices must account for expected mortality as well as expected future productivity, whereas hire rates reflect current productivity.

To estimate past hire rates at various ages for former slaves alive in 1860, one must consider patterns over time as well as across age groups. Chart 8 shows just how important time trends are: this graph portrays hire rates and an index of average prices as well as a wage index for common laborers in the South Atlantic region, all corrected for changes in the underlying price level.[28] The three series move generally in tandem, with a sharp runup (particularly for slave prices) just before the Panic of 1837, followed by a drop during the recession years of the late 1830s and early 1840s, then another increase up to the end of the 1850s. What the graph makes clear is that slave hire rates in real terms varied substantially across the years. To calculate

---

[28] The wage rates are from Margo, *Wages and Labor Markets*, table 3A.5.

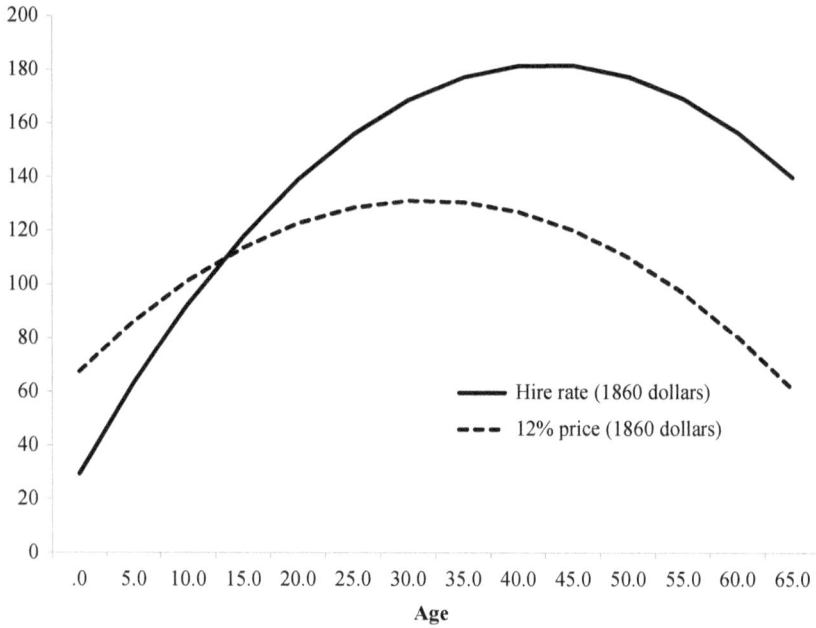

CHART 7. Age-specific hire rates and price index, male slaves, 1850s (1860 dollars). Source: Fogel and Engerman, ICPSR 7421 and 7422 data.

lost wages to slaves alive in 1860, one must account for the differences in hire rates over time.

Calculating Aggregate Losses: Reverse Age the Population and Apply Age-Specific Hire Rates for the Relevant Time Period

Table 2 offers the basic data used to calculate the losses to former slaves from forgone net wages. I obtained the population of slaves in each age group in 1860 from the federal census; each total is roughly half male and half female, as Chart 3 shows. I then "reverse aged" the 1860 population to show what age group these individuals fell into for each prior census year. For example, the 697,498 slaves aged twenty to twenty-nine in 1860 would have been ages ten to nineteen in 1850 and zero to nine in 1840. Note that the number of slaves in each age group for years before 1850 does not represent the entire population of slaves of those ages in that year, but rather only those who lived until at least 1860. The weighted average age in 1860 for slaves

CHART 8. Average slave prices, slave hire rates, and wages, 1811–60 (1860 dollars).
Sources: Tables Bb209–214, Cc1–2, Susan B. Carter, Scott Sigmund Gartner, Michael R. Haines, Alan L. Olmstead, Richard Sutch, and Gavin Wright, eds., *Historical Statistics of the United States, Earliest Times to the Present: Millennial Edition* (New York, 2006); Robert Margo, *Wages and Labor Markets: 1820–1860* (Chicago, 2000), Fogel and Engerman, ICPSR 7422 data.

with known ages was 21.5 years, so I simply assigned this age to the 697 slaves recorded in the 1860 census with unknown age.

Table 2 also reports estimated annual age-specific real (1860 dollars) hire rates for each decade (averaged across males and females). To find these, I started with the hire rates estimated from the actual hiring data.[29] As a check on these figures, I applied the 1850 hire/price ratio by age to the estimated age-specific real sale prices for the given census year.[30] For

---

[29] See note 27 and the appendix for the estimation methodology. I adjust for the differences across region as well.

[30] The hire/price ratios for 1850 are generally smaller than those for earlier census years. I adjusted for price differences across region. Something I could not adequately account for was the possibility that a particular slave moved from one region to another at some point in his or her life. Because prices and hire rates tended to be somewhat higher

Table 2 Base figures for estimating forgone wages to slaves living in 1860.

	1860	1850s	1850	1840s	1840	1830s	1830	1820s	1820
	N	Hire	*N*	Hire	*N*	Hire	*N*	Hire	*N*
<10	1,228,394	78	989,110	43	697,498	55	438,533	45	279,530
10–19	989,110	118	697,498	97	438,533	98	279,530	97	155,509
20–29	697,498	145	438,533	108	279,530	127	155,509	131	90,233
30–39	438,533	160	279,530	120	155,509	141	90,233	145	31,109
40–49	279,530	163	155,509	115	90,233	137	31,109	136	9,943
50–59	155,509	153	90,233	88	31,109	112	9,943	94	3,031
60–69	90,233		31,109		9,943		3,031		1,570
70–79	31,109		9,943		3,031		1,570		
80–89	9,943		3,031		1,570				
90–99	3,031		1,570						
100+	1,570								
unknown	697								

Sources: University of Virginia, Geospatial and Statistical Data Center, http://fisher.lib.virginia.edu/collections/stats/histcensus/index.html; regression results from the appendix; Fogel and Engerman ICPSR 7421 and 7422 data.

example, the first method yields an estimated annual hire rate of $124 (in 1860 dollars) for twenty-five-year-old slaves in the 1840s, but the second generates an estimate of $108. I used the smaller of the two figures to generate the conservative estimates of yearly hire rates reported in table 2.[31]

A numerical example is helpful: Consider a slave fifty years old in 1860. This slave would have generated aggregate benefits to a slave owner roughly equivalent to the market hire rate for the relevant age for the

---

in the Cotton South and because the slave population was more heavily represented in the Cotton South in later years, the figures calculated here may slightly overstate lost wages.

[31] Compare these to the figures for annual hire rates during the 1840s reported in Evans, "The Economics of American Negro Slavery," tables 31–32, 38–39: rates for the Upper South ranged from $60 to $160 and for the Lower South from $72 to $250. The case of *Pryor et al. v. Ryburn*, 16 Ark. 671 (1856), refers to a hire rate of $120 for a prime male slave in 1848, which translates to a rate of $126 in dollars of 1860. The rates I choose are therefore conservative ones.

1810s Hire	1810 N	1800s Hire	1800 N	1790s Hire	1790 N	1780s Hire	1780 N	1770s Hire	1770 N	1760s Hire	1760 N	1750s Hire
43	155,509	36	90,233	12	31,109	20	9,943	10	3,031	10	1,570	10
83	90,233	72	31,109	50	9,943	70	3,031	44	1,570	44		
110	31,109	95	9,943	75	3,031	92	1,570	65				
125	9,943	108	3,031	83	1,570	104						
128	3,031	110	1,570	72								
109	1,570	82										

last forty-five years or so. Table 3 shows that the estimated value of these benefits would have been over $5,000 (in 1860 dollars), even if the real interest rate were zero. At a more reasonable estimate of 1 percent for the real interest rate, the estimated value increases to nearly $6,500 (in 1860 dollars).

To come up with an aggregate number for lost wages for all slaves alive in 1860, I conservatively assume that slaves under age six and over age fifty-nine would have earned nothing.[32] I also recognize that older slaves within an age category would have earned the hire rate pertaining to their age group for most years of the preceding decade, but younger ones mostly would have earned the hire rate associated with the next-younger age group. For example, slaves aged twenty-nine in 1860 would have

[32] The Fogel/Engerman data (ICPSR 7422) include contracts for a sixty-two-year-old hired in 1858 at an annual rate of $140 and a sixty-one-year-old hired in 1857 at an annual rate of $150, for example.

Table 3 Example of lost wages for a slave aged 50 in 1860.

Decade	Forgone hire (1860 dollars) 0% real interest rate	Forgone hire (1860 dollars) 1% real interest rate
1850s	1,630	1,713
1840s	1,200	1,393
1830s	1,270	1,629
1820s	970	1,374
1810s	215	336
Total	5,285	6,446

Source: Table 2
Note: Assume hire rate of 0 for ages lower than 6.

earned wages in the 1850s pertaining to the twenty- to twenty-nine-year-old age category for nine of the years and wages pertaining to the ten- to nineteen-year-old category for one year. A rough estimate of the real wages earned over the previous decade for each age group thus would equal the number of slaves in the age group multiplied by five times the annual wage for that age group plus five times the annual wage for the next-younger age group.

Incorporating the Time Value of Money

A simple aggregation of these sums yields a figure of about $7.9 billion (in 1860 dollars). Although this figure does account for general price-level changes over time, it does not incorporate the time value of money.[33]

Suppose the real interest rate were 1 percent. The aggregate number would increase to about $9.3 billion. At a real interest rate of 3 percent, the

---

[33]The time value of money simply refers to the benefit of having resources in hand earlier rather than later. Interest rates therefore tend to be positive even when inflation is zero. The difference between the nominal, or market, interest rate and (expected) inflation is typically termed the real interest rate.

figure jumps to about $13.6 billion. All of these figures are in 1860 dollars. To put these numbers into perspective, note that U.S. GDP at the time was $4.35 billion and public debt was $64.8 million.[34]

What About Previously Freed Persons and the Timing of Emancipation?

One group not included in this calculation is persons freed before abolition who were still living at the time of abolition. Nor have I addressed the issue of exactly when abolition occurred and why using the 1860 population of slaves is reasonable. Yet including previously manumitted slaves and projecting forward to 1863 or 1865 would not change my figures significantly.

Here is why: According to decennial census records, slaves constituted 88 percent of the "colored" population in 1850 and 89 percent in 1860. Many free blacks in 1860 had been born free or manumitted years earlier; only about 3,000 manumissions occurred in 1860 and about 20,000 throughout the decade of the 1850s.[35] Like slaves emancipated by nationwide abolition, manumitted slaves lost out on their potential hire value. Yet this loss, while real, is minuscule compared to the aggregate losses suffered by those still in bondage when abolition occurred. What is more, the population of "colored" persons enumerated in the census grew very little from 1860 to 1870 (from 4,427,924 to 4,435,562). These figures suggest that using the number of slaves alive in 1860 is a reasonable approximation for the base population of newly freed persons at the time of emancipation.

Relevance of This Work to the Reparations Literature

My calculations of losses to former slaves fits nicely into the literature concerning reparations to black Americans—payments to compensate them for the suffering of their ancestors under slavery and Jim Crow laws. General William Tecumseh Sherman offered the first plan for reparations to former

---

[34]For GDP, see *HSUS*, table Ca9–19; for debt, see table Ea650–661 in the same source.
[35]Evans, "The Economics of American Negro Slavery," p. 226.

slaves shortly after the Civil War ended: his order—soon rescinded—set aside land on the coasts of Georgia and South Carolina for the newly freed.[36] Since 1989, Michigan Representative John Conyers has repeatedly introduced legislation (H.R. 40 in each Congress since 1997) to set up a commission to study reparations proposals. A recent lawsuit filed against several U.S. companies claims that over eight million Africans and their descendants were enslaved from 1619 to 1865, and from 1790 to 1860 the U.S. economy reaped benefits of as much as $40 million in unpaid labor. Unfortunately, the plaintiffs' brief appears to have a typographical error, in that the source for this number cites a figure of $40 billion.[37]

A more rigorously calculated estimate of the loss to slave laborers appears in work by James Marketti. Marketti estimated the losses for the period 1790–1860 to range from $448 to $995 billion in current dollars. By discounting at a rate of 3 percent, these figures translate to $19 to $42 billion in dollars of 1860.[38] Other researchers have calculated larger figures, ranging from $60 to $300 billion in dollars of 1860.[39]

My estimate is considerably less than those reported elsewhere. Why? Recall that I am estimating losses only to those living—and therefore those with unambiguous legal standing—in 1860. By taking the number of slaves enumerated in the census in various years and assuming that the length of

---

[36]Special Field Orders No. 15, Headquarters Military Division of the Mississippi, Jan. 16, 1865, Orders & Circulars, ser. 44, Adjutant General's Office, Record Group 94, National Archives and Records Administration.

[37]*In re: African-American Slave Descendants Litigation* (2006). The defendants in the case are successor businesses to banks, railroads, and insurance companies that allegedly profited from slavery. The source for the number quoted is Tim Wise, "Breaking the Cycle of White Dependency," June 22, 2002, http://www.timwise.org/2001/05/breaking-the-cycle-of-white-dependence-a-modest-call-for-majority-self-help/.

[38]Marketti uses slave prices rather than hire rates to make his calculations. He used different interest rates for the pre- and postwar eras—either 5 or 6 percent prewar and 3 percent postwar. To my knowledge, no one else has explicitly utilized hire rates to calculate lost wages. James Marketti, "Black Equity in the Slave Industry," *Review of Black Political Economy* 1, no. 2 (1972):43–66.

[39]Julian Simon and Larry Neal, "A Calculation of the Black Reparations Bill," *Review of Black Political Economy* 4 (1974):75–86, estimate a loss of $96.3 billion to $9.7 trillion, which yields something like $3 billion to $300 billion in dollars of 1860. Marketti, "Estimated Present Value of Income Diverted during Slavery," has also put forth a number of $4 trillion (in dollars of 1990), and Richard America suggests something between $5 and $10 trillion (presumably in 1999 dollars) in reparations. These figures discounted at 3 percent yield estimated losses in 1860 around $60 to $70 billion.

time between generations is approximately thirty years, I find that roughly 40 percent of all slaves who ever resided in the United States were living in 1860. Does this mean that my figure should be 40 percent of existing estimates? No: 41 percent of the 1860 slave population was under age ten, so abolition meant that these individuals arguably were entitled to the fruits of their labor throughout most of their lifetimes. This suggests that my number should be perhaps one-quarter of the loss sustained by slave laborers throughout the entire antebellum period. Because I deliberately constructed my estimate using conservative assumptions about slave hire rates, my figure of less than $14 billion thus is somewhat smaller than what others might have estimated had they focused solely on slaves alive in 1860. Nevertheless, it is still a staggering number.

Concluding Thoughts

The abolition of slavery in the United States could be cast in terms of a taking, but the direction of the taking is ambiguous. A traditional interpretation of the takings clause of the U.S. Constitution would concentrate on the property loss incurred by former slave owners. But an alternative view would consider slavery itself a taking, with abolition representing the undoing of this illegitimate regime.[40]

The focus of this research has been pecuniary losses. Yet one could argue that much more was lost, particularly by slaves. Wrongful-death and personal-injury lawsuits often include an estimate for hedonic damages, or the lost enjoyment of life, as well as pecuniary losses.[41] A recent practice manual for lawyers suggested that total damages in a personal-injury

---

[40] This is the main argument put forth by Wenger, "Slavery as a Takings Clause Violation."

[41] Adding in an element of damages for the lost "enjoyment of life" was popularized by economist Stan Smith, who first introduced the idea in the case of *Sherrod v. Berry*, 629 F. Supp. 159 (N.D.Ill. 1985); Affm'd, 827 F.2d 195 (7th Cir. 1987); rev'd on other grounds, 856 F.2d 802 (7th Cir. 1988). This method has met with considerable criticism. For a set of opposing views, see O'Hara, "Hedonic Damages for Wrongful Death"; Eric A. Posner and Cass R. Sunstein, "Dollars and Death," *University of Chicago Law Review* 72 (2005):537–98; and W. Kip Viscusi, "The Flawed Hedonic Damages Measure of Compensation for Wrongful Death and Personal Injury," *Journal of Forensic Economics* 20 (2007):113–35.

lawsuit might equal some multiple of economic damages, to compensate plaintiffs for reduced (or eliminated) quality of life.[42] Likewise, total losses to slaves could arguably have equaled some multiple of forgone wages to compensate them for lost freedom.

What about additional losses under a traditional takings argument? Did slave owners lose more than the market value of their property? Antebellum southern masters successfully brought some lawsuits in courts of equity for slaves unlawfully taken or sold, arguing that damages could not fully compensate them.[43] Yet these cases rested on the notion that bonds of love tied masters and slaves, and "no damages can compensate; for there is no standard by which the price of affection can be adjusted, and no scale to graduate the feelings of the heart."[44] Losing slaves due to abolition may have generated anger and frustration at the loss of coercive power, which is a far different sort of loss—one for which American courts would be unlikely to compensate.

One final point: Suppose we adopt the alternative view that slavery itself was a taking. Whom could former slaves have sued for their losses? Those held unlawfully in slavery sued the persons who posed as their masters.[45] Abolition made former slave owners virtually judgment-proof, as many of them lost the bulk of their wealth when they lost their power to own other persons. But casting slavery as a taking suggests that the appropriate defendant is the federal government, which had allowed slavery to thrive lawfully for so many years.[46]

Could the government have afforded the bill? Estimated pecuniary losses to living slaves as of 1860 were at least double the entire GDP of the United States at the time. Suppose, however, that the U.S. government had issued bonds with a face value of around $8 billion, which is

---

[42]Michael Brookshire, Frank Slesnick, John Ward, and George Barrett, *The Plaintiff and Defense Attorney's Guide to Understanding Economic Damages* (Tucson, Ariz., 2007).

[43]For discussion of specific cases, see Jenny Bourne (Wahl), *The Bondsman's Burden: An Economic Analysis of the Common Law of Southern Slavery* (New York, 1998), pp. 45ff.

[44]*William v. Howard*, 3 Murph. 74, 80 (N.C. 1819).

[45]*Hickham v. Hickham*, 46 Mo. App. 496 (Ct. App. 1891), is a case in point.

[46]Wenger, "Slavery as a Takings Clause Violation," pp. 218ff, offers several arguments showing why the federal government helped perpetrate and significantly benefited from slavery.

something it did a half century after the Civil War was over.[47] By extracting in taxes a mere 6 percent of GDP for each of the years from 1860 to 1876, it could have paid off the bonds in full the year before Reconstruction officially ended.[48]

---

[47] Federal debt jumped by nearly $9.5 billion between 1917 and 1918. In 1860 dollars, this translates to about $5.3 billion. Debt figures are reported in table Ea650–661, price indices in table Cc1–2, and GDP in table Ca9–19, *HSUS*.

[48] This would have increased the federal government's share of the economy considerably: federal revenues were only about 1.2 percent of GDP in 1860, with most of those derived from import tariffs. By comparison, federal tax revenue has been between 15 and 20 percent of GDP for the last fifty years in the United States, with the largest single source of revenue being the individual income tax. For a brief review of the numbers, see *HSUS*, tables Ca9–19 (GDP) and Ea584–587 (revenue), and http://www.taxpolicycenter.org/briefing-book/background/numbers/revenue.cfm (current data).

Appendix

Sale regression (dependent variable: sale price).				
Variable	Coefficient	Std. Error	Mean	Std. Dev.
(Constant)	260.65	4.67		
Age	22.85	.31	24.34	16.71
Age squared	−.40	.00	871.77	1,101.80
Dummy: Male	−53.68	5.50	.56	.50
Male*age	13.72	.42	14.16	17.56
Male*age squared	−.18	.01	508.57	931.08
Dummy: Cotton South	183.43	2.66	.623	.485
Dummy: 1770s	−481.74	12.48	.007	.086
Dummy: 1780s	−472.31	9.11	.015	.121
Dummy: 1790s	−477.72	6.36	.034	.182
Dummy: 1800s	−384.80	5.80	.041	.199
Dummy: 1810s	−318.33	4.50	.075	.264
Dummy: 1820s	−340.78	3.97	.105	.306
Dummy: 1830s	−220.64	3.94	.100	.300
Dummy: 1840s	−279.08	2.86	.243	.429
Dummy: 1860s	222.56	4.33	.073	.261
Adjusted R^2	0.612			
N	55,288			

Source: Fogel and Engerman, ICPSR 7421 data.

Hire regression (dependent variable: hire rate in 1860 dollars).

Variable	Coefficient	Std. Error	Mean	Std. Dev.
Constant	68.12	15.93		
Age	3.19	1.14	24.97	14.5
Age squared	−0.05	0.02	833.27	985.48
Dummy: Male	−28.66	19.91	0.64	0.48
Age*male	3.97	1.48	16.92	17.71
Age squared* male	−0.04	0.02	599.13	962
Dummy: Old South	−70.92	6.94	0.81	0.39
Dummy: Year contract	−0.43	7.00	0.8	0.4
Dummy: Before 1810	−42.21	45.5	0.0027	0.05
Dummy: 1810–19	−34.71	10.94	0.0546	0.23
Dummy: 1830–39	−2.96	17.21	0.0219	0.15
Dummy: 1840–49	−20.99	5.55	0.3033	0.46
Dummy: 1860 and later	−18.91	10.66	0.0574	0.23
N	366			
Adjusted R^2	0.515			

Source: Fogel and Engerman, ICPSR 7422 data.
Note: No hire rates for slaves with known age and gender were present for the decade 1820–29.

Matthew Pinsker

Mr. Spielberg Goes to Washington

WHEN FRANK NUGENT, the film critic for the *New York Times*, wrote his glowing review of Frank Capra's *Mr. Smith Goes to Washington* (1939), he observed tartly that the director had gone after "the greatest game of all, the Senate," in a fashion that subjected "the Capitol's bill-collectors to a deal of quizzing and to a scrutiny which is not always tender." Nugent was wise enough, however, to see through Capra's faux cynicism about the institution, commenting that the great director was "a believer in democracy" who had created an American cinematic masterpiece that was "a stirring and even inspiring testament to liberty and freedom."[1]

If such a judgment seems almost trite today, it was not so back then. In the wake of the movie's release in late 1939, many politicos balked angrily at what they considered to be over-the-top depictions of senatorial corruption. Future vice president Alben W. Barkley (D-Ky.) was shocked that a major Hollywood movie could show "the Senate as the biggest aggregation of nincompoops on record!" Future Supreme Court justice and secretary of state James F. Byrnes (D-S.C.) coolly informed the *Christian Science Monitor* that the film portrayed "exactly the kind of picture that dictators of totalitarian governments would like to have their subjects believe exists in a

---

A version of this essay was delivered as a talk at the 2014 U.S. Capitol Historical Society Symposium; sections of this text have also appeared online at the *Unofficial Teacher's Guide to Spielberg's Lincoln*, http://housedivided.dickinson.edu/sites/emancipation/spielberg/.

[1] Frank S. Nugent, "The Screen in Review," *New York Times*, Oct. 20, 1939.

democracy."[2] The controversy even injected an element of drama into a stalled antitrust bill—the Neely anti–block booking bill—which aimed to break up studio-owned movie theater chains. Proponents of the measure started arguing in public soon after the movie's October release that such legislation would make it possible to limit the distribution of an anti-American film like *Mr. Smith*. Capra was appalled. "Can you imagine that?" he exclaimed to a journalist, "With all those things they've got to do down there, with the neutrality bill, and social legislation, with war breaking loose in Europe . . . the whole majesty of the United States Senate has to move against one moving picture. It's amazing!"[3]

When Steven Spielberg released his movie *Lincoln* following the 2012 midterm elections, there were a few such dustups, but nothing like the kind of fierce resistance that Capra had experienced.[4] This was despite the fact that Spielberg was going after what might be called the second "greatest game of all"—the U.S. House of Representatives—with his gritty account of the behind-the-scenes efforts to secure passage of the Thirteenth Amendment. To most critical observers, Spielberg appeared as Nugent had described Capra, an ardent "believer in democracy," despite taking plenty of sharp jabs at Capitol Hill and the American political process. Spielberg's somewhat misnamed movie is really about the moral complexity of the legislative process, with Abraham Lincoln as a not-so-innocent protagonist (Mr. Smith as Great Emancipator) who overcomes a contentious House Chamber full of very Capra-esque characters. Yet *Lincoln* is an even darker movie than *Mr. Smith*, because President Lincoln engages in no gallant, Hollywood-style filibuster to save the day. Instead, according to the film, he manages one of the noblest achievements in American legislative history through implicit bribery and explicit deception.

It is remarkable that more critics have not focused on that darkness at the center of the *Lincoln* movie, especially since it is a film that seems almost

---

[2]Barkley and Byrnes, both quoted in Richard L. Strout, "Congress's Response to 'Mr. Smith Goes to Washington,'" *Christian Science Monitor*, Oct. 17, 1939, http://xroads.virginia.edu/~ma97/halnon/capra/smithrev.html. The Neely bill never became law.

[3]Quoted in Joseph McBridge, *Frank Capra: The Catastrophe of Success* (1992; reprint ed., Jackson, Miss., 2011), p. 422.

[4]For a summary of the critical reaction to the movie, especially among historians, see "Historians React to the 'Lincoln' Movie," *Unofficial Teacher's Guide to Spielberg's Lincoln*, http://housedivided.dickinson.edu/sites/emancipation/2013/02/07/historians-react-to-the-lincoln-movie/.

designed for classroom use. Teachers at the secondary and undergraduate level will be showing clips from *Lincoln* for years to come. For that reason alone, it deserves our toughest scrutiny, especially since almost all of the scenes involving political intrigue and corruption have been thoroughly fictionalized.

A film like Spielberg's *Lincoln* must be considered a work of fiction, even though it is inspired by historical events and adapted from Doris Kearns Goodwin's *Team of Rivals*, a real work of history.[5] The reason the movie itself cannot be filed under "nonfiction" is that the figures involved in the production take significant artistic license in order to create an engaging drama. They invent characters, dialogue, and scenes. They rearrange chronology. They borrow from various types of sources without documenting any of them. They also take big interpretive leaps of faith based more on instinct than on evidence. Yet artists such as scriptwriter Tony Kushner, filmmaker Steven Spielberg, or actors such as Daniel Day-Lewis can appear almost as historians because they go to such great lengths to try to "get it right" by recreating period details. The result, however, is confusing for many audiences—especially for students—who want to know exactly what is real and what is invented. Although this chapter does not claim to establish what really happened with regard to the Thirteenth Amendment, it does highlight the most revealing examples of artistic license within the *Lincoln* film, especially those concerning Lincoln's role in the lobbying effort.

There is no denying that the film opens in the most artistic way possible—a cinematic version of the Lincoln Memorial with Daniel Day-Lewis as President Lincoln seated, not in a marble temple, but rather on a dark wooden platform in the cold, wet Washington Naval Yard. We then overhear the president in conversation with a kind of Greek chorus of fictional soldiers (two black and two white) who gather around him and in the course of their politically charged conversations end up reciting portions of the Gettysburg Address. That ten-sentence speech has long been a sacred national text, but it was not one that Americans were reciting to each other in January 1865. There was not even yet an established single text for the address—the version quoted by the soldiers (the so-called "Bliss Copy," which appears on the wall of the memorial) was not the one Lincoln

---

[5]Doris Kearns Goodwin, *Team of Rivals: The Political Genius of Abraham Lincoln* (New York, 2005).

actually delivered at Gettysburg.[6] The scene is almost totally implausible from a strictly historical perspective, but it does create a memorable and dramatic framework for the movie—especially when you realize that the film does not end with Lincoln's assassination, but rather with a flashback to his Second Inaugural Address, the other text that graces the interior walls of the Lincoln Memorial.

The movie then launches into its main narrative with a dream sequence. In this case, the filmmakers have Abraham Lincoln describe an ominous-looking vision to Mary Lincoln, one that involves him standing alone on the deck of a ship. Yet this eerie dream derives from an account that appeared in the diary of Gideon Welles, who served as Lincoln's secretary of the navy. Welles's entry, dated April 14, 1865 (but written a few days afterward) described the president as telling his cabinet officers on the very day that he was assassinated about a recurring dream in which "he seemed to be in some singular, indescribable vessel, and that he was moving with great rapidity [toward an indefinite shore]." The president claimed to have had this dream before "nearly every great and important event of the War."[7] Tony Kushner's script alters the language of this account somewhat and puts it into an exchange between husband and wife preceding a "revelation" about his intention to fight for passage of an amendment to abolish slavery during the January 1865 lame-duck session of Congress.[8] In this plot-setting scene, Mary Lincoln (Sally Field) appears shocked by such news and argues vociferously against it, saying to her husband:

> No one's loved as much as you, no one's ever been loved so much, by the people, you might do anything now. Don't, don't waste that power on an amendment bill that's sure of defeat.[9]

In reality, however, Lincoln had already announced plans to push for a January vote on the abolition amendment—a measure that almost everyone

---

[6]See Matthew Pinsker, "Lincoln's Gettysburg Addresses," Google Cultural Institute, https://www.google.com/culturalinstitute/exhibit/lincoln-s-gettysburg-addresses/wReow-98.
[7]Diary entry, Apr. 14, 1865, in *The Civil War Diary of Gideon Welles: Lincoln's Secretary of the Navy*, ed. William E. Gienapp and Erica L. Gienapp, (Urbana, Ill., 2014), p. 623.
[8]Tony Kushner, *Lincoln*, p. 8; the final script is available online via the Internet Archive, http://web.archive.org/web/20130120042546/http://www.dreamworkspicturesawards.com/SSPublicationScriptLincoln12.20.2011.pdf.
[9]Ibid., p. 9.

expected to pass eventually. Following his party's landslide November election victories, the president's annual message to Congress in early December 1864 had predicted in public and with great confidence that "the next Congress will pass the measure [abolishing slavery] if this does not." Lincoln then bluntly suggested that since there was "only a question of time as to when the proposed amendment will go to the States," why "may we not agree that the sooner the better?"[10] The tone of this passage is already triumphant. Regardless, the president's plan to push one more time for an abolition amendment in the outgoing Thirty-Eighth Congress was certainly not secret. Yet the movie pretends that his wife and nearly everyone else in the capital was somehow unaware of all this and that many were opposed to it. Here is how artistic license works in Hollywood movies. Filmmakers strive to establish compelling conflicts at the outset of their work so that they can proceed to resolve them with a suspenseful plot that also reveals essential traits of the main characters along the way. That's just Scriptwriting 101. History, of course, is messier.

Even though the movie runs quite long at 150 minutes, time constraints require numerous simplifications of this sort. Consider the sweeping conflations regarding Civil War–era partisanship. There were deep divisions within the Republican Party during the 1860s that have traditionally been identified as a split between Radicals and Conservatives, but those factions were not arguing over abolition in January 1865 as the script repeatedly tries to maintain. Key figures such as Secretary of State William Henry Seward, Republican Party elder statesman Francis Preston Blair Sr., and Radical congressmen including James Ashley and Thaddeus Stevens may have despised each other (as the movie demonstrates), but by that point in the war they were all more or less in agreement that the Constitution had to be amended in order to eradicate the final underpinnings of the peculiar institution. This in itself was a pretty remarkable shift for some of these Republican politicians (Lincoln included) and was not at all apparent at the beginning of the conflict—but it was self-evident by 1865.[11]

---

[10]Annual Message to Congress, Dec. 6, 1864, in *The Collected Works of Abraham Lincoln*, ed. Roy P. Basler, 9 vols. (New Brunswick, N.J., 1953–55), 8:149.

[11]The most sophisticated recent portrayal of Republican divisions over abolition and Reconstruction comes from James Oakes, *Freedom National: The Destruction of Slavery in the United States, 1861–1865* (New York, 2013).

Yet the film leaves a much different impression. There's no mention whatsoever of the president's aggressive December 1864 message. Instead, a determined Lincoln has to endure a series of mini-lectures and complaints from his stunned Republican colleagues during the first third of the film, once he starts "revealing" to them his plans for the abolition amendment. A skeptical Secretary Seward (David Strathairn) asks Lincoln pointedly, "since when has our party unanimously supported anything?" Yet the correct answer to that question would have been the last time the abolition amendment had appeared in the House (June 1864), when the only Republican to vote against it was Rep. James Ashley, the sponsor, who did so on technical grounds so that he could bring it back later for reconsideration.[12] The cabinet did once argue over the timing and merits of presidential emancipation, as the movie suggests in one very teachable scene, but that was in the summer of 1862, not in early 1865. And Montgomery Blair may well have been pushed out of the president's cabinet in September 1864 as part of a deal with radicals, but Preston Blair (Hal Holbrook) surely never told Lincoln, as he does in the film, "Our Republicans ain't abolitionist." By that point in the war, almost everybody in the Republican Party was an abolitionist. Both Maryland and Missouri (Border States and key Blair strongholds) had already abolished slavery on their own initiative by early 1865. Yet Tony Kushner, the scriptwriter, has Blair sound almost like a Copperhead as he admonishes a beleaguered Lincoln: "We can't tell our people they can vote yes on abolishing slavery unless at the same time we can tell 'em that you're seeking a negotiated peace."[13] Not only is that a false note coming from someone like Blair, but also it's not even entirely clear that the elderly and perpetually controversial figure had any "people" left in the House now that his other son Frank (Francis Preston Blair Jr.), a former congressman, was back in the Union army. All of the so-called "Conservative Republicans" with speaking parts in this film and identified as being under Blair's sway are fictional characters.

The conservative element of the Republican Party was not an obstacle to passage of the amendment. Rather, the challenge for the amendment's backers was to win over Democratic votes, presumably lame-duck ones from

---

[12]Kushner, *Lincoln*, p. 12. On this point, see Michael Vorenberg, *Final Freedom: The Civil War, the Abolition of Slavery, and the Thirteenth Amendment* (Cambridge, 2001), pp. 138–39.

[13]Kushner, *Lincoln*, p. 22.

the Lower North, as well as a few stray Border State Unionists who had never really identified as Republicans. This was the great concern in January 1865, and one that fully engaged Lincoln. He personally lobbied Border State congressmen such as James Rollins from Missouri, who had originally come to Washington in 1861 as a Constitutional Unionist. Rollins had been reelected in 1862, defeating a Radical Republican, but then had declined to run for reelection in 1864. The Missouri Unionist did not call himself a Republican during the war and had typically voted against Republican antislavery measures, including the abolition amendment in June 1864, but now, under the changing political circumstances, he appeared open to casting his ballot with the forces of history.[14] The story of Lincoln's subsequent lobbying effort with Rollins is well known to historians, but strangely omitted from this movie. Instead, the filmmakers create a fictional congressman from Missouri named Josiah "Beanpole" Burton, whom they explicitly label in the script as an "undecided" Republican.[15] They then have some of his fictional constituents, a memorable couple named Mr. and Mrs. Jolly, visit the White House just as Lincoln and Seward are arguing about whether passage of the amendment was even possible during the lame-duck session. Skeptical of what he considers to be Lincoln's unrealistic plans, the Seward character then artfully guides the Jollys through a conversation that exposes their latent racism, leaving viewers to appreciate just how daunting the prospect of black equality really was in 1865. It's a compelling scene, perhaps necessary to help educate a modern moviegoing audience about the grim reality of nineteenth-century racial views, but it is the kind of fiction that does some real damage to the complexity of the historical record.

Still, by far the worst damage to the historical record comes from the film's humorous but deeply cynical depiction of the lobbying effort orchestrated in the movie by an amusing trio of corrupt political hired guns. Robert Latham (John Hawkes), Richard Schell (Tim Blake Nelson), and William N. Bilbo (James Spader) were real nineteenth-century political figures authorized by Secretary of State Seward in the winter of 1864–65 to help promote passage of what ultimately became the Thirteenth Amendment. Historians typically describe these men (and sometimes a few others)

---

[14]On Rollins, see Leonard L. Richards, *Who Freed the Slaves? The Fight over the Thirteenth Amendment* (Chicago, 2015), p. 151. On the Rollins–Lincoln relationship, see David Herbert Donald, *Lincoln* (New York, 1995), p. 554.

[15]Kushner, *Lincoln*, p. 17.

as the "Seward Lobby," but they disagree over exactly how they lobbied for the amendment and to what degree President Lincoln was aware of their activities. Still, there's no doubt that Latham and Schell were leading financiers and old friends of Seward's and that Bilbo was a prominent southern attorney and businessman who had switched sides during the war. Bilbo was mysterious but memorable, "known," according to historians John and LaWanda Cox, "for his elaborate waistcoats, his long sideburns, and his elegant manners."[16] Bilbo was also important enough that he had met with President Lincoln just after the 1864 election and then corresponded with him later (when he got arrested, no less, for being an alleged spy). While visiting the nation's capital that winter, he roomed with a Democratic congressman. When in Manhattan, he stayed in the city's finest hotel. Yet the movie introduces these characters as seedy outsiders, completely unknown to the president and forced to rent rooms in a "squirrel-infested attic," as Bilbo (James Spader) puts it so memorably, because Seward was keeping them on such a tight retainer.[17] Nothing could have been further from the truth. These were well-connected men of affairs who had volunteered their services in the final effort to secure a constitutional revolution. After passage of the Thirteenth Amendment, Latham waxed indignant when the secretary of state tried to have the men reimbursed for some of their expenditures. He wrote to Seward's son Frederick, "A Gentleman called to have me give an acct of expenses. *Which amt to nothing* [emphasis added]," before generously offering that, "At any time that I can be of service to the Hon Sec of State or yourself I will do all I can but at my own expence."[18]

The movie portrays the men in much different light—as very rough figures (Bilbo/Spader even says directly to President Lincoln at one point, "Well, I'll be fucked") who spread bribes easily. In fairness, however, this type of characterization does not just come out of thin air. Over the years, various historians have suggested that some kind of corruption was probably behind the amendment. Doris Kearns Goodwin did not write about the Seward Lobby in *Team of Rivals*, but she did claim in her work that

---

[16]LaWanda Cox and John H. Cox, *Politics, Principle, and Prejudice, 1865–66: Dilemma of Reconstruction America* (New York, 1963), p. 6. Bilbo's letter to Lincoln, thanking him for help after his arrest in New York, was not featured in the movie, but is available online: William N. Bilbo to Abraham Lincoln, Jan. 26, 1865, Abraham Lincoln Papers at the Library of Congress, http://memory.loc.gov/mss/mal/mal1/402/4026800/001.jpg.

[17]Kushner, *Lincoln*, p. 33.

[18]Cox and Cox, *Politics, Principle, and Prejudice*, p. 24.

Lincoln had made it perfectly "clear to his emissaries" that they could offer a range of "plum assignments, pardons, campaign contributions, and government jobs" for any Democratic members who would switch their votes.[19] The only specific example, however, that Goodwin identifies for this type of quid pro quo corruption was Moses Odell, a New York Democrat, who became the naval officer for the port of New York soon after the war. Odell (not mentioned in the movie) did vote in favor of the amendment in January 1865, but it was surely not because of any last-minute patronage promise. He had also voted for the abolition measure back in June 1864. That was one reason why he was a lame duck. Local Democrats had dumped him for repeatedly breaking ranks, especially over the all-important slavery question. More important for his job-seeking prospects, however, was the fact that he had been the only House Democrat who had served on the Joint Committee on the Conduct of the War. In that position, he had proven to be quite an ardent reformer, often willing to criticize Democratic generals, as well as someone who had become "warm personal friends" with then fellow committee member Sen. Andrew Johnson (D-Tenn.), the president who eventually appointed him to the New York post in late 1865.[20]

The scholars who have focused most directly on corruption in the antislavery lobbying effort, such as the Coxes or Michael Vorenberg, have been far more cautious about drawing conclusions from the limited, mostly recollected evidence that remains.[21] In truth, there are just a few secondhand, often decades-old, claims about shady patronage offers—none of which can be corroborated with contemporary evidence. The only notable direct testimony for corruption comes from a letter in Seward's papers, written by Robert Latham. At one point, in early January, Latham wrote, "Money will certainly do it, if patriotism fails."[22] It's a great line—one that really should have been in the movie—but the context of the letter suggests that Latham was probably joking.

---

[19]Goodwin, *Team of Rivals*, p. 687.

[20]Leonard L. Richards describes Odell's politics succinctly in *Who Freed the Slaves?*; see pages 180–82. For a good description of Odell's connections to Andrew Johnson, see *New York Times*, "Our Federal Relations; Changes in the Government Blue Book," Sept. 1, 1865. Johnson named Odell a naval officer with a recess appointment in the summer of 1865, but the former congressman did not last long in the job. He suffered from throat cancer and died in June 1866.

[21]Cox and Cox, *Politics, Principle, and Prejudice*, p. 28; Vorenberg, *Final Freedom*, p. 204.

[22]Cox and Cox, *Politics, Principle, and Prejudice*, p. 17.

Every lobbying scene in the film involves fictional congressmen and purely invented interactions. None of it is real, not even recollected reality. The best example of this imaginary corruption concerns Rep. Clay Hawkins of Ohio (Walton Goggins), who Bilbo (Spader) initially switches over to favor the amendment with the promise of a postmastership in Millersburg, Ohio, following some memorably boozy hunting outings. The movie has President Lincoln himself commenting on this news by remarking, "He's selling himself cheap, ain't he?"[23] That line, in particular, seems unwarranted by the historical record. There was a single lame-duck Democratic congressman from Ohio who switched his vote in favor of the antislavery amendment in January 1865, but his name was Wells A. Hutchins and he did not receive any postwar patronage appointment in the federal government. Nor was he much recognizable in the character of Clay Hawkins. In real life, Hutchins was a reasonably tough, independent-minded Democrat who had voted to support the abolition of slavery in the District of Columbia in 1862 and who had backed the Lincoln administration on several controversial issues during the war, including the suspension of habeas corpus and other civil liberties—an issue that was especially unpopular among Ohio Democrats.[24] Understanding this background helps explain why he was a lame duck in 1865 and why he was such a natural target for supporting the amendment. It had nothing to do with hunting, drinking, or patronage.

There's also no significant evidence connecting the Seward lobbyists to Hutchins or any Democrats outside the Mid-Atlantic region. According to LaWanda and John Cox, the lobbyists, especially Bilbo, spent most of their time in New York (not Washington), generally attempting to persuade influential Democratic newspapers (such as the *New York World*) and the state's Democratic governor (Horatio Seymour) to send signals that would allow wavering lame-duck Democrats in the region to feel more confident about switching their votes.[25] In his more recent work on this subject, historian Leonard Richards agrees that the "main task" of the Seward Lobby "was to get support of the six New Yorkers" on Congressman Ashley's list of

---

[23]Kushner, *Lincoln*, p. 47.
[24]For a good, short profile of Hutchins, a relatively obscure nineteenth-century congressman, see Nelson Wiley Evans and Emmons B. Stivers, *A History of Adams County, Ohio* (West Union, Ohio, 1900), pp. 314–16 (via Google Books).
[25]Cox and Cox, *Politics, Principle, and Prejudice*, pp. 19–25.

persuadable Democratic lame ducks. Yet Richards is not even convinced they were pivotal in that limited effort.[26]

That is why perhaps the most telling example of artistic license in the whole film involves an amusing race between Bilbo (Spader) and White House aide John Hay (Joseph Cross) during the day of the final House vote on January 31, 1865. The movie has the two figures running desperately to get Lincoln's response to some damning reports of impending peace talks—a leak which the script claims would threaten to jeopardize the entire lobbying effort. The younger Hay beats out the noticeably winded Bilbo, and then President Lincoln proceeds to draft an evasive reply that allows the final roll call to proceed and victory to be achieved. It is a powerful climax with political machinations and social justice converging in ways that illustrate the film's major insight about Lincoln—that he understood how to bend a flawed, messy democratic process toward moral consequences. However, in real life, Bilbo was in New York at the time of the vote. There was an evasive message from the president, but certainly no footrace from the Capitol and no significant presence in Washington at all by those Seward lobbyists during the final fight to win House passage of the amendment. It turns out this dramatic moment is just another one of those fabled Hollywood chase scenes.

Another type of film tradition seems to lurk behind much of the *Lincoln* movie's approach to the Radical Republicans and their ostensible leader, Thaddeus Stevens (R-Pa.). The script describes the setting in Stevens's Capitol Hill office as "redolent of politics, ideology (a bust of Robespierre, a print of Tom Paine), long occupancy and hard work."[27] Such characterizations would strike most historians as heavy-handed and utterly out of date. Older generations of scholars sometimes referred to the Radicals as "Jacobins," but in recent years historians of the period have been more attentive to the complexities of wartime partisanship. That scene in the office also establishes Thaddeus Stevens as the central radical figure organizing the amendment's passage, even more so than the measure's somewhat hapless sponsor, James Ashley. This is not how most historians have characterized their respective roles. As chairman of the House Committee

---

[26]Richards, *Who Freed the Slaves?* p. 210. According to Richards, the Seward Lobby should really be identified as Bilbo, Emanuel B. Hart, Latham, and George O. Jones.

[27]Kushner, *Lincoln*, p. 30.

on Ways and Means, Stevens was undoubtedly an important figure, but probably not the central one in securing passage of the Thirteenth Amendment. The chairman had only four index entries in Doris Kearns Goodwin's *Team of Rivals* (2005), a nearly 800-page book from which the screenplay was adapted. Stevens plays a somewhat larger role in Michael Vorenberg's more compact *Final Freedom* (2001), with seven index entries, but even there he is clearly superseded by other figures such as Ashley and Senator Lyman Trumbull (R-Ill.), who is not even mentioned in the film. The latest and most comprehensive study of wartime abolition policies—James Oakes's *Freedom National* (2012)—contains a mere six index entries for Stevens.

By contrast, Stevens (Tommy Lee Jones) has about forty-five speaking parts in the Spielberg film, second only to Abraham Lincoln. He looms large as a counterweight to the president—Lincoln's near opposite in both style and policy. Their confrontation in the White House kitchen following a reception upstairs organized by Mary Lincoln—and about exactly halfway through the script—proves to be one of the movie's most gripping scenes. Yet in that revealing encounter, Kushner seems to be investing many older and quite hostile ideas about Stevens into the film. The scriptwriter contrasts Lincoln's calculated, pragmatic approach with Stevens's far more rigid, ideological worldview. Nor is he subtle about where his sympathies lie. He actually has Stevens (Jones) saying at one point, in defense of his sweeping plans for revolutionizing the South, "Ah, shit on the people and what they want and what they are ready for! I don't give a goddamn about the people and what they want! This is the face of someone who has fought long and hard for the good of the people without caring much for any of 'em."[28] Such lines (minus the cursing) would be perfectly at home within the captions of D. W. Griffith's groundbreaking and controversial silent film *Birth of a Nation* (1915). Griffith's film depicted Reconstruction as an utter failure, in part because of the unyielding attitudes of radicals like Austin Stoneman (the character based on Stevens). In the kitchen debate between Lincoln and Stevens, Kushner essentially embraces this view. He has Lincoln commenting drily on Stevens's outburst about the "people" by calling it, "the untempered version of Reconstruction," and "not exactly" what he intends. Nor does that comment appear to have been an accident. Kushner

---

[28]Ibid., p. 59.

pointedly informed one interviewer, after the movie's release, "The abuse of the South after they were defeated was a catastrophe, and helped lead to just unimaginable, untellable human suffering."[29]

Nonetheless, Spielberg's *Lincoln* is no Lost Cause film. Instead, the few Reconstruction-inspired stereotypes that might lurk within the script come across in the actual film more as accommodations to time constraints than as a result of any concerted political agenda. Stevens is "untempered" because such views are just easier to establish than more complicated realities. He is the boss of both radical congressman and senators, because it would be too difficult to flesh out characters like Benjamin "Bluff" Wade, identified in the script as "formidable Senator BLUFF WADE (R-MA), who's never smiled."[30] Old Bluff provides some passing comic relief in the film, grousing with Stevens in the chairman's office and then grimacing at Mrs. Lincoln during the White House reception, but otherwise the powerful radical from Ohio (not Massachusetts, his native state) gets no serious attention for his ambitious alternative to the abolition amendment, the so-called Wade-Davis bill, which Lincoln had pocket-vetoed the previous summer. Curiously, there is no Congressman Henry Winter Davis in the film either. Instead, the filmmakers present a fictional character named Asa Vintner Litton (Stephen Spinella), described in the script as a lame-duck Radical Republican from Maryland. In the film, Litton appears as the embodiment of pure radicalism and believes more deeply in Ashley's amendment than anybody else—even in some ways more than Ashley himself—calling it "abolition's best legal prayer."[31] Yet Henry Winter Davis, a radical lame duck from Maryland, was much more ambivalent about the amendment. He had missed the June 1864 vote (intentionally, according to historian Michael Vorenberg) because he considered his omnibus reconstruction plan preferable to the separate measures for abolition and reconstruction that had been introduced by Ashley at the end of the first session and were now being debated again in January 1865. Ultimately, Davis voted for the amendment in January, but the quirky and utterly fictional combination of

---

[29]"Kushner's 'Lincoln' Is Strange, but Also Savvy," NPR, Nov. 15, 2012, http://www.npr.org/2012/11/15/165146361/kushners-lincoln-is-strange-but-also-savvy.

[30]Kushner, *Lincoln*, p. 30.

[31]Ibid., p. 31.

Bluff Wade and Asa Linton offers none of these nuances of the historical record.[32]

There were more than time constraints, however, involved in the film's simplistic explanation of how Lincoln finally won Stevens over to the more tempered approach to abolition. According to the movie, about two weeks after the White House reception, Stevens (Jones) finally decided to restrain himself and ended up endorsing a limited approach to civil rights, at least while the outcome of the amendment vote was in jeopardy. He says repeatedly through gritted teeth, in the face of fierce race-baiting from Copperhead leader Fernando Wood, "I don't hold with equality in all things only with equality before the law and nothing more." This concession to pragmatism prompts Mary Lincoln (Field) in the House gallery to remark to her black dressmaker, Elizabeth Keckley (Gloria Reuben), "Who'd ever guessed that old nightmare capable of such control?" To this, Keckley excuses herself angrily and leaves with tears welling in her eyes.[33] It's a compelling scene, but one full of artistic license. The excerpts from the House debates are not real quotations from the *Congressional Globe*. They appear instead to be a creative collage of materials pulled together by Tony Kushner from a variety of secondary sources. Michael Vorenberg, for example, quotes Stevens earlier in that month claiming that he "never held to that doctrine of negro equality . . . not equality in all things—simply before the laws, nothing else." Yet that remark was made on January 5, 1865—ten days before the kitchen scene. And, in fact, Stevens and other radicals had made similar statements in the past. Nor is there any evidence that Mary Lincoln ever attended those House debates. Instead, what the filmmakers have done by rearranging events and inventing selected details is to attribute what looks like Stevens's newfound pragmatism to Lincoln's timely intervention. That's not historical fact, but it is critical to the plot.

According to the movie's narrative, Friday, January 27, 1865, was an action-packed and pivotal day. It was the day of Thaddeus Stevens's surprisingly controlled performance in the House. It was a day marked by Abraham Lincoln's bitter argument with his oldest son and then his subsequent

---

[32]For a careful analysis of Davis's complicated views on the abolition amendment, see Vorenberg, *Final Freedom*, p. 129.

[33]Kushner, *Lincoln*, pp. 78–79.

clash with his wife Mary after he revealed that he had finally decided to allow their eldest son Robert to join the Union army. That decision then leads Mary Lincoln, after her bitter outburst, to suddenly change her mind about the abolition amendment. She informs her husband while they are attending the theater that night that if the amendment will truly help end the war, then she wants him to do whatever it takes to make it happen. Upon returning to the White House from that very theater outing, Lincoln also has a timely encounter with one of the few black characters in the film, dressmaker Keckley, who also urges the president to provide greater leadership in the fight for the antislavery amendment. All of these "events" are fictional, but they prove essential for explaining the film's point of view—namely, that Lincoln interjected himself at the end of the battle for the constitutional amendment in a way that proved decisive.

The next several scenes show Lincoln in urgent action. He meets for the first time with the Seward lobbyists and helps plot their final, hardball strategy. He cajoles support for the amendment by himself and with Secretary Seward. Then finally, on the night of Sunday, January 29, 1865, he presides over an intense strategy session in the White House with Rep. James Ashley, Preston and Montgomery Blair, Secretary of State Seward, and aides John Nicolay and John Hay. This is one of the key scenes featured in the movie's trailer, showing an angry, forceful Lincoln demanding action by shouting, "Now, now, now!" and memorably declaring, "I am the President of the United States, *clothed in immense power!*"[34]

Ironically, this un-Lincolnian-sounding statement is one of the few quotations in the movie that has roots in a real primary source. Rep. John B. Alley (R-Mass.) claimed more than twenty years after the fact that he had heard from some unnamed person that during the battle for the amendment the president had called into his office a pair of unidentified congressmen in order to tell them that only two more votes were needed for passage and that they "must be procured." Then Alley's recollection provided a lengthy verbatim quotation of eighty-six words, which he attributed to Lincoln, and which culminated with the ringing phrase, "I am President of the United States, clothed with immense power" (note that the script silently changes "clothed with" to "clothed in"—a more fitting usage). Yet this quotation cannot be taken seriously. Alley was recalling events from two decades past

---

[34]Ibid., p. 99.

that he had apparently heard about second- or even thirdhand. There are no names, no dates, and the only specific detail—two votes short of the required two-thirds majority—seems suspiciously like the final vote tally.[35] Regardless, nobody can be trusted to remember verbatim quotations of such length. Yet Doris Kearns Goodwin quotes the entire passage in her book *Team of Rivals*, and it appears it was from this account that Kushner got the raw material for his script, which he then embroidered by placing it at the very end of the lobbying effort and in a meeting with several of the movie's principal characters, not simply two unnamed congressmen.[36]

The vote for what ultimately became the Thirteenth Amendment to the U.S. Constitution did occur on January 31, 1865, and the *Lincoln* filmmakers work diligently to recreate that moment in its full historical grandeur. But they also employ here, as elsewhere, various types of artistic license. None of the floor exchanges from the movie actually match with the official accounts in the *Congressional Globe*. Instead, the movie takes as its dramatic centerpiece the behind-the-scenes story of President Lincoln's evasive reply about impending peace talks—a minor deception or "lawyer's dodge" as the script labels it—but one that helps smooth the way toward final passage. This was a real story, but one that comes mostly from a recollection made shortly after the war by Rep. Ashley.[37] According to Ashley, prior to the final vote, he had sent Lincoln a dire warning that rumors of peace talks were interfering with the likelihood of their success. He wrote:

> Dear Sir, The report is in circulation in the House that Peace Commissioners are on their way or are in the city, and is being used against us. If it is

---

[35]John B. Alley in Allen Thorndike Rice, ed., *Reminiscences of Abraham Lincoln by Distinguished Men of His Time* (New York, 1886), p. 586. Michael Vorenberg has a good dissection of this shaky recollection in *Final Freedom*, p. 198.

[36]Goodwin, *Team of Rivals*, p. 687; Kushner, *Lincoln*, pp. 97–99.

[37]Kushner, *Lincoln*, p. 104. James M. Ashley to William H. Herndon, Nov. 23, 1866, in Douglas L. Wilson and Rodney O. Davis, eds., *Herndon's Informants: Letters, Interviews, and Statements about Abraham Lincoln* (Urbana, Ill., 1998), pp. 413–14. Ashley included a copy of his correspondence with Lincoln in his message to Herndon, claiming John G. Nicolay had delivered it. However, Elizabeth Peabody, a noted educator from Massachusetts, visited the White House in early February 1865 and heard a slightly different version of the story from President Lincoln, who told her about the notes after she complimented him on the passage of the amendment. See Elizabeth Peabody to Horace Mann Jr. [February 1865], in Arlin Turner, "Elizabeth Peabody Visits Lincoln, February 1865," *New England Quarterly* 48 (March 1975):119–20.

true, I fear we shall loose [*sic*] the bill. Please authorize me to contradict it, if not true. Respectfully, J. M. Ashley.

This was a reference to Confederate envoys who were at that moment on their way to Hampton Roads, Virginia, where in a few days they would have an unprecedented meeting with President Lincoln. On the reverse side of Ashley's note, Lincoln decided to acknowledge none of this, but instead wrote:

> So far as I know, there are no peace Commissioners in the City, or likely to be in it. Jan. 31, 1865. A. Lincoln

The filmmakers present this exchange in the most dramatic fashion possible, having Democratic leader George Pendleton (D-Ohio) disrupt the morning's proceedings, allegedly waving "affidavits from loyal citizens" confirming the existence of secret peace talks. This creates some considerable chaos on the floor of the House that leads fictional "conservative" Republican Aaron Haddam to indicate (after receiving a critical nod from Preston Blair, perched conveniently in the gallery) that the "conservative faction of border and western Republicans" could not support the amendment "if a peace offer is being held hostage to its success."[38] What follows is that mad footrace from the Capitol to the White House described earlier, the one that involved Lincoln's aides and the Seward lobbyists, who have now somehow magically appeared from their hotel rooms in New York City.

At the White House, the drama only intensifies as John Hay, the president's young assistant private secretary, heatedly warns him against "making false representation" to Congress. Lincoln, however, crafts his deceptive answer and hands the note to Bilbo (Spader), the seasoned lobbyist, ignoring the warnings from Hay about this "impeachable" action. Bilbo subsequently delivers the message to Rep. Ashley, who reads it with a flourish to the entire House. There is no record of any of this in the official proceedings, nor does it match with Ashley's postwar description of how he shared the note with his colleagues. Bilbo was not even in Washington at the time, and there was almost certainly no footrace. Nor does any contemporary account have Preston Blair in the gallery giving directions to conservative congressmen. Aaron Haddam is

---

[38]Kushner, *Lincoln*, p. 101.

a fictional character, listed as a Republican from Kentucky, with no obvious historical counterpart. All of these details are included in the film merely for dramatic effect.

Yet these details matter, because the film asserts throughout that peace and abolition were two aspirations that appeared to be in utter collision to almost everybody at that time except Lincoln. At one point, Seward (Strathairn) actually tells the president, "It's either the amendment or this Confederate peace, you cannot have both."[39] That is arguably the central premise of the movie, and helps explain why the now-obscure February 3, 1865, encounter with Confederate envoys Alexander Stephens, John A. Campbell, and Robert M. T. Hunter at Hampton Roads plays such an unexpectedly large role in the narrative. That encounter was a real event—the only time in the war that Lincoln and Secretary Seward met with Confederate politicians to discuss the possibility of ending the conflict. The five men sat together for a couple of hours on board the steamboat *River Queen* in Union-controlled waters near Fortress Monroe. Nothing came of their meeting, however, and the war itself ended in a matter of weeks anyway, following Confederate army surrenders in the field. Moreover, no transcript exists for the Hampton Roads conversations, but former Confederate Vice President Alexander Stephens famously wrote about the episode in his postwar reminiscences. Stephens made some pretty wild claims about Lincoln's alleged concessions that seem totally out of character for the president. Partly for this reason, many Civil War historians dismiss the Hampton Roads talks as little more than a sideshow—one of several improbable and failed efforts undertaken in the last year of the war to end the conflict. These varied efforts appear so improbable in retrospect because both Jefferson Davis and Abraham Lincoln had become implacable in their positions by that point. Lincoln had clearly established his preconditions for peace from July 18, 1864, forward—an end to the rebellion, the restoration of the union, and the abandonment of slavery. Those three conditions never changed in the final year of the conflict, making true peace talks impossible. Yet other historians have been more willing to take the Hampton Roads conference seriously. Doris Kearns Goodwin takes the conference quite seriously in *Team of Rivals* (2005), which probably helps explain its importance in the

---

[39]Ibid., p. 49.

movie. The film, however, takes liberties with the narrative of this final peace effort that Goodwin does not.[40]

The movie has Lincoln meeting with Preston Blair and his children at the Blair House in early January, reluctantly agreeing to authorize the elder Blair to undertake a secret trip to Richmond in exchange for the family's support for the antislavery amendment. This January deal is what essentially results in the February meeting at Hampton Roads. In reality, Blair and Lincoln had met alone at the White House in December to discuss the proposed journey. At that time, Lincoln authorized a pass for Blair to travel into enemy lines, yet it's not at all clear what the two men agreed on in terms of peace talks. What we do know is that the elder statesman began his journey on January 3, 1865, arriving in Richmond by January 12, and that once in front of Davis, he proceeded to outline a wild scheme to end hostilities by initiating a joint expedition of former Confederate and Union troops into Mexico in order to remove the French occupation and restore the Monroe Doctrine. This was not any kind of plan ever endorsed by President Lincoln. Davis also rejected most of Blair's ideas outright, but he did agree to try to open talks for ending hostilities between what he termed the "two countries." Blair returned to Washington on January 16 and met with Lincoln on January 18, 1865. The president agreed merely that the administration would receive envoys willing to secure peace for "our one common country." Three days later, Blair then brought this message back to Richmond. Davis subsequently met with Alexander Stephens on January 27 and appointed him and former Supreme Court Justice Campbell and Senator Hunter as his personal envoys. Some historians consider this a pretty good sign that Davis wasn't serious himself about these potential talks, since all three men had become highly critical of his leadership. It appeared instead that he was trying to show up his critics by demonstrating once and for all

---

[40]For a good representation of how most historians dismiss the Hampton Roads peace talks, see James M. McPherson, *Battle Cry of Freedom: The Civil War Era* (New York, 1988), pp. 812–14. Goodwin spends more space on Hampton Roads than on the actual fight for the amendment, but neither gets more than a handful of pages; see *Team of Rivals*, pp. 690–96. A more thorough revisionist account of the failed peace talks, which argues for their importance, comes from William C. Harris, "The Hampton Roads Peace Conference: A Final Test of Lincoln's Presidential Leadership," *Journal of the Abraham Lincoln Association* 21 (Winter 2000):30–61. See also James B. Conroy, *Our One Common Country: Abraham Lincoln and the Hampton Roads Peace Conference of 1865* (Guilford, Conn., 2014).

that they would come back with nothing from the unyielding Union leader. Regardless of the motives of the respective presidents, however, the Confederate envoys traveled toward Union lines on January 29 and met with General Grant on January 30, before they eventually spent the morning of February 3 with Lincoln and Seward.[41]

The movie accelerates and rearranges this timeline pretty ruthlessly. It ignores the fact that Blair made two trips to Richmond that occupied most of the month of January, and instead depicts him reporting back to Lincoln on or about January 10, 1865, with news that Davis had already appointed his three peace commissioners. Lincoln then agrees to proceed with the talks if Blair (Holbrook) will lobby for his antislavery amendment. Blair objects to the "horsetrading," but accepts the condition. The next day, Seward (Strathairn) reveals to Lincoln that he has found out about this deal with Blair and that he resents it bitterly. That's when he confronts Lincoln with the stark choice: abolition or peace.[42] Yet once again, this type of simplistic contrast is only made evident to the movie audience by the rearranging and omitting of a host of details.

The movie also ducks the biggest historical controversy over Stephens's postwar account of Hampton Roads—one that definitely undermines a key element of the Spielberg message. According to the former Confederate vice president, Lincoln offered to allow Southern states to reenter the union by ratifying the Thirteenth Amendment "prospectively," suggesting that they could take up to five more years to put it into effect.[43] Stephens also claimed that Lincoln proposed Union payments of up to $400 million for the South to abandon slavery. Campbell and Hunter also asserted after the war that Lincoln had offered at least some kind of compensation in their talks on February 3. There is no corroboration for Stephens's outlandish claim about prospective ratification (which would be utterly unconstitutional), but there is contemporary evidence that Lincoln did consider in effect paying the Southern states to end the war and abandon slavery. He actually drafted such a proposal and presented it to his cabinet on February 5, 1865; the cabinet unanimously opposed it, and Lincoln then dropped the

---

[41]Harris provides the best chronology of the Blair role in his article, "The Hampton Roads Peace Conference."

[42]Kushner, *Lincoln*, pp. 41–49.

[43]Alexander H. Stephens, *A Constitutional View of the Late War between the States*, 2 vols. (Philadelphia, 1870), 2:614.

plan. Whether or not he was serious remains an open question. But it is revealing that this idea does not appear in the *Lincoln* movie at all. Doris Kearns Goodwin addresses it in *Team of Rivals*, but here is a good illustration of the difference between works of history and historical fiction. The former are almost always more complicated, and, in some ways, less satisfying.[44]

This insight also helps explain the matter of the final roll call vote on January 31, 1865. It was an unusual affair by any account. The House galleries were crowded, anticipation was high, and the celebration afterward was unprecedented. Newspapers and magazines all took note of the revolutionary nature of the moment. Even the *Congressional Globe* invested this particular roll call with special drama, recording, as it rarely did, outbursts of "considerable applause" when certain lame-duck Democratic members, such as Rep. James English (D-Conn.), voted "aye" for the amendment.[45] Yet the *Lincoln* movie ignores this fact. Instead, two fictional congressmen from Connecticut cast the very first movie votes on the amendment—both nays. This was a mistake on multiple levels. Nineteenth-century House roll-call votes proceeded in alphabetical order by congressman (not by state), and the entire four-man Connecticut delegation voted in favor of abolition. Such discrepancies might seem trivial, but modern-day Connecticut congressman Joe Courtney was enraged enough to demand a public apology from Steven Spielberg and to request a correction for the DVD edition of the movie. *New York Times* columnist Maureen Dowd then sided with the congressman with a tough op-ed headlined "The Oscar for Best Fabrication."[46] More important, this flap played out right in the middle of Academy Award season, and while it lacked the intensity of the original backlash against Capra's *Mr. Smith*, it may well have impacted the

---

[44]For the possibility of compensation, see ibid., 2:617; Draft Resolution, Feb. 5, 1865, in Basler, ed., *Collected Works*, 8:260–61; Goodwin, *Team of Rivals*, pp. 694–96. In his article "The Hampton Roads Peace Conference," William C. Harris carefully analyzes the other lesser-known recollected accounts of the meeting from Campbell and Hunter. Neither Lincoln nor Seward produced an account of the conversations.

[45]*Congressional Globe*, 38th Cong., 2d sess., Jan. 31, 1865, p. 531.

[46]Lyneka Little, "Congressman Says 'Lincoln' Got Connecticut's Slavery Vote Wrong," *Wall Street Journal*, Feb. 7, 2013. Maureen Dowd, "The Oscar for Best Fabrication," *New York Times*, Feb. 16, 2013. It's worth noting, however, that Congressman Courtney appeared to be utterly unaware that James English had switched his vote between June 1864 and January 1865. In other words, the historical fiction of the movie captured something truthful about Connecticut's divisions over abolition that attempts to "correct the record" were distorting.

relatively disappointing results for the film (only Daniel Day-Lewis received an Oscar).

When *Lincoln* scriptwriter Tony Kushner responded in public to the criticism from Congressman Courtney, he used the occasion to outline his theory about how to distinguish history from historical drama. "Here's my rule," he wrote. "Ask yourself, 'Did this thing happen?' If the answer is yes, then it's historical. Then ask, 'Did this thing happen precisely this way?' If the answer is yes, then it's history; if the answer is no, not precisely this way, then it's historical drama."[47]

The problem with this line of defense is that it's too simple-minded in its description of history. Historians are not really capable of deciding how things happened "precisely." They argue over matters large and small, almost endlessly, because their method is totally dependent on evidence—and evidence changes. Historians routinely find new evidence, even for topics as familiar as Lincoln and the Civil War. Sometimes they discover new ways of looking at old evidence. Once in a while, sadly, they lose evidence. But it's all about telling stories with the evidence—at least for historians. For dramatists, the storytelling is accomplished in other ways, usually with the artistry of plot and character. They are not bound, as historians are, by the rules of evidence. That is the fundamental difference between history and historical fiction, and no amount of getting some things "right" can make up for inventing or rearranging other things. But it's not clear that Kushner acknowledges this reality. He seems to think that he was true to the historical evidence in the *Lincoln* movie. In his response to Rep. Courtney, Kushner offered a sweeping defense of his script as historical in nature:

> The Thirteenth Amendment passed by a two-vote margin in the House in January 1865 because President Lincoln decided to push it through, using persuasion and patronage to switch the votes of lame-duck Democrats, all the while fending off a serious offer to negotiate peace from the South. None of the key moments of that story—the overarching story our film tells—are altered.[48]

Yet, as this essay demonstrates, Kushner and Spielberg altered many "key moments" in this profoundly important historical story. Pointing them out

---

[47]Christopher John Farley, "Tony Kushner Fires Back at Congressman's 'Lincoln' Criticism," *Wall Street Journal*, Feb. 8, 2013.
[48]Ibid.

does not condemn the movie, certainly not as drama, but it serves as a reminder to students (and perhaps future filmmakers) that when you read or invoke the phrase "Based on a true story," that means it's not a true story and should neither be judged nor defended as one.

This is something that Steven Spielberg himself once seemed only too happy to acknowledge. In November 2012, he was invited to deliver the Dedication Day address at the Soldiers' National Cemetery in Gettysburg. Speaking on the 149th anniversary of the Gettysburg Address, Spielberg was eloquent and quite profound on the differences between history and historical fiction. "One of the jobs of art is to go to the impossible places that other disciplines like history must avoid," he said explicitly, calling films like his "an illusion," "a fantasy," and "a dream," before adding, rightly, that nevertheless, "dreams matter." He noted with some poignancy that "among the reasons I wanted to make this film" was that he had hoped almost "impossibly to bring Lincoln back from his sleep of one and a half centuries, even if only for two and a half hours, and even if only in a cinematic dream."[49]

The challenge for educators is that some of Spielberg's historical dreams have a nightmarish quality. It's not just that Bluff Wade was a senator from Ohio instead of Massachusetts, or that Thaddeus Stevens delivered some remarks on January 5 instead of January 27. It's not even about who knew what when regarding Lincoln's intentions to push for an antislavery amendment. It's about integrity. Spielberg's cinematic tour of Civil War Washington is dramatic because it is so full of corruption, intrigue, and deception. More important, it's a movie that describes how Abraham Lincoln navigated this ethical morass through a series of increasingly dark compromises. According to Spielberg's vision, Lincoln had to be deceptive, condoning forms of corruption in order to succeed. That may have been so, but the record doesn't really support it. When Daniel Day-Lewis comments acidly that "He's selling himself cheap, ain't he?" about the bribing of a fictional congressman, that particular dream really does matter if American students end up believing it was President Lincoln who said that. Great filmmakers, like Capra and Spielberg, should never have to be tender about whatever political games they go after, but in doing so they must realize they are teaching powerful—and sometimes disturbing—lessons about democracy and leadership.

---

[49]Steven Spielberg, Dedication Day Address, Nov. 19, 2012, Gettysburg, Pa.

Contributors

L. Diane Barnes is professor of history at Youngstown State University and editor of *Ohio History*. She specializes in U.S. nineteenth-century social history, slavery and abolition, and documentary editing. She has served as associate editor on three volumes of the Frederick Douglass Papers and has authored two books on Douglass: *Frederick Douglass: Reformer and Statesman* (Routledge, 2012) and *Frederick Douglass: A Life in Documents* (University Press of Virginia, 2013).

Jenny Bourne is professor of economics at Carleton College in Northfield, Minnesota. She previously held positions at St. Olaf College, George Mason University, and the U.S. Treasury Department. She is the author of *The Bondsman's Burden: An Economic Analysis of the Common Law of Southern Slavery* (Cambridge University Press, 1998); her current research includes a study of the financial legacies left by the Thirty-Seventh Congress and a book manuscript on the Granger movement.

Michael Burlingame holds the Chancellor Naomi B. Lynn Distinguished Chair in Lincoln Studies at the University of Illinois at Springfield. He previously taught in the History Department at Connecticut College in New London from 1968 until he retired in 2001 as the May Buckley Sadowski Professor of History Emeritus. He is the author of *Abraham Lincoln: A Life* (2 vols.; Johns Hopkins University Press, 2008) and *The Inner World of Abraham Lincoln* (University of Illinois Press, 1994). In addition, he has edited several important volumes of Lincoln primary source materials.

Orville Vernon Burton is Creativity Professor of Humanities, professor of history and computer science at Clemson University, and the director of the Clemson CyberInstitute. He was the founding director of the Institute for Computing in Humanities, Arts, and Social Science (I CHASS) at the University of Illinois, where he is emeritus University Distinguished Teacher/Scholar, University Scholar, and professor of history, African American studies, and sociology. He has twenty authored or edited books and more than two hundred articles. *The Age of Lincoln* (Hill and Wang, 2007) won the Chicago Tribune

Heartland Literary Award for Nonfiction and was selected for the Book of the Month Club, History Book Club, and Military Book Club.

Seymour Drescher is Distinguished University Professor of History at the University of Pittsburgh, where he teaches courses on slavery and antislavery, modern France, and Atlantic history. He is the author of several important studies of slavery and abolition, including *Capitalism and Antislavery* (Oxford University Press, 1986), *From Slavery to Freedom* (New York University Press, 1999), *The Mighty Experiment* (Oxford University Press, 2002), and *Abolition: A History of Slavery and Antislavery* (Cambridge University Press, 2009).

Paul Finkelman is a senior fellow at the Penn Program on Democracy, Citizenship, and Constitutionalism at the University of Pennsylvania and a scholar-in-residence at the National Constitution Center. He has taught law and history at several universities, including Albany Law School (President William McKinley Distinguished Professor of Law and Public Policy and senior fellow in the Government Law Center), University of Tulsa College of Law (Chapman Distinguished Professor of Law, 1999–2006), and University of Akron School of Law (John F. Seiberling Professor, 1998–99). He is the author of more than thirty books and a hundred fifty scholarly articles.

Amy S. Greenberg is Edwin Erle Sparks Professor of History and Women's Studies at Penn State University. Her most recent book, *A Wicked War: Polk, Clay, Lincoln and the 1846 U.S. Invasion of Mexico* (Alfred A. Knopf/Vintage Books, 2012), was a main selection of the History Book of the Month Club as well as a selection of the Book of the Month Club and the Military Book of the Month Club.

James Oakes is Distinguished Professor of History and Graduate School Humanities Professor at the Graduate Center of the City University of New York. He taught previously at Princeton University and Northwestern University. His most recent books are *Freedom National: The Destruction of Slavery in the United States, 1861–1865* (W. W. Norton, 2012) and *The Scorpion's Sting: Antislavery and the Coming of the Civil War* (W. W. Norton, 2014).

Beverly Wilson Palmer is a documentary editor whose many projects include *The Selected Letters of Charles Sumner* (Northeastern University Press, 1990) and *The Selected Papers of Thaddeus Stevens* (University of Pittsburgh Press, 1997, 1998), as well as microform publications of the papers of Charles Sumner and the papers of Thaddeus Stevens. Other documentary editions include *Selected Letters of Lucretia Coffin Mott* (University of Illinois Press, 2002), *A Woman's Wit and Whimsy: The 1833 Diary of Anna Cabot Lowell Quincy* (Northeastern University Press, 2003), and with Kathryn Kish Sklar, *The Selected Letters of Florence Kelley, 1869–1931* (University of Illinois Press, 2009).

Matthew Pinsker is associate professor of history and Pohanka Chair in American Civil War History at Dickinson College in Carlisle, Pennsylvania. He also serves as codirector of Dickinson's House Divided Project, an innovative effort to build digital resources on the Civil War era. He is the author of two books: *Abraham Lincoln* (CQ Press, 2002), a volume in the American Presidents Reference Series, and *Lincoln's Sanctuary: Abraham Lincoln and the Soldiers' Home* (Oxford University Press, 2003).

Index

abolition: British, 10, 13–20; continental, 13; French, 20–29; political, 130; United States, 9, 29–36. *See also* antislavery
abolitionist movement, 62–65
abolitionists, opposition to Mexican War, 50
Abraham Lincoln 1808–1858 (Beveridge), 46
Adams, John Quincy, 63
African Americans, and military service in Civil War. *See* black soldiers in Civil War
Africans, and British abolitionism, 15–16
African slave trade. *See* slave trade
Age of Revolution, 9
Alabama, secession, 82, 86
Algeria, 25
Alley, John B., 250
American Anti-Slavery Society, 32, 136, 146
American Revolution, 9, 62, 102, 202
Amis des Noirs, 20, 22
Andrew, John A., 115, 119, 120, 136
Anthony, Susan B., 119
Antietam, Battle of, 175, 207
antislavery: economic context of, 9–12; free blacks, participation in, 33; political context of, 12–13; riots, 34; varieties of, 12–13; women, participation in, 33. *See also* abolition
Arizona, 50
Arkansas, 191
Ashley, James, 119, 240, 241, 245–46, 247–48, 250–52
Ashmore, John, 89–90
Ashmun Amendment, 55
Averill, Charles, 48, 49, 60

Bailey, Gamaliel, 156
Baja California, 58
Baker, Edward, 55
Baker, Frank, 177
Ball's Bluff, Battle of, 189
Baltimore, Maryland, 174
Baltimore Sun, 157
Barkley, Alben W., 236

Basler, Roy P., 90
Bates, Edward, 70, 94
Bear Flag Revolt (1846), 51
Beauregard, Pierre Gustave Toutant, 103
Bennett, Lerone, 175
Beveridge, Albert, 46, 47
Bibb, Henry, 125
Bigelow, Jacob, 157
Bilbo, William N., 242–43, 245–46, 252
Bird, Francis, 110
Birth of a Nation (1915), 247
black soldiers in Civil War, 6, 118, 133–34, 136–39, 201–2. *See also* Douglass, Frederick: and black troops, recruitment of; Fifty-Fifth Massachusetts Infantry Regiment; Fifty-Fourth Massachusetts Infantry Regiment
Blair, Francis Preston, 92, 240, 241, 250, 252, 254
Blair, Francis Preston, Jr., 241
Blair, Montgomery, 117, 118, 204–51, 255
Blair House, 254
Blight, David, 132, 133
"Bliss Copy," 238
blockade runners, 190
Border States, 63, 114–15, 173–74, 183, 185–88, 192
Boritt, Gabor, 47
Boston Journal, 116
Breckinridge, John C., 178
Bright, John, 105, 112, 116, 117, 118, 120
British Emancipation Act, 32
Brown, John, 102, 140
Browning, Orville, 78, 92, 186
Buchanan, James, 100, 101, 178
Buell, Don Carlos, 190
Buena Vista, Battle of, 51
Bugeaud, Thomas Robert (Marshall), 25
Bull Run, First Battle of, 111, 133, 189
Bull Run, Second Battle of, 163, 207
Burke, Edmund, 18
Burton, Josiah, 242
Bush, George W., 81

263

Butler, Benjamin F., 178, 180–82, 191, 199
Byrnes, James F., 236

cahiers de doléances (1789), 21
Calhoun, Andrew Pickens, 88
Calhoun, John C., 34, 42, 85–86, 95
California, 50, 51
Cameron, Simon, 112, 181, 182
Campbell, John A., 253, 254
Capra, Frank, 236, 237, 256, 258
Carey, M. B., 178, 180
Catholic clergy (French) and emancipation, 25
Cerro Gordo, Battle of, 51
Chamber of Deputies. *See* French Chamber of Deputies
Channing, William, 77
Chaplin, William L., 157
Chapman, Maria Weston, 136
Chapultepec Castle, 51
Charleston, South Carolina, 189
Charleston Mercury, 63
Chase, Salmon P., 84, 110, 157, 173
Chicago, Illinois, 174
Chicago Tribune, 44
Chihuahua, Mexico, 57
Child, Lydia Maria, 120
Christian Science Monitor, 236
Cincinnati, Ohio, 174
Civil Rights Act of 1965, 122
Civil War (United States), 6, 36, 76–80, 101. *See also* black soldiers in Civil War; *under names of battles*
Clarkson, Thomas, 22, 31
Clay, Henry, 52–54, 85, 86, 91, 98, 147
Clay, Henry, Jr., 52
Clifford, Nathan, 173
Cobden, Richard, 105, 112
Collected Works of Abraham Lincoln, The (Basler), 91, 92
Colonial Committee, Constituent Assembly. *See* French Constituent Assembly: Colonial Committee
colonization, 91, 92, 192–93, 201
Colorado, 50
compensated emancipation. *See* emancipation: compensated
Confederacy, illegality of, 172
Confederate Congress, 190
Confederate States of America, 64. *See also* Constitution of the Confederate States of America

Confederation (United States), 30
Confiscation Act. *See* First Confiscation Act (1861); Second Confiscation Act (1862)
Congress. *See* United States Congress
Congressional Globe, 249, 251
Conscription Act, 139
Constitution. *See* United States Constitution
Constitutional Convention, 30–31
Constitution of the Confederate States of America, 96–98
Continental Congress, 30, 31
contraband: policy, 178, 180–82, 184, 187; runaway slaves as, 180, 200–201
Conyers, John, 230
Cooper Union (Institute), 89, 110, 112
Corwin, Thomas, 72
Corwin amendment, 72
Courtney, Joe, 256
Cox, John, 243, 244, 245
Cox, LaWanda, 243, 244, 245
Cox, Samuel, 122
Crittenden, John J., 71
Crittenden Compromise, 71
Cross, Joseph, 246
Cumberland River, 190
Curtis, Newton, 48, 49

Danton, Georges-Jacques, 24
Dartmouth College, 105
Davis, David Brion, 16
Davis, Garrett, 42
Davis, Henry Winter, 248
Davis, Jefferson, 64, 70, 83, 254
Day–Lewis, Daniel, 238, 257, 258
Declaration of Independence, 1, 30, 82, 83, 85
Declaration of the Rights of Man and Citizen (1789), 21
Delany, Martin R., 125, 132
Delaware, 172, 174, 181
Demerara (Guyana), 16
Democrats, congressional, 241, 246
Disquisition on Government (Calhoun), 86
District of Columbia Compensated Emancipation Act, 192, 201
Douglas, Stephen A., 43, 144, 145
Douglass, Charles, 136
Douglass, Frederick, 33, 177, 200; and black troops, recruitment of, 136–39; and colonization, 135; and emancipation, 123–42; and Emancipation Proclamation, 134–35; and Lincoln, Abraham, 123,

Index 265

129–30, 131, 132, 134, 135, 139–41, 160; and Washington, D.C., emancipation in, 135
Douglass, Lewis, 136
Douglass, Rosetta, 132
Douglass' Monthly, 131
Dowd, Maureen, 256
Dred Scott v. Sandford (1857), 74, 83, 167, 173
Du Bois, W.E.B., 128
Duncan, Joseph, 147
Du Pont, Samuel Francis, 189

E.I. du Pont de Nemours and Company, 174
Electoral College, 2
emancipation: British, 13–20; comparative, 8–38; compensated, 92, 114–15, 157–59; economic impact of, 211–23l, French, 20–29; gradual, 30, 62, 79, 91, 92, 158; international, impact of, 37–38; military, 62–65, 79–80, 112–13, 178, 180–82; preconditions for, 171–76; in United States, 29–38. *See also* self-emancipation
Emancipation Act (British, 1833), 19
Emancipation Day, 208
Emancipation League, 134
Emancipation Proclamation, 6, 129, 144, 162, 164, 201; first draft of, 203–4; Marx, Karl, on, 208, 210; preliminary, 207–8. *See also* Preliminary Emancipation Proclamation
Engerman, Stanley, 213, 222
English, James, 256
Everett, Edward, 148

Fehrenbacher, Don, 45
Field, George, 77
Field, Sally, 239, 249
Fifth Amendment, 167, 168, 172, 173, 183, 192
Fifty–Fifth Massachusetts Infantry Regiment, 137
Fifty–Fourth Massachusetts Infantry Regiment, 136
Final Freedom (Vorenberg), 247
First Confiscation Act (1861), 6, 112, 118, 175, 183–87, 191–92
First Congress, 31
first world's antislavery conference (1840), 18
Florida, 82
Fogel, Robert, 213, 222
Foner, Eric, 121
Fort Donelson, 190
Fort Henry, 190
Fortress Monroe, 178, 180, 253

Fort Sumter, 76, 78, 103, 110, 132, 133, 170, 176
Fourteenth Amendment, 83
Fox, Charles James, 18
France. *See* abolition: French
Francis, Simeon, 149
Franklin, Benjamin, 31
Frederick Douglass' Civil War (Blight), 132
Fredericksburg, Battle of, 163
Free Democrats, 130
Freedom National (Oakes), 247
Free Soil Party, 130
Frémont, John C., 51, 113, 134, 139, 171, 184–89
French Abolitionist Society, 28
French Chamber of Deputies, 25
French Constituent Assembly, 28; Colonial Committee, 21
French Constitution (1791), 21
French Convention, 23, 24
French National Assembly, 22, 30
French Revolution (1789), 22, 102
French Revolution (1848), 102
fugitive slave clause, 31, 172, 178, 199
Fugitive Slave Law of 1850, 2, 67, 71, 73, 170, 172, 176–78

gag rule, 34
Gales, Joseph, 155
Garibaldi, Giuseppe, 102, 103–4
Garnett, Henry Highland, 125
Garrison, William Lloyd, 32, 61, 100, 155; and Douglass, Frederick, 125, 127, 130, 136
Gay, Sydney Howard, 159
General Order No. 11, 194
General Order No. 143, 137
Georgia, 82
Gettysburg Address, 103, 104, 238, 258
Giddings, Joshua R., 153, 156, 159, 160
Goggins, Walton, 245
Gott, Daniel, 152, 153, 155
gradual emancipation. *See* emancipation: gradual
Grant, Ulysses S., 190, 202, 255
Great Britain, 112, 163. *See also* abolition: British
Great Depression, 81
Greeley, Horace, 100, 155, 157, 205
Griffith, D. W., 247
Guadalupe Hidalgo, Treaty of, 49, 50, 58, 60
Guelzo, Allen C., 144

266   *Index*

guerrilla warfare, 191
Guizot, François, 28

Haddam, Aaron, 252
Haiti, 132; creation of, 24; independence, 26; revolution, 26
Halleck, Henry W., 114, 182
Hampton Roads conference, 252–55
Harney, William S., 180
Harpers Ferry, Virginia, 88–89
Harper's Weekly, 170
Harvard University, 105
Hawkes, John, 242
Hawkins, Clay, 245
Hay, John, 246, 250, 252
Helper, Hinton Rowan, 99
Henderson, John B., 119, 122
Henry, Anson G., 54, 55, 56
Herndon, William, 47, 54, 55, 159–60
Hickham v. Hickham (1891), 221
Hilton Head, South Carolina, 202
Hofstadter, Richard, 164, 208
Holbrook, Hal, 241, 255
House Committee on Ways and Means, 108, 246–47
House Divided speech (Lincoln), 5
House of Commons, 18
Hunted Chief; or Female Ranchero, The (Curtis), 48
Hunter, David, 113, 194–98
Hunter, Robert M. T., 253, 254

Illinois, 149, 174
Illinois Anti-Slavery Society, 149
Illinois General Assembly, 146, 168
Illinois State Journal, 149
Illinois State Register, 43, 49, 57
immediatism, 61
Impending Crisis, The (Helper), 99
Indiana, 174
Indianapolis, Indiana, 174
Indianapolis Daily Journal, 68
Indian Territory, 172
Interesting Narrative of the Life of Olaudah Equiano (Equiano), 15–16
Inter-University Consortium for Political and Social Research, 213
Invasión Norteamericana, La, 39
Iowa, 174
Iowa State Register, 69
Island No. 10, 191

Jackson, Andrew, 85, 115
Jamaica, slave uprising in, 16
Jefferson, Thomas, 1, 2, 30, 91
Jim Crow, 229
Johannsen, Robert W., 143
John Brown's raid, 88–89
Johnson, Andrew, 108, 244
Johnston, John, 150
Joint Committee on the Conduct of the War, 244
Jones, Tommy Lee, 247
Jones County, Mississippi, 98
Julian, George W., 155

Kansas–Nebraska Act of 1854, 3
Kearny, Stephen W., 51
Keckley, Elizabeth, 249, 250
Kentucky, 172, 173, 175, 181, 186, 187, 190
Kentucky legislature, 190
Kushner, Tony, 238, 239, 241, 247–48, 249, 257

Lamon, Ward Hill, 150
Lancaster, Pennsylvania, 105, 116
Latham, Robert, 242–43, 244
Lester, Julius, 143
Liberty Party, 62, 130
Lieber, Francis, 117, 121
Lincoln (motion picture, 2012), 237–58
Lincoln, Abraham: on Brown, John, 89; and Butler, Benjamin F., 181–82; Clay, Henry, as beau ideal, 52, 54, 147; congressional term of, 39–60, 52–60, 168; and Constitution and slavery, 4, 61, 83, 165–69, 171–73, 199; Cooper Union speech, 89; and Douglass, Frederick, 123, 129–30; and Dred Scott decision, 74; and election of 1860, 86; and emancipation, 77, 81–104, 143–44; and emancipation, compensated, 197–98; and emancipation, gradual, in Washington, D.C., 43, 192–93; and emancipation, military victory as precondition for, 199–200; and Emancipation Proclamation, 199, 203–4; family of, 94–96, 151; and First Confiscation Act, 184; first inaugural address of, 71–76, 83–84, 87, 163, 165, 168; and Frémont, John C., 134, 186–89; and fugitive slave issue, 73; and Greeley, Horace, 205–6; and Hunter, David, 196–98; in Illinois legislature, 168; and

Polk, James K., 56–58; and Preliminary Emancipation Proclamation, 207–8; and rule of law, 93; and secession, 5–6, 81–104, 172; second inaugural, 140–41, 151, 176, 239; and slavery, hostility to, 4, 144–61; and slavery, ultimate extinction of, 35, 63; and Union, preservation of, 4–5, 170. See also *Collected Works of Abraham Lincoln, The* (Basler); Gettysburg Address; House Divided speech (Lincoln); *Lincoln* (motion picture, 2012); Spot Resolutions
Lincoln, Mary Todd, 94, 141, 239, 247, 249, 250
Lincoln, Robert, 250
Lincoln, Thomas, 150
Lincoln–Douglas debates, 91–92
Lincoln Memorial, 162, 238, 239
Lincoln penny, 162
Litton, Asa Vintner, 248–49
lobbying, 242
London *Times*, 79, 100
Longfellow, Henry Wadsworth, 110
Louisiana, 82, 174

Mallory, Charles K., 177, 180
Mallory, Shepard, 177
Manifest Destiny, 50
Marcy, William L., 148
Marketti, James, 230
Martin, Waldo, 127, 128
Martineau, Harriet, 112, 113
Marx, Karl, 209–10
Maryland, 172, 174, 181
Matamoros, 57, 58
McClellan, George, 120, 180, 190
Memphis, Tennessee, 191
Mexican Ranchero, The (Averill), 48
Mexican War, 39–40, 48, 49–51
Mexico City, Mexico, 51, 57
Middlebury College, 147
military emancipation. *See* emancipation: military
Militia Act, 137, 201–3
Minnesota, 174
Mississippi, 82
Mississippi River, 191
Mississippi Valley, 190
Missouri, 171–73, 175, 180–81, 184, 187, 191
Missouri Compromise of 1820, 2
Monterey, 57
Moore, Matilda Johnson, 150

Mr. Smith Goes to Washington (1939), 236, 237, 256
My Bondage and My Freedom (Douglass), 124
Myers, Peter C., 132

Napoleon, 14, 24, 26
Narrative of the Life of Frederick Douglass (Douglass), 124
Nashville, Tennessee, 190
National Intelligencer, 155
Nat Turner's slave rebellion, 16–17
Nebraska, 172
Neely, Mark S., 47
Neely anti–block booking bill, 237
Nelson, Tim Blake, 242
Nevada, 50
New Mexico, 50, 51
New Orleans, Louisiana, 174, 191
New York Times, 82, 236, 256
New York Tribune, 159, 160, 205
Nicolay, John, 250
North Star (Rochester, N.Y.), 124
Nugent, Frank, 236, 237
Nullification Crisis, 85

Oakes, James, 144, 247
Obama, Barack, 81
Odell, Moses, 244
Ohio, 174
Ohio River, 174
Orr, James L., 90
Oxford Democrat (Paris, Me.), 78

Panic of 1837, 223
Pantagraph (Bloomington, Ill.), 69
Parks, Samuel C., 149
Pasha of Egypt, 27
Pax Brittanica, 15
Pea Ridge, Battle of, 191
Pendleton, George, 252
Pennington, William, 95
Pennsylvania Abolition Society, 31
"Petition from the Women of Paris" (1847), 25
Philadelphia Evening Journal, 76
Phillips, Wendell, 111, 113, 132, 136, 146, 156, 159
Pickens, Francis, 34
Pinckney, Charles Cotesworth, 3, 166
Pitt, William, 18
Pittsburgh, Pennsylvania, 174
Polk, James K., 39–40, 43, 50, 51, 57–60

Port Royal, South Carolina, 189
Preliminary Emancipation Proclamation, 117, 134, 175–76, 177, 207
Prelude to Greatness (Fehrenbacher), 45

Quaker societies, 31
Queen Victoria, 15

Radical Abolitionist Party, 131
Radical Republicans: and First Confiscation Act, 110–11; Spielberg's *Lincoln*, depiction in, 246–50; Stevens, Thaddeus, and Sumner, Charles, as, 105
Ranchero Spotty, 39, 43, 44, 48
Raynal, Abbé, 8–9
Reconstruction, 79, 141
reparations, 212, 229–31
Republican Banner (Nashville, Tenn.), 71
Republican Party: and abolition and emancipation, 62, 63, 72, 79–80, 125, 186, 188, 204–5; divisions within, 240–41; and Douglass, Frederick, 128–42; and Frémont, John C., 186; platform (1860), 72, 165. *See also* Radical Republicans
Reuben, Gloria, 249
Revolution of 1848, 33
Rhett, Robert Barnwell, 87, 89
Richards, Leonard, 245
Richmond Enquirer, 63
Rio Grande, 57, 58
River Queen (steamboat), 253
Roanoke Island, 189
Rochester, New York, 130
Rollins, James, 24
Roosevelt, Franklin D., 81
Ruffin, Edmund, 102
runaway slaves, 200–201. *See also* contraband
Russell, William Howard, 79

Saint-Domingue, 24, 25
Saint-Domingue Revolution (1791), 9, 22–23
Santa Anna, Antonio López de, 51
Savannah, Georgia, 189
Saxton, Rufus, 202
Schell, Richard, 242–43
Schoelcher, Victor, 25, 28
Schurz, Carl, 95
Scott, Winfield, 51
Seaton, William, 155
secession, 5–6, 35; and abolition, 61–80; arguments for, 87–88; crisis of, 94; and emancipation, 81–104; movement, 64, 81; slavery as cause of, 169; in South Carolina, 82, 85, 89; southern opponents of, 70
secessionists, 95
Second Confiscation Act (1862), 6, 115, 202–4
Second Seminole War (1835–42), 62
Seddon, James A., 202
self-emancipation, 163, 176–77
Senate. *See* United States Senate
Senate Foreign Relations Committee, 108
Seward, Frederick, 143
Seward, William H., 64–68, 141, 157, 173, 198, 240–42, 250, 253, 255
Seward Lobby, 243, 245
Seymour, Horatio, 245
Sherman, William T., 229
Shiloh, Battle of, 191
slaveowners, monetary losses to due to emancipation, 218–20
Slave Power, 128, 134
slave prices, 212, 221
slave productivity, 215
slave rebellions, 67, 69–70. *See also* Haiti: revolution; Nat Turner's slave rebellion; Saint-Domingue Revolution
slavery: French, 10; Spanish, 10; United States, 10–12, 29–30
slaves: American Revolution, status of, 1; constitutional framework for freeing, 171–73; economic losses to, due to enslavement, 220, 227–28; female, value of, 215; hire rates and wages of, 220–29; numbers and locations of, 213–14. *See also* contraband; Haiti: revolution; runaway slaves; Saint-Domingue Revolution; slave rebellions; slave trade
slave trade: British, 10, 14; domestic (United States), 71; transatlantic, 10, 27, 31; in Washington, D.C., 34
Smith, Adam, 8
Smith, Caleb B., 153
Smith, Gerrit, 113, 127, 130, 131, 134, 136
Soldier's National Cemetery (Gettysburg, Pennsylvania), 258
Sonthonax, Léger Felicité, 24
South Carolina, 61, 64
South Carolina Agricultural Society, 88
South Carolina House of Representatives, 166
South Carolina Ordinance of Secession (1861), 82, 85

South Carolina Sea Islands, 189
South Carolina secession convention, 5
Spader, James, 242, 243, 245, 246, 252
Speed, Joshua, 85, 144, 145
Spielberg, Steven, 237, 238, 248, 256, 258
Spooner, Lysander, 166
Spot Resolutions, 39, 40–42, 45, 54–60
Springfield, Illinois, 95, 148
Stanton, Edwin M., 113, 137, 139, 202
Stearns, George L., 137–39
Stephens, Alexander, 94, 169, 253, 254
Stevens, Thaddeus: Civil War, justification of, 109; and emancipation, 105–22; Lincoln, Abraham, support of, 110; Spielberg's *Lincoln*, depiction in, 240, 246–49; Sumner, Charles, compared to, 105–8
St. Louis, Missouri, 174, 191
Stone, Dan, 146, 147, 148
Stoneman, Austin, 247
Strathairn, David, 241, 253, 255
Strong, George Templeton, 70
sugar riots, 23
Sumner, Charles: Civil War, justification of, 109; and emancipation, 105–22; Lincoln, Abraham, support for, 110, 188; Stevens, Thaddeus, compared to, 105–8
Supplemental Civil Rights Act, 121–22
Supreme Court. *See* United States Supreme Court

Taney, Roger B., 74, 166, 167, 173, 188, 208
Tappan, Lewis, 136
taxation populaire, 23
Taylor, Zachary, 39, 51, 56, 57
Tazewell (Illinois) *Whig*, 54
Team of Rivals (Goodwin), 238, 243, 247, 251, 253, 255
Tennessee, 190
Tennessee River, 190
Texas, 82, 85
Texas v. White (1869), 84
Thirteenth Amendment, 7, 36, 80, 83, 105, 119–21, 141, 201, 237–58
Thirtieth Congress, 40, 49–51
Thirty-Eighth Congress, 115, 240
Thomas, Lorenzo, 139
Townsend, James, 177
Trafalgar, Battle of, 14
Trafalgar Square, 19
Trefousse, Hans, 122
Trist, Nicholas, 49, 57, 58, 60

Trumbull, Lyman, 100, 109, 111, 247
Twentieth Amendment, 81

Underground Railroad, 140, 157
Unionists, Border State, 186, 242
United States Colored Troops, 134, 137
United States Congress: and compensated emancipation, 198; and emancipation in the territories, 194; and emancipation in Washington, D.C., 192. *See also* First Congress; Joint Committee on the Conduct of the War; Thirtieth Congress; Thirty-Eighth Congress; United States House of Representatives; United States Senate
United States Constitution: Douglass, Frederick, on, 130; Lincoln's interpretation of on slavery, 171–73; and slavery, 30–31, 61, 67, 83, 125, 165–69, 199; takings clause, 231; three-fifths clause, 2
United States House of Representatives, 2, 31, 237–58. *See also* House Committee on Ways and Means
United States Senate, 2–3. *See also* Senate Foreign Relations Committee
United States Supreme Court, 3, 84, 166, 167, 173, 188, 199, 208. See also *Dred Scott v. Sandford* (1857); *Texas v. White* (1869)
University of Illinois, 143
University of Massachusetts–Amherst, 143
Utah, 50, 172

Van Dorn, Earl, 191
Vera Cruz, Mexico, 51
Vicksburg, Mississippi, 139
Vorenberg, Michael, 244, 247, 248, 249

Wade, Benjamin, 246
Wade–Davis bill, 120, 248
Walker, Peter F., 127
War Department, 182
War of 1812, 62, 202
Washburne, Elihu, 100
Washington, D.C.: abolition of slavery in, 71, 114–15, 146, 152, 192–93; slavery in, 3, 167, 168–69, 172. *See also* District of Columbia Compensated Emancipation Act
Washington Navy Yard, 238
Waterloo, Battle of, 27
Webster, Daniel, 32
Welles, Gideon, 198–99
Westminster Abbey, 19, 32

West Virginia, 7, 98
Whig Party, 44
Wilberforce, William, 18, 19, 32
Wilmington, North Carolina, 189
Wilmot, David, 50
Wilmot Proviso, 55
Wilson, Henry, 114
Wilson, William H., 45
Winthrop, Robert C., 159

women. *See* antislavery: women, participation in
Women's National League, 119
Wood, Fernando, 249
Worcester, Massachusetts, 111
Worcester Palladium, 69
Wyoming, 50

Yamasee War (1715–18), 202